A FIELD GUIDE TO THE
MAMMALS OF BORNEO

Junaidi Payne
Charles M. Francis
illustrated by
Karen Phillipps

The Sabah Society
with
World Wildlife Fund Malaysia
1985

The Sabah Society
P.O. Box 10547
88806 Kota Kinabalu
Sabah, Malaysia

World Wildlife Fund Malaysia
P.O. Box 10769
Kuala Lumpur

ISBN: 967-99947-1-6

Printed in Kuala Lumpur by Pencetak Weng Fatt Sdn. Bhd.
Lot 8243, Jalan 225, Section 51A, 46100 Petaling Jaya, Selangor.

CONTENTS

3

ILLUSTRATIONS

Figures:

7

 **WWF** WORLD WILDLIFE FUND   MALAYSIA

FOREWORD BY THE PRESIDENT, WORLD WILDLIFE FUND MALAYSIA

As Mankind alters the natural world to improve his own life, space available for wildlife decreases and, unless special efforts are made to prevent it, species go extinct. As people become more urbanised, however, their interest in wild animals and plants tends to increase and, fortunately, both in Malaysia and adjacent countries, natural areas have been set aside for conservation in the form of National and State Parks, Wildlife Reserves and Sanctuaries.

World Wildlife Fund (WWF) Malaysia attaches particular importance to the establishment of such conservation areas, and raises money and provides various forms of assistance where required to help fulfil this primary aim. It has been associated with the establishment of several important conservation areas in recent years, especially in Sabah and Sarawak.

Another large part of the work of WWF Malaysia may be summarised by the word "education". All of us - not only children - need to be educated that conservation means management of water supplies and soil, sustained production of renewable forest resources and preservation of species for both economic purposes and pleasure.

A vital part of the education process is to have available up-to-date and reliable written and pictorial material. This book, A Field Guide to the Mammals of Borneo, provides such a service, with a succinct yet comprehensive text and delightful yet functional illustrations. It will be useful to a wide range of residents and visitors in Sabah and Sarawak, as well as in the neighbouring areas of Brunei and Kalimantan. I hope that it will stimulate interest in wildlife generally, aid the amateur naturalist and be a source of information for those whose work or studies involves wildlife.

Kair Johari

Kuala Lumpur
27 June 1985

M. Khir Johari
President
World Wildlife Fund Malaysia

8

Telefon: 660811

Telegram: "FORESTS SANDAKAN"

Telex: MA 82016

JABATAN HUTAN,

PETI SURAT 311

SANDAKAN

SABAH, MALAYSIA

FOREWORD BY THE CONSERVATOR OF FORESTS AND CHIEF GAME WARDEN, SABAH

Forests depend on land, rainfall and sunshine for their existence while, equally, animals depend on forests. The past two decades have seen an enormous increase in the rate of forest exploitation· in Sabah, Sarawak and Kalimantan, and much of the island of Borneo is in the process of experiencing inevitable and permanent change. This occurs in the form of forest clearance for agriculture, replacement of natural forest with forest plantations, and selective logging of native trees for timber. Rightly, concern has been expressed over the effects of these changes on wildlife, and some observers have painted a bleak picture of species extinctions.

Several developments in recent years, however, suggest a much brighter future. Firstly, the authors of this field guide have discovered a number of extensions to the known range of various mammals in Sabah, as well as three new species of bats, indicative that there are generally more mammals than is readily apparent. Secondly, it has become clear that selective logging as practised in Sabah, and presumably elsewhere in Borneo, may result in smaller population sizes for many species, but there is no evidence that it results in species extinction. Thirdly, in 1984, an area amounting to nearly one half of Sabah was legally established as permanent Forest Reserve, Wildlife Reserve, Park and National Park. Similarly large conservation areas have been and are being established elsewhere in Borneo.

Undoubtedly, not everything is perfect from a conservation viewpoint: for example, hunting of wild mammals, a tradition among all peoples in Borneo, is difficult to regulate, and most lowland forest must give way to agriculture as a more productive form of land use. Nevertheless, I believe that the basis for conservation of mammals and other wildlife in Borneo is now satisfactory. I hope th. this field guide, with its emphasis on illustrations and succinct text, will contribute to the most important factor in conservation, namely interest and understanding among all sections of our society.

S. ℎ. ℛ... [signature]

Datuk Haji K M Mastan
Conservator of Forests and
Chief Game Warden
Sabah

PREFACE

The idea of this book was conceived in Sabah, where we frequently felt a need for a book like it ourselves. We intend it as a field guide useful to everyone, including the zoologist or specialist, and we hope that the somewhat technical language necessary in some cases will not discourage the general reader.

We wish to thank the following people for contributing in one way or another towards its production. Many other people have helped in numerous small ways, and we regret that space does not permit us to mention everyone.

Staff of the Sabah Forest Department were particularly helpful and we are especially grateful to P. M. Andau, the Assistant Chief Game Warden, for providing facilities and allowing us to work at Sepilok and the Forest Department headquarters. Assistant Game Ranger Simon Ambi caught an impressive number of mammals of all sorts, making the task of illustrating the guide much easier than would otherwise have been the case.

The Director and Assistant Director of Sabah Parks, Lamri Ali and Rahim Sidek, kindly provided permission and facilities to work at Kinabalu Park, where we were able to obtain live examples of species not readily available elsewhere. The Park Ecologist, Anthea Phillipps, and other Parks staff helped out with field work and accomodation.

Additional assistance was provided in Sabah from the Agriculture Department and the Sabah Museum. We appreciate the considerable input received from members of the Western Foundation of Vertebrate Zoology bird study group, especially Fred Sheldon and Jody Kennard, while they were working in Sabah.

Special thanks to Susan Phillipps, Tony Lamb of the Agricultural Research Station, Tenom and Ron and Ann Greening at Sepilok who kindly permitted us to use their homes as bases for field work.

In Sarawak, much useful material was made available to us at the Sarawak Museum, by courtesy of the Director, Lucas Chin, and Zoologist, Charles Leh, who provided excellent assistance. The Director of the Sarawak Forest Department and Paul Chai P. K., head of the National Parks and Wildlife Office, kindly provided permission and facilities to work at Samunsam Wildlife Sanctuary. Staff at Samunsam, especially CUSO volunteer Bob Basiuk, made field work there enjoyable. Assistance and accommodation in Sarawak were provided by Michael Kavanagh and were much appreciated.

Material from Brunei Darussalam was made available by courtesy of the Brunei Museum and special thanks are due to Mohd. Jaya Hj. Sahat, Curator of Natural History, for data from Tasek Merimbun.

In Kuala Lumpur, unpublished data, especially valuable body size measurements, were made available by K. Inder Singh, head of the Medical Ecology section at the Institute for Medical Research.

We are indebted to the Earl of Cranbrook (formerly Lord Medway) for laying out the taxonomic groundwork on which this field guide is based. Without his *Mammals of Borneo*, our task would have been much greater and more tedious. Much of the information on species distribution was provided by him, as were numerous helpful comments.

11

The staff of the Mammal Section, Department of Zoology, British Museum (Natural History) were always helpful during the time we spent working there. John E. Hill freely gave advice on the taxonomy of bats and other small mammals, even after we had returned to Sabah.

G.G. Musser (American Museum of Natural History) and R.W. Thorington (National Museum of Natural History) helped with the taxonomy of rats and squirrels.

Lyall Watson and Tom Ritchie kindly gave us permission to redraw the illustrations of whales, dolphins and porpoises from their book *Sea Guide to Whales of the World*.

Mike Sparks drew four of the maps at a time when he was exceptionally busy. Nico van Strien provided a very useful contribution in the form of his drawings of footprints: all those in this field guide are based on his "A guide to the tracks of mammals of Western Indonesia".

Several of the people mentioned above also made very useful comments on the text, special thanks to Elizabeth Bennett and Julian Caldecott.

Support while we were working on the book came from several quarters. Datuk Hj. K.M. Mastan, Conservator of Forests, backed the idea at a time when both authors had other duties in the Sabah Forest Department.

Junaidi Payne was employed by World Wildlife Fund Malaysia throughout most of the period when the book was being prepared, and the Fund's executive director, Ken Scriven, was supportive from the beginning. Charles M. Francis was employed by the Wildlife Section of the Sabah Forest Department under arrangement with the Canadian development agency, CUSO, and was permitted by the Assistant Chief Game Warden to work on the book as part of his studies.

The Sabah Society provided a stimulus and funds for travel after agreement was reached that the Society would publish the field guide. The Society's president, Richard Dingley, and treasurer, Chio Cheng Leng, took a keen and constant interest in seeing it to completion, and frequently helped us with design of the book and logistical problems.

Introduction

The primary aim of this field guide is to provide a convenient means for both the general public and professional scientists to identify all of the mammals currently known to occur in Borneo. We hope that people using this book will be able to identify any mammal they find by looking through the colour plates and reading the corresponding text descriptions.

A number of books have been published on Bornean mammals in the past including Banks (1949), Davis (1962), Harrison (1964), Hose (1893) and Medway (1977). Of these, Medway's *Mammals of Borneo* is the most complete, but it is primarily a checklist with only limited keys for identification. These keys are difficult for non-scientists to use as very few mammals are illustrated. Since it was published many new species have been added to the Bornean list, and much additional information has been learned. As a result we felt there was a strong need for a new and comprehensive book on the mammals of Borneo.

This book describes every species of wild mammal presently known to occur in Borneo and its offshore islands. Approximately 221 species of wild land mammals have been recorded in Borneo, of which 92 species are bats. Also included are descriptions of the more commonly encountered domestic animals which might be confused with wild mammals, as well as a few species which have not definitely been recorded in Borneo but which are likely to be found in the area.

Sea mammals, including the cetaceans (whales, dolphins and porpoises) and the Dugong, are also included. Little is known about these in Bornean waters, as few people have studied them and, until recently, there were few books available describing them. The only species definitely known to occur are those for which stranded specimens have been obtained. Only 10 species have been confirmed in this way, although a further 5 have been reported from sight records. To encourage more people to study cetaceans, we have included all species found in nearby seas which are likely to occur in Bornean waters.

Every mammal is illustrated in colour, with the exception of a few which so closely resemble another species as to be indistinguishable by sight, or for which no adequate specimens or descriptions were available. Several of the more distinctive subspecies are also illustrated.

With the exception of the cetaceans, most of the mammals were drawn either from live animals or from freshly collected specimens. However, in a few cases it was necessary to use older museum specimens. If we felt the specimens might have altered or faded significantly with age, this is indicated in the text. The illustrations of cetaceans are based on Lyall Watson and Thomas Ritchie's *Sea Guide to the Whales of the World*, with the kind permission of the authors.

The colour illustrations together with the brief notes on the facing page will be adequate for many people. For those who wish to learn more about each species, or confirm their identifications, greater detail is given in the text. The text highlights identification characters easily visible on the live animal, but for groups such as bats and shrews which can be difficult to identify, we have also included technical details on dentition or skull shape.

Brief notes are given on the ecology, habitat, and distribution of each species. This information is often helpful for finding mammals and studying them, but also highlights how little is known about most of the mammals in Borneo. The basic ecological requirements are known for only a very few mammals. For most species almost nothing is known, yet data on the habits, habitat, food and distribution of each species are essential for wise management or conservation. We hope this book will encourage more people to watch mammals and study them, and perhaps fill some of the gaps in our knowledge.

If anybody finds new information, knows of publications we have missed, or finds errors in the text, we hope that they will inform us. Changes and additions can then be included in future editions of the book and made available to everyone. Please write to the authors at the following address:

The Sabah Society
P.O. Box 10547
88806 Kota Kinabalu
Sabah, Malaysia

How to identify mammals

What is a mammal? Mammals are distinguished from other animals by several features. All species (except a few in Australia and New Guinea) give birth to live young and feed their young on milk. Most mammals have fur or hair, although in sea mammals the hairs are scattered and inconspicuous. All species are warm-blooded and share many features of internal anatomy. Most have four limbs — two hind legs and two front legs, wings or arms. A few mammals somewhat resemble other types of animals and might cause confusion. Bats are often thought to be birds because they can fly, but they have fur rather than feathers, teeth instead of beaks and give birth to live young. Whales, dolphins and porpoises are often confused with fish, but they are actually mammals which have lost most of their hair and their hind legs and replaced their front legs with flippers. They still breathe air, give birth to live young and feed them on milk. The pangolin somewhat resembles a reptile because of its scales and long tongue, but the scales are actually formed from packed hairs, and it has all the remaining features of a mammal.

Classification and Naming. To provide some order to the large number of animals in the world and to indicate their relationships, animals are classified at different levels. Individuals which can interbreed freely and produce fertile offspring are considered to belong to one species. Closely related species are put in the same genus. Genera (plural of genus) which share many features are grouped in families which, in turn, are grouped into orders.

Every species of animal known to science has an officially designated scientific name. These names are usually based on Latin or Greek, and are accepted by scientists all over the world regardless of their own language. Scientific names are always written in italics to distinguish them. The name is composed of two parts, indicating the genus and the species. If populations of a species in different geographical areas can be consistently distinguished from each other by measurements or colour, then they are given subspecies names. For example, *Callosciurus* is the genus name for several species of similar medium-sized squirrels. *Callosciurus prevosti* refers specifically to the Prevost's Squirrel. *Callosciurus prevosti pluto,* sometimes abbreviated *C. p. pluto,* is the form of Prevost's Squirrel found in Sabah, while *C. p. caroli* is the form in northern Sarawak.

The relationships between many animals are still not well understood and, as a result, not everyone agrees on the taxonomy. A common problem is determining relationships between closely related animals from different geographical areas. Some people might consider them all the same species and use the same name for all of them, while others consider each a separate species, using a different name for each population. Depending on the author's viewpoint, books sometimes differ in the name used for a particular animal.

The classification and names, both scientific and English, used in this book generally follow Medway (1977). However, some things have been altered to conform with more recent opinions. The tree-shrews are placed in their own order, Scandentia. Bats, many of which are not included in Medway, follow Hill (1983) or Hill and Francis (1984). The English name of the leaf monkeys has been changed to langurs. Cetaceans follow Leatherwood and Reeves (1983), although the alternative English names used by Watson and Ritchie (1981) are given as well. For names which differ from Medway and might confuse the reader, the old name is given in parentheses.

English names for bats are a particular problem. Scientists generally use only the scientific name, so many species have never been assigned an English name. Some common species have many different names proposed by each person who has written a book, while others have names which are used for many totally unrelated species in different parts of the world. Some names are based on localities where a species is now rare or no longer found.

In choosing names for this book we have used names already in the literature if they seemed suitable, otherwise we have invented new names. Names which describe a distinctive character of the bat were preferred. In order to prevent confusion over these new names for bats, the scientific name is given together with the English name throughout the text.

Identification of mammals. The colour plates are the most important aid to identification for most mammals. When a mammal is encountered, the illustrations should be studied first until the closest match is found. With practice, and by reading the text, the main family groups can be recognized readily and the search reduced.

The key identification features are summarized on the caption pages opposite the plates. Some species have more variation than is indicated in the drawings, especially in coloration, so the text should always be consulted to confirm identifications. In addition, a small number of mammals were drawn from old museum specimens in which the colours may have altered, so live animals may appear slightly different.

Size is important for distinguishing many mammals. This is indicated by scale on the plates and measurements in the text. The measurements are based on standard techniques for measuring museum specimens (see the next section). However, the apparent size of a live animal may vary depending on its posture. If it hunches its back, the body seems shorter and the tail proportionately longer. Since individuals within a species vary in size, a range of measurements is given, but some particularly large or small individuals might fall outside the range.

The "Similar species" section highlights distinctions from other mammals with which the species might be confused. The list is not exhaustive but concentrates on the most similar species and those which appear different in the illustrations but sometimes look similar in life.

Many of the larger mammals can be identified from a distance, but smaller species often have to be captured for close examination. Rodents caught in cage traps can usually be identified without handling them. If they need to be held, heavy gloves can be useful to avoid being bitten. Anaesthetics such as chloroform are sometimes used, but care must be taken not to give an overdose.

For some species, such as bats or shrews, the teeth need to be examined to confirm the identity. These can usually be seen in a live bat by gently prying open the mouth with a toothpick or similar tool. A hand lens is often necessary to see the smallest teeth.

The number and arrangement of teeth is sometimes given as a "dental formula". This is a shorthand way of indicating the number of teeth in one side of the upper and lower jaws. The teeth are always given in the order: incisors, canines, premolars and molars (see Figure 5). For example, the dental formula for most *Myotis* bats is: $\frac{2}{3} \frac{1}{1} \frac{3}{3} \frac{3}{3}$, indicating 2 incisors, 1 canine, 3 premolars and 3 molars on each side of the upper jaw, and 3 incisors, 1 canine, 3 premolars and 3 molars on each side of the lower jaw for a total of 38 teeth.

Some teeth are very small, and could be easily overlooked. To show the patterns of the teeth and their relative sizes, diagrams are provided of the tooth rows for many species. Occasionally teeth are missing or have fallen out. Usually if this happens, there is a gap where the tooth used to be or the two sides of the jaw are not symmetrical, but sometimes the result is quite confusing.

With present knowledge, some species can only be positively identified after museum preparation of the skull. For the benefit of scientists using this book, diagnostic characters of the skull of these species are included. In the future, when more field studies have been done, other distinctive features may be found which help to identify these species in life.

Details of skulls are also useful for identifying dead mammals or their remains (for example, during feeding studies of predators). Experts can often determine the identity of a mammal using only its skull. Diagrams of the main skull types are included in the text along with measurements for many species. Although not all skulls are described, it should be possible to determine the group to which a skull belongs. For confirmation, the specimen can be sent to a reputable museum for comparison with skulls of known species.

Young mammals can be difficult to identify, as they often differ in both size and coloration from adults. The young of larger mammals are often seen with adults, but in smaller species, such as rodents or bats, the young are likely to be trapped alone. Rats are a particular problem, as fur colour is important for identification. The young often have fluffier and darker fur than adults, and can sometimes be recognized by their fresh, unworn teeth which have not fully erupted from the gums. Young bats can usually be recognized by their greyer fur and incompletely formed wing bones — if held to the light the joints of the wings appear banded where the cartilage has not yet turned to bone.

Measurements. For most mammals a series of standard measurements are provided. Unless otherwise indicated, these are taken from Bornean specimens, except for the cetaceans which follow Leatherwood and Reeves (1982). The animal is straightened but not stretched before taking each measurement. The range covers the usual variation found in adults, but not necessarily the extremes. Skull measurements are also given for some species. Although it may occasionally be possible to measure the teeth on a live mammal, most skull measurements can only be taken on museum specimens. Body measurements can be taken with a ruler or tape measure, but skulls should be measured with calipers. Depending on the type of mammal or the purpose of the study, several different measurements are taken on animals. The measurements used in this book are as follows:

Figure 1. Body measurements of land mammals other than bats.

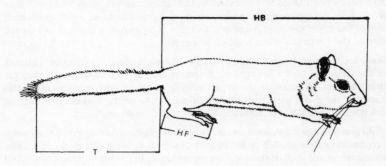

Figure 2. Measurements of bats.

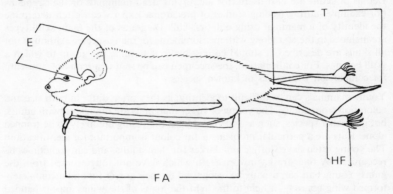

Body measurements (see Figures 1-2)

Head-and-body length (HB) — measured from the anus to the front of the nose

Tail (T) — measured to the tip of the tail excluding long fur or hairs which project beyond the end

Hind foot (HF) — from the heel to the end of the longest toe, excluding the claws

Ear length (E) — measured from the external opening to the tip

Forearm (FA) — (in bats) from the outside of the elbow to the outside of the wrist in the bent wing

Total length (TL) — (in whales and dolphins) from the front of the head to the notch in the tail flukes

Figure 3. Skull measurements of rodents.

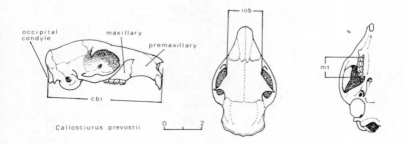

Callosciurus prevostii

Figure 4. Skull measurements of shrews.

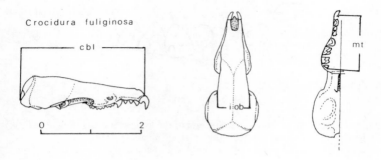

Crocidura fuliginosa

Figure 5. Skull measurements and dentition of bats.

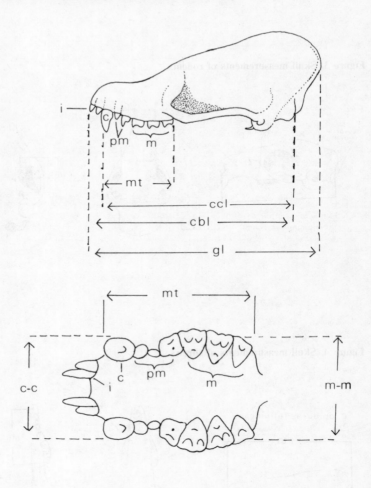

Skull Measurements (see Figures 3-5)

Greatest length (gl) — the longest distance from the back of the skull to the front, excluding the teeth

Condylobasal length (cbl) — from the back of the occipital condyles to the front of the premaxillary bone

Condylocanine length (ccl) — from the back of the occipital condyles to the front of the canines

Interorbital breadth (iob) — the least width across the top of the skull between the position of the eyes (orbits); this can sometimes be hard to define on shrews

Maxillary toothrow (mt) — the length of the upper toothrow from the back of the molars to the front of the canines (excluding the incisors); usually this is measured to the base of the canine, but for bats this extends to the front of the curve of the canine; for rodents, which have no canines, this includes only the molars and premolars (3 teeth in rats, 4 in squirrels — the tiny premolar at the front is excluded); for shrews the relationships of the teeth are unclear, and the whole toothrow is measured, including the incisor at its base.

Molar width (m-m) — the width across the outside of the upper molars (at the bases).

Canine width (c-c) — the width across the outside of the base of the canines.

Finding and studying mammals. Although mammals are generally more difficult to observe than birds, there are many different ways to see and study them. The best approach depends on the types of mammals involved and their preferred habitat. In Borneo, most mammals species occur in lowland dipterocarp rain forest, with somewhat fewer species in swamp forest or kerangas forest. Some species are restricted to higher elevations in hill or montane forest. Many species appear to survive in altered habitats, and often can be most easily seen in freshly logged and secondary forests or even plantations, where the vegetation is less dense and the visibility better. The edges between forests and plantations or gardens often support relatively high densities of animals.

During the day, monkeys, apes, some squirrels and treeshrews are found in trees, while other squirrels and larger mammals such as pigs, deer, mongooses, bears and otters are active on the ground. Many of the larger mammals are quite shy and difficult to approach closely. They need to be stalked very quietly, and a lot of luck is required to see the wary or less common species. Some animals, such as monkeys, can be gradually accustomed to a human observer, but time and patience are required. Binoculars are a very useful aid to watching many of the tree dwelling animals and are often essential to see the diagnostic features of some of the smaller squirrels.

Most other mammals, including the flying squirrels, civets, rats, mice and bats, are active mainly at night.Large terrestrial mammals such as pigs and elephants can be active at any time of day. Many mammals are less wary at night than during the day, making them easier to observe. The best way to locate them is using a headlamp or spotlight. Their eyes usually reflect a red or green glow in the light. A 30 or 50 watt spotlight is especially useful for observing animals in trees, although it is sometimes too bright for mammals that are close and scares them away. A red lamp (easily constructed by placing red cellophane over a spotlight) is less harsh and is useful for observing animals over a long period of time. Portable spotlights can be powered by a small motorcycle-sized 12V wet cell, although this must be carried carefully; dry cells, if available, are easier to use.

Mammals are most easily seen in relatively open areas. Good places to search are along rivers, in small open clearings, along wide paths or on disused logging roads. Many mammals can be located by the noise of their movements — crashing of branches, or rustling of leaves. Some species have distinctive calls, including many of the primates, some squirrels, and barking deer. With practice many of these mammals can be identified based only on the call. Calls are hard to describe in words, but an attempt has been made to do so for species where it might aid identification. Unfortunately very little is known about the calls of many of the nocturnal animals such as the flying squirrels.

Figure 6. Cage trap for catching small mammals.

Tracks of animals are often useful for study. Carefully counting and measuring tracks of some of the larger ungulates can give information on population numbers and age structure. Illustrations of typical mammal tracks are included at the back of this book.

Many of the smaller mammals need to be captured for identification or study. One of the most commonly used traps for small mammals such as rats, squirrels and treeshrews, is the cage trap (Figure 6). This can be set on the ground or tied to fallen trees, branches or lianas. Many different foods are suitable for bait, including fruits and salt fish. Small ripe bananas are one of the easiest to obtain and most effective baits. A larger version baited with raw meat or fish and set on the ground by a stream or a path can be used to catch some mustelids and viverrids.

The smallest mammals, such as shrews and ground-dwelling mice, can be caught in pit-fall traps. These consist of any smooth-sided container dug into the ground so that the edges are level with the ground. They must be deep enough that the animals can not jump out and escape. Small fences made of branches or wire mesh can be useful to guide animals into the traps. Drainage holes should be placed in the bottom so that animals do not drown in heavy rain, and the traps should be checked frequently.

Bats are particularly difficult to find and study. Because most species are small and fly at night, they are hard to identify in flight. Even experienced bat biologists can rarely identify more than a few species at a distance. As a result it is usually necessary to capture them.

One of the most effective ways to catch bats is with a "harp" trap (Figure 7). This stops the bats in flight with vertical strands of fishing line and lets them slide into a holding bag with funnel-like plastic sides. These traps should be placed across flyways such as narrow paths or small streams. Very fine nets, called mist nets, are also used to catch bats and are particularly effective with frugivorous species which have no echolocation. They have the disadvantage that many species can detect and avoid them with their sonar, while those which do get caught often rapidly escape by chewing holes in the net unless the net is closely watched. Occasionally tarsiers and small flying squirrels are caught in mist nets as well.

Figure 7. Harp trap for catching bats.

With the advent of portable electronic "bat detectors" it is possible to identify many bats in flight by their echolocation calls. Bats (except most of the fruit bats, Pteropodidae), have a sophisticated form of sonar or echolocation to find their way in the dark. They emit short pulses of sound through their mouth or nostrils and listen for the echo to learn about obstacles or food in front of them. These calls are mostly of a very high frequency (20-200 Khz) which we are unable to hear, although a few have components in the audible range. Each species of bat has a unique frequency pattern enabling it to be identified if the call can be detected. "Bat detectors" transform this sound to a form we can understand, either an audible sound or a graph on an oscilloscope or paper. In the future, when the calls of the Bornean bats have been better studied, it may be possible to include their descriptions in field guides such as this one.

Basic known habitat preferences as well as a summary of the known ecology are given for each species in the "Ecology and Habitat" section. This section includes mainly information which might be helpful in finding or identifying a mammal, or learning more about its ecology. For many species, especially the bats and other small mammals, very little is known, and the only information available is the site of capture of the few specimens that have been collected. For large mammals, which are better known, only a summary of the available information has been included. Further information may be found in the publications listed in the bibliography.

Describing the habitat preferred by a mammal presents difficulties because there are many names available to describe different sorts of forest, yet none are precisely defined. In this text, two basic divisions in forest type are described by the terms "tall" and "secondary". "Tall" means forest which shows little or no sign of disturbance in recent times. Often, such forest is referred to as "primary", meaning untouched by man, but forest which was felled or selectively logged a long time ago has a very similar appearance. "Secondary" means forest which has been totally or partially felled fairly recently, and the tree canopy is still mainly low and broken. The term "belukar" is often used within Malaysia to refer to this type of forest. The term "logged" is used for dipterocarp forest which has been recently selectively logged. "Gardens" includes land with fruit trees, shrubs and patches of secondary forest, a common habitat in rural areas. "Plantations" refers to cocoa, oil palm and rubber plantings unless otherwise stated.

Distribution of mammals

Extra-limital distribution. Although the area included in this book is confined to Borneo and its offshore islands, many species are much more widely distributed in the region. For the benefit of people working in adjacent areas who might be using this book, the known world range of each species is described. However, caution is necessary when using this book outside Borneo, as subspecies often differ considerably, and only the Bornean forms are described and illustrated here. Information on the world range has been drawn largely from published secondary sources including Honacki *et al* (1982), Lekagul and McNeely (1977), and Medway (1978). As a result, some recent records may have been inadvertently omitted, while any published errors may have been perpetuated.

A variety of terms have been used to simplify the range descriptions. "South-east Asia" includes Burma, Laos, Thailand, Cambodia, Vietnam, and Peninsular Malaysia. "Indochina" includes Laos, Cambodia (Kampuchea) and Vietnam. The major Indonesian islands are usually listed separately, but many of the smaller islands are not listed. "Philippines" includes any number of islands within the Philippine archipelago. "New Guinea" includes both Irian Jaya and Papua New Guinea.

Bornean distribution. This is given following the world distribution. For species with more than one described subspecies, the name of the Bornean form is given first followed by a description of its range. If more than one subspecies occurs in Borneo, the range of each is listed in turn. All of the place names may be found on Maps 1 or 5, or in the gazetteer at the end of the book.

For large and distinctive mammals the range is usually fairly well known, but for many of the smaller species very little information is available. In these cases it has been necessary to merely list the known locations where the species has been recorded. Most of the detailed collecting and studying has been done in Sabah and Sarawak with relatively little work in Kalimantan. It seems likely that many species will prove to be much more widely distributed than is presently realised. We hope that people will be encouraged to study mammals in other areas, to learn more about their actual distribution before they become threatened or endangered.

The information in this section has been largely drawn from Medway (1977), with additional records from more recent publications as listed in the bibliography. Some unpublished data from the Brunei Museum, the Sarawak Forest Department (on Samunsam Wildlife Sanctuary), and the Game Branch of the Sabah Forest Department (particularly recent bat records) have also been used.

Geography and vegetation of Borneo

With an area of over 700,000 square kilometres, Borneo is the third largest island in the world, stretching from about 4° south of the equator to 7° north. Politically, Borneo is divided amongst three countries: Malaysia (the states of Sabah and Sarawak), Indonesia (the provinces of West, Central, South and East Kalimantan) and Brunei (Map 1).

Large tracts of Borneo, particularly the southern and eastern regions, consist of hilly lowlands and swampy plains. The central and north-western regions are dominated by rugged mountain ranges with peaks rising to between 1000 and 2000 m above sea level. G. Kinabalu, at 4101 m, is the highest peak between the Himalayas and New Guinea.

Most of the island consists of geologically young sedimentary rocks, including sandstones, mudstones and limestones. There are some old volcanic rocks in south-eastern Sabah, but no active volcanoes. The Meratus mountains in South Kalimantan, the Schwaner mountains which straddle the boundary between inland Central and West Kalimantan, and scattered mountains in Sabah are of igneous rocks.

MAP 1 MAJOR GEOGRAPHICAL FEATURES OF BORNEO

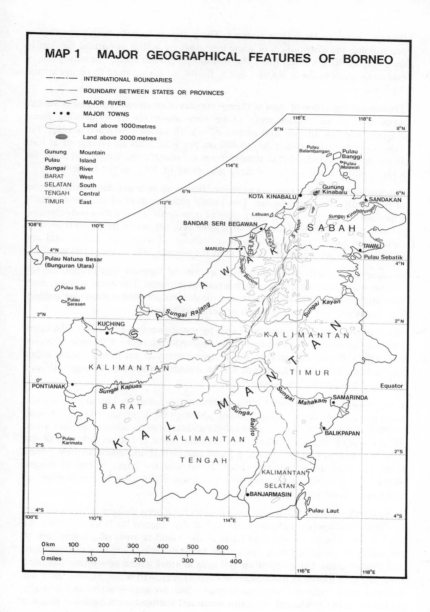

Borneo has many large river systems. These appear to have been important in determining the distribution of some mammals by acting as natural barriers to their spread. Rivers often mark the boundary between species or subspecies of mammals, such as the S. Kapuas and S. Barito, which separate the Bornean and Agile Gibbons.

The natural vegetation of most of Borneo consists of evergreen rain forest of various types. Soil characteristics seem to be very important in influencing forest composition. The amount and pattern of rainfall varies from place to place, but most areas receive between 200 to 400 cm per year, with an average of at least 10 cm in most months. Mean temperatures are roughly the same in all areas, for a given altitude, with a typical daily maximum of 30°C in the lowlands.

Tall lowland and hill forests up to about 1000 m altitude are dominated by trees of the family Dipterocarpaceae. This family includes most of the commercially important timber trees. Many other types of trees occur, along with woody climbing plants. Small flowering plants and ferns grow as epiphytes on the larger trees. This dipterocarp forest supports the highest diversity of mammals, and coastal and riverside areas are generally richer than the steeper hills in the interior.

In some areas, particularly substantial sections of Sarawak and Brunei, the soil consists mainly of coarse silica which is poor in nutrients. The forest is lower, more open and more uniform in structure, and the streams are often stained dark reddish. Few mammals live in these heath or kerangas forests.

Much of the coast of Borneo is fringed by mangrove and nipah palm. In many areas further inland, extensive freshwater swamp forests occur. Peat swamp forests, where the soil consists largely of acidic organic material, are found in some areas, especially between the S. Kapuas in West Kalimantan and the S. Tutong in Brunei. This forest supports few mammals.

Lower stature montane forest replaces dipterocarp forest on hills and mountains at an average altitude of about 1000 m, although the interface is lower on small mountains, and higher in extensive ranges and on large mountains. In some areas the division between dipterocarp and montane forest is distinct, while in others there is a more gradual reduction in forest stature with increasing altitude. Many small mammals are restricted to high altitudes on the larger mountain ranges, although their distribution in terms of habitat actually overlaps both true montane and upper dipterocarp forest.

Traditionally, most of Borneo's native peoples have been shifting cultivators, both in coastal and lowland riverine areas and in the uplands far from the coast. As a result, the vegetation in many parts of the island consists of a patchwork of essentially undisturbed forest, low stature forest in various stages of regeneration, and cleared areas. On many steep and upland areas where agriculture has been tried, the thin topsoil is inadequate to support regrowth of forest, and there are now extensive tracts of coarse lalang grass which are unproductive and virtually useless for both wildlife and Man. In some areas, attempts are being made to make such land productive again by planting exotic trees tolerant of poor conditions.

The most extensive and rapid change in Borneo's vegetation has occurred over the past 20 years or so through selective logging of the dipterocarp forests. Selective logging involves the removal of only the largest trees from the forest, but in the process many smaller trees are killed or damaged. Regeneration of selectively logged forest to a state approaching its original condition may take decades.

Permanent agriculture is practised only in the lowlands and more fertile upland valleys in Borneo. It takes many forms, ranging from wet rice paddies and small-holdings with mixed crops including fruit trees, vegetables and pepper, to large-scale plantations of cocoa, oil palm and rubber.

Future of wildlife in Borneo

The need for conservation. With the rapid rate of development in Borneo, increasing concern is being generated over future prospects for wildlife. Three main factors are potentially affecting mammals: hunting, selective logging and forest clearance.

Mammals undoubtedly have been hunted in Borneo since Man first arrived on the island. Most species have survived without adverse effects, although some may have suffered reductions in population or geographical distribution. With the advent of firearms, the opening of the forest for logging and easier access to the forest by road, hunting pressure has been increased greatly. Despite this, apart from a few localised areas, it seems that most species are not yet threatened with extinction by hunting, except for a few of the larger mammals which exist at low density and breed slowly. The species most severaly threatened in this way are the Two-horned Asian Rhinoceros, *Dicerorhinus sumatrensis,* and the Tembadau, *Bos javanicus.*

The Rhinoceros is in the most serious condition with only a small remnant breeding population in eastern Sabah, and scattered individuals elsewhere in Sabah, and probably in interior Borneo. All of these are under threat from poaching. The horn and other parts of the body fetch very high prices on the black market for medicine in Chinese shops throughout Asia. The Tembadau is more numerous, but breeds slowly and is a prime target for meat. Its habitat is being opened up and consequently becoming more accessible for hunting.

The Asian Elephant, *Elephas maximus,* although not threatened by poaching in Borneo, is restricted to a very small part of the island, much of which has been allocated for permanent agriculture.

Selective logging is widespread throughout Borneo and affects large numbers of mammals. Apart from the immediate loss of shelter and food sources for small mammals, and the disturbance caused during the actual logging, the long-term effects are not known. General observations over the past five years in Sabah suggest that most of the larger species can still survive in logged forests, although the densities may be reduced due to loss of food and other requirements.

Forest clearance for agriculture and other purposes is a much more serious threat for mammals and other wildlife. Although certain animals make use of plantations, most remain tied to neighbouring patches of forest and cannot survive without them. Clearing of land and change is an inevitable consequence of an increasing human population, but the opportunity to conserve wild populations of all of Borneo's mammal species still exists. Adequately large areas of forest need to be set aside in the form of gazetted reserves. Already such areas have been created in most regions of Borneo. Many are quite large, and if adequately managed, will enable future generations to observe and enjoy the mammals of Borneo.

Parks and Reserves in Borneo. Reserves have been created throughout Borneo, but only a few are developed for visitors and readily accessible. Those which are of the greatest interest to people studying mammals are described briefly below:

Sabah: For information on Parks contact the Sabah Parks Office, P. O. Box 626, Kota Kinabalu. Other Reserves and Sanctuaries are administered by the Chief Game Warden, Forest Department, P. O. Box 311, Sandakan. Sepilok and Kinabalu are open to visitors, while the remainder have been set aside for wildlife but are not readily accessible to the public.

Sepilok Forest Reserve. (4,300 ha). This area of tall lowland dipterocarp forest in eastern Sabah is the location of an Orang-utan rehabilitation centre run by the Sabah Forest Department. Young Orang-utans are trained to live in the forest and released to join the wild population. Most mammal species characteristic of lowland forest can be found here. No accomodation is available but the Reserve is easily accessible by road from Sandakan town.

Kinabalu Park. (75,000 ha). All of the montane mammals known from Borneo can be found here including a number of locally endemic species. Some lowland mammals can be found in the lower areas of the Park, such as Poring. A wide range of accomodation is available at the Park for visitors, who should contact the Sabah Parks office in advance for bookings.

Tabin Wildlife Reserve. (120,521 ha). The only protected area in Borneo with a known breeding population of the Asian Two-horned or Sumatran Rhinoceros, as well as Elephants and other large mammals.

Danum Valley Conservation Area. (42,755 ha). A large area of undisturbed lowland and hill dipterocarp forest with a field studies centre for scientific researchers.

Crocker Range National Park. (139,919 ha). Hill and montane forest with many montane species endemic to Borneo.

Gomantong Forest Reserve. (3,600 ha). Limestone caves with colonies of over one million swiftlets and two million bats.

Kulamba Wildlife Reserve. (20,682 ha). Coastal swamp forest with Tembadau and large colonies of Flying Foxes.

Brunei: At present, there are no legally established conservation areas, but one area — Tasek Merimbun — has been proposed as a National Park. This is an inland lake with many small mammal species in the surrounding forest. Research is being conducted by the Curator of Natural History, Brunei Museum.

Sarawak: Parks and Sanctuaries are administered by the National Parks and Wildlife Office, Forest Department, Jalan Gartak, Kuching. Niah and Bako have facilities for visitors, but the remaining areas described below are not easily accessible to the public.

Niah National Park. (3,100 ha). There are many limestone caves in Borneo containing large colonies of bats. Niah is one of the largest and most accessible, with an estimated 300,000 bats. The caves are also of archaeological and cultural interest. Hostel accomodation is available nearby.

Bako National Park. (2,700 ha). An area of great botanical interest, this Park attracts many visitors because of its proximity to Kuching. Several species of monkeys may be seen in the Park, and small caves in cliffs hold some unusual bats. Accomodation must be booked in advance in Kuching.

Gunung Mulu National Park. (52,900 ha). An important conservation area with a wide range of mammals in lowland and montane habitats. Spectacular limestone hills and caves, but few large mammals.

Lanjak-Entimau Wildlife Sanctuary. (168,000 ha). One of the largest protected areas in Malaysia, important for Orang-utans.

Samunsam Wildlife Sanctuary. (6,100 ha). An area of nipah, mangrove and lowland forest notable for Proboscis Monkeys and many small mammals.

Kalimantan: There are over seventy existing and proposed Parks and Reserves in Kalimantan, most of which are remote and can be visited only with very great difficulty. Some of the most important conservation areas include (F.A.O., 1981):

Sungai Kayan — Sungai Mentarang. (1.6 million ha; proposed). In interior East Kalimantan.

Kutai. (about 200,000 ha). In East Kalimantan, with parts damaged by exploitation.

Pleihari Martapura. (30,000 ha). In South Kalimantan, part of the Meratus Range.

Tanjung Puting. (300,000 ha). In Central Kalimantan, coastal swamp and dryland forest with Orang-utans and Proboscis Monkeys.

Bukit Raya. (170,000 ha). In Central Kalimantan, includes the highest mountain peak (2,278 m) in southern Borneo.

Gunung Palung. (30,000 ha). In West Kalimantan.

Gunung Bentung and Karimun. (600,000 ha). In West Kalimantan, adjacent to Sarawak's Lanjak-Entimau Wildlife Sanctuary.

Glossary

adult — sexually mature

alveolus — the socket of a tooth

anterior — towards the front

arboreal — living in trees

arthropod — invertebrate animals with a hard, jointed exoskeleton, including insects, spiders and crustaceans

bell-hole — small rounded indentations in the roof of a cave

buff — very pale yellowish-brown

bukit (Bt.) — (Malay) hill

canines — pointed, usually long teeth behind the incisors (see Figure 5)

canine width (c-c) — width across the outside of the base of the canines (see Figure 5)

cheek teeth — the chewing teeth; the molars and premolars combined

condylobasal length (cbl) — length of the skull from the back of the occipital condyles to the front of the premaxillae (see Figures 3 - 5)

condylocanine length (ccl) — length of the skull from the back of the occipital condyles to the front of the canines (see Figures 3 - 5)

cusp — a raised point on a tooth

deciduous teeth — the first set of "milk" or "baby" teeth which are shed before the permanent teeth grow in

decurved — curved downwards

dental formula — a shorthand notation for indicating the arrangement and number of teeth (see page 17)

digit — finger or toe

diastema — a natural gap between adjacent teeth

diurnal — active during daylight

dorsal — relating to the back or upper surface

feral — domestic animals which have escaped from captivity and breed in the wild state

forearm (FA) — the part of the arm between the elbow and the wrist (see Figure 2)

greatest length (gl) — the greatest length from the back to the front of a skull excluding the teeth

grizzled — dark coloration with white or pale specks

gua — (Malay) cave

guard hairs — hairs which are longer than the main coat of hairs

gunung (G.) — (Malay) mountain

hallux — big toe on the hind foot

incisors — the front teeth (see Figure 5)

infant — baby animal entirely dependent on its mother

interfemoral membrane — (in bats) membrane between the hind legs, often enclosing the tail

interorbital breadth (io) — the least width across the top of the skull between the position of the eyes or orbits (see Figures 3 - 4)

juvenile — young animal, partially or totally independent of its mother

maxilla — the bone in the skull which supports all of the upper teeth except the incisors

maxillary toothrow (mt) — the length of the upper toothrow from the back of the molars to the front of the canines (see page 21)

metacarpal — bone between the wrist and the finger bones (see Figure 12)

molars — the relatively large posterior cheek teeth, distinguished from the premolars by not having deciduous precursors or "baby" teeth (see Figure 5)

32

molar width (m-m) — the width across the outside of the upper molars at the bases (see Figure 5)

muzzle — the part of an animal's face in front of its eyes

nocturnal — active only or mainly at night

olive — a greenish-brown colour

orbit — the area in the skull where the eyes are

palate — the upper part (roof) of the mouth

phalanx (plural **phalanges**) — finger bones

posterior — towards the rear

prehensile — referring to a tail with a tip that can curl and grasp branches

premaxilla — the small bones at the front of the skull which support the incisors — vary greatly in size and shape, especially within the bats

premolars — teeth between the molars and the canines which are preceded by "baby" teeth which are shed (see Figure 5)

pulau (P.) — (Malay) island

rostrum — the narrower part of the skull in front of the position of the eyes

sungai (S.) — (Malay) river

tanjung (Tg.) — (Malay) promontory or peninsula

teluk (T.) — (Malay) bay

terrestrial — active on the ground

tragus — a flap of skin inside the ear of most bats

ulu — (Malay) upper reaches of a river system

underparts — the throat, chest, belly and insides of the legs

upperparts — the back or "top" of a mammal including the outsides of the legs.

List of Abbreviations

HB — Head and Body length
T — Tail length
TL — Total length
FA — Hind foot length (excluding claws)
Wt — Weight
gl — Greatest length of skull
cbl — Condylobasal length of skull
ccl — Condylocanine length of skull
io — Interorbital breadth
mt — Maxillary toothrow length
c-c — canine width
m-m — molar width
Bt. — Bukit (Hill)
G. — Gunung (Mountain)
P. — Pulau (Island)
S. — Sungai (River)
T. — Teluk (Bay)
Tg. — Tanjung (Promontory or Peninsula)

ha — hectare (= 100 x 100 m or 2.47 acres)
km — kilometre (1000 m)
m— metre (= 100 cm)

Note: unless otherwise stated, all measurements are in millimetres (mm), and all weights are in grams (g) although **the scale bars on plates and figures are in centimetres (cm).**

34

Plate 1

MOONRAT, LESSER GYMNURE AND SHREWS

1. MOONRAT *Echinosorex gymnurus*   p. 156
    Predominantly white; nocturnal.

2. LESSER GYMNURE *Hylomys suillus*   p. 156
    Mountains; very short tail.

3. SAVI'S PIGMY SHREW *Suncus etruscus*   p. 159
    Very small; tail short; 9 upper teeth;
    skull (cbl) less than 15 mm.

4. BLACK SHREW *Suncus ater*   p. 158
    Small; 9 upper teeth; skull (cbl) about 21 mm.

5. HOUSE SHREW *Suncus murinus*   p. 157
    Medium size; tail thick at base; often lives in houses.

6. SOUTH-EAST ASIAN WHITE-TOOTHED SHREW   p. 159
    Crocidura fuliginosa
    Small; tail long; 8 upper teeth; skull (cbl) 21-25 mm.
    a) *C. f. foetida.* Tail shorter than body; short hair.
    b) *C. f. kelabit.* Tail longer than body.
    c) *C. f. baluensis* — not illustrated. Tail shorter
    than body; long hair).

7. SUNDA SHREW *Crocidura monticola*   p. 159
    Very small; tail length moderate; 8 upper teeth;
    skull (cbl) 15-17.5 mm.

8. HIMALAYAN WATER SHREW   p. 160
    Chimarrogale himalayica
    Feet with a fringe of short, stiff hairs;
    lives in mountain streams

Plate 1

Plate 2

TREESHREWS

(see also plate 5)

1. SLENDER TREESHREW *Tupaia gracilis* p. 163
Tail long; hind foot 37-43 mm.

2. LESSER TREESHREW *Tupaia minor* p. 163
Hind foot 29-34 mm.

3. COMMON TREESHREW *Tupaia glis* p. 161
Lowlands and hills; upperparts plain; tail hairs with pale and dark bands.

4. PENTAIL TREESHREW *Ptilocercus lowii* p. 161
Nocturnal; feather-like hairs on tail.

Plate 2

1

2

3

4

0   4

Karen Phillipp

Plate 3

TREESHREWS
(see also Plate 5)

Plate 3

Plate 4

TREESHREWS
(see also Plate 5)

1. LARGE TREESHREW *Tupaia tana*   p. 164
    Large size; long muzzle; colour varies with subspecies.
    (T. t. paitana illustrated)

2. PAINTED TREESHREW *Tupaia picta*   p. 164
    Smaller; muzzle shorter; colour varies with subspecies.
    (T. p. picta illustrated)

3. RUDDY TREESHREW *Tupaia splendidula*   p. 162
    Upperparts reddish or dull brown; tail hairs pure dark red.
    (T. s. carimatae illustrated).

Plate 4

Plate 5

TREESHREWS: DORSAL VIEW

1. LESSER TREESHREW *Tupaia minor* p. 163
2. SLENDER TREESHREW *Tupaia gracilis* p. 163
3. COMMON TREESHREW *Tupaia glis* p. 161
4. MOUNTAIN TREESHREW *Tupaia montana* p. 162
5. PAINTED TREESHREW *Tupaia picta* p. 164
6. RUDDY TREESHREW *Tupaia splendidula* p. 162
7. STRIPED TREESHREW *Tupaia dorsalis* p. 164
8. LARGE TREESHREW *Tupaia tana* p. 164
   a) *T. t. paitana*
   b) *T. t. nitidus*
   c) *T. t. chrysura*

Plate 5

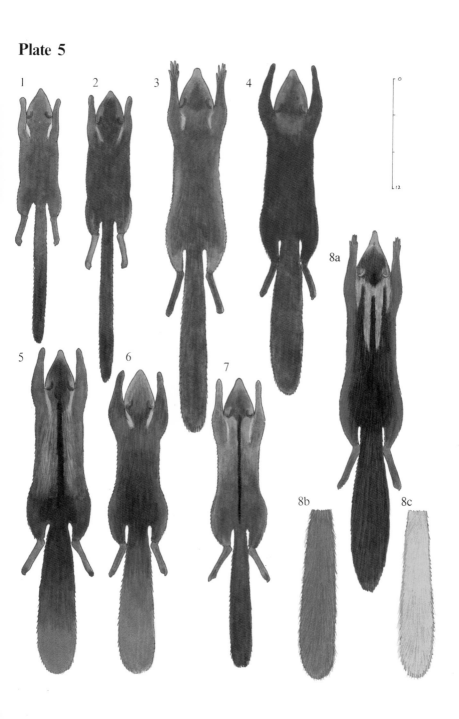

Plate 6

FRUIT BATS

Medium to large species with distinct tails.

1. SHORT-NOSED FRUIT BAT *Cynopterus brachyotis* (male) p. 173
   a) roosting (x ½), b) head. Forearm 55-65.
   White rims to ears; two pairs of lower incisors;
   female less brightly coloured.

2. HORSFIELD'S FRUIT BAT *Cynopterus horsfieldi* (male) p. 174
   Forearm 68-76. White rims to ears; cheek teeth square
   with cusps or ridges. Collar of female more yellowish.

3. GREATER SHORT-NOSED FRUIT BAT p. 174
   Cynopterus sphinx (male)
   Forearm 65-76. White rims to ears; cheek teeth rounded.
   Collar of female more yellowish; fur greyer.

4. DUSKY FRUIT BAT *Penthetor lucasii* p. 175
   a) head b) roosting (x ½). Forearm 57-62.
   No bright collar; one pair of lower incisors.

5. DAYAK FRUIT BAT *Dyacopterus spadiceus* p. 176
   Forearm 77-81. Large; thick head and short muzzle;
   large cheek teeth.

6. GEOFFROY'S ROUSETTE *Rousettus amplexicaudatus* p. 171
   a) back (x ½), b) head of female; male similar to 7b.
   Forearm 78-87. Muzzle moderately long;
   claw on second digit; wings not joined.

7. BARE-BACKED ROUSETTE *Rousettus spinalatus* p. 171
   a) back (x ½), b) head of male; female similar to 6b.
   Forearm 83-89. Wings joined down middle of back.

Plate 6

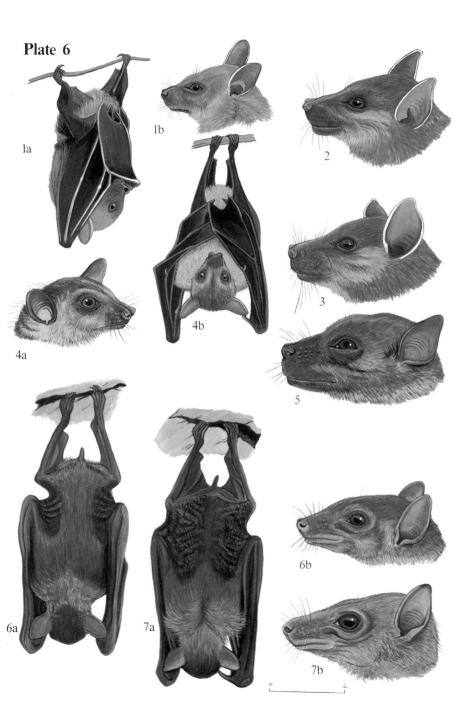

1a

1b

2

4a

4b

3

5

6a

7a

6b

7b

Plate 7

FRUIT AND NECTAR BATS

The first five species are fairly small and lack visible tails; the remaining three species eat nectar and have long muzzles and long tongues.

1. SPOTTED-WINGED FRUIT BAT *Balionycteris maculata* p. 177
   a) resting (x ½), b) head. Forearm 40-45.
   Pale spots on wings and head.

2. BLACK-CAPPED FRUIT BAT *Chironax melanocephala* p. 177
   a) resting (x ½), b) head. Forearm 43-46.
   Dark brown or black head;
   pale underparts usually with yellow tufts;
   two pairs of lower incisors.

3. GREY FRUIT BAT *Aethalops alecto* p. 178
   a) head, b) resting (x ½). Forearm 42-46. Muzzle narrow;
   interfemoral membrane thickly furred;
   one pair of lower incisors.

4. TAILLESS FRUIT BAT *Megaerops ecaudatus* p. 176
   Forearm 51-58. Muzzle short; no tail;
   interfemoral membrane thinly furred;
   one pair of lower incisors.

5. WHITE-COLLARED FRUIT BAT *Megaerops wetmorei* p. 176
   Forearm 46-51. Muzzle short; white tufts on side of neck
   (may sometimes be lacking).

6. CAVE NECTAR BAT *Eonycteris spelaea* p. 178
   Forearm 62-70. Muzzle narrow; no claw on second digit.

7. GREATER NECTAR BAT *Eonycteris major* p. 178
   Forearm 71-80. Muzzle long and narrow;
   no claw on second digit.

8. LONG-TONGUED NECTAR BAT *Macroglossus minimus* p. 179
   a) feeding on banana flower (x ½), b) head profile.
   Forearm 38-42. Muzzle long; tongue narrow; small.

Plate 7

Plate 8

FLYING FOXES AND FREE-TAILED BATS

Flying foxes are the largest bats in the world — they are drawn at half the scale of other bats to fit on the page.

1. LARGE FLYING FOX *Pteropus vampyrus*   p. 172
   a) hanging from branch (x ¼), b) head (x ½).
   Forearm 185-200. Large; orange collar.

2. ISLAND FLYING FOX *Pteropus hypomelanus*   p. 172
   a) hanging from branch (x ¼), b) head (x ½).
   Forearm about 120. Medium large; usually on islands.

Free-tailed bats can be distinguished from other insectivorous bats by the thickened tail which protrudes from the end of the interfemoral membrane.

3. WRINKLE-LIPPED BAT *Tadarida plicata*   p. 222
   a) roosting in cave (x ½), b) head. Forearm 40-44.
   Ears joined over head; skull relatively small;
   an extra small upper premolar.

4. FREE-TAILED BAT *Tadarida mops*   p. 221
   Forearm 43-46. Ears joined over head;
   skull large with only one upper premolar.

5. NAKED BAT *Cheiromeles torquatus*   p. 220
   a) head, b) hanging from branch (x ½). Forearm 74-83.
   Almost hairless; ears separate.

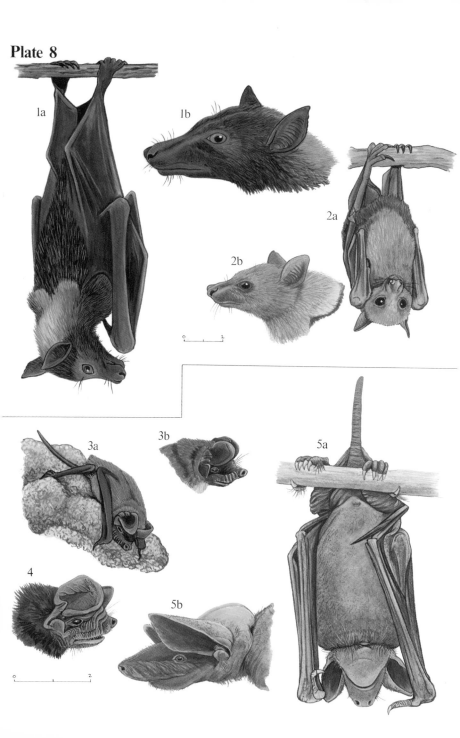

Plate 8

Plate 9

SHEATH-TAILED BATS

These can be separated from other bats by form of the tail which protrudes from the middle of the interfemoral membrane.

1. LESSER SHEATH-TAILED BAT *Emballonura monticola*   p. 182
   a) roosting (x ½), b) head. Forearm 43-45. Small;
   dark brown; balances on wrists.

2. GREATER SHEATH-TAILED BAT *Emballonura alecto*   p. 182
   Forearm 45-48. Like Lesser Sheath-tailed Bat,
   but slightly larger (see text).

3. POUCHED TOMB BAT *Taphozous saccolaimus*   p. 183
   a) head profile, b) chin, c) roosting in house (x ½),
   d) stretched wings (not to scale). Forearm 71-78.
   Wings very white; no wing (radiometacarpal) pouch;
   chin pouch in both sexes.

4. BLACK-BEARDED TOMB BAT *Taphozous melanopogon*   p. 184
   a) at roost on rock (x ½), b) head profile,
   c) chin of female, d) chin of male. Forearm 60-63.
   Wing pouch well developed; chin furred in both sexes,
   sometimes with a black beard; tail thickened at tip.

5. LONG-WINGED TOMB BAT *Taphozous longimanus*   p. 184
   a) head profile, b) female chin, c) male chin.
   Forearm 54-58. Wing pouch well developed in both sexes;
   chin naked, with a distinct pouch in males; tail tapered at tip.

Plate 9

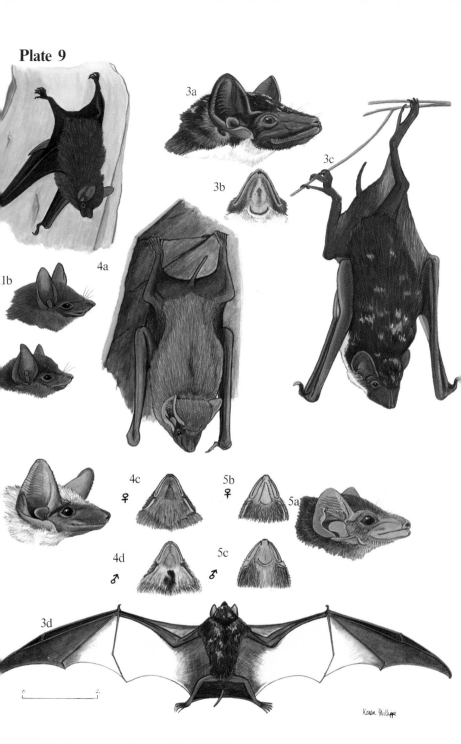

Karen Phillips

Plate 10

HORSESHOE BATS

Profile of noseleaf drawn beside each face. See Figure 19 for diagram of typical noseleaf and its parts.

All species on this page lack lateral lappets at base of sella.

1. PHILIPPINE HORSESHOE BAT *Rhinolophus philippinensis*
    a) wings spread (not to scale), b) head. Forearm 48-53.   p. 191
    Ears very long; sella long with cup-like base.

2. CREAGH'S HORSESHOE BAT *Rhinolophus creaghi*   p. 190
    Forearm 46-51. Conical tuft of hairs instead of
    connecting process.

3. ACUMINATE HORSESHOE BAT *Rhinolophus acuminatus*
    Forearm 48-50. Connecting process pointed.   p. 190

4. ARCUATE HORSESHOE BAT *Rhinolophus arcuatus*   p. 189
    Forearm 46-48. Sella broad; connecting process rounded,
    originating at tip of sella.

5. BORNEAN HORSESHOE BAT *Rhinolophus borneensis*   p. 189
    Forearm 40-44. Moderately small.

6. LEAST HORSESHOE BAT *Rhinolophus pusillus*   p. 189
    Forearm 37-40. Very small.

7. INTERMEDIATE HORSESHOE BAT *Rhinolophus affinis* p. 190
    Forearm 49-54. Sella narrow; connecting process rounded,
    originating from back of sella.

Plate 10

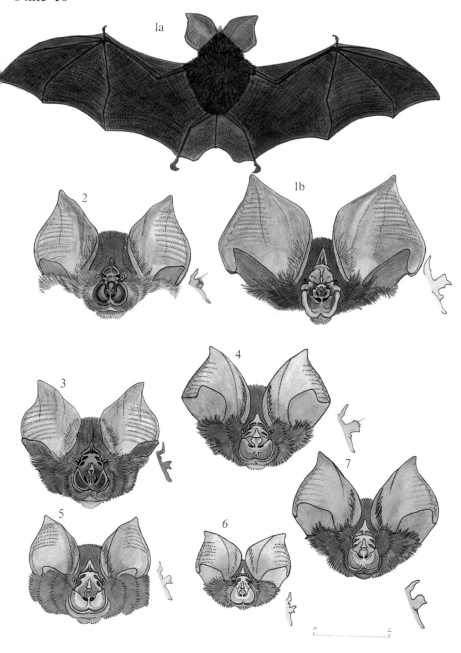

1a

1b

2

3

4

5

6

7

0   2

Plate 11

HORSESHOE BATS, HOLLOW-FACED BAT AND FALSE VAMPIRE

1. GREAT WOOLLY HORSESHOE BAT *Rhinolophus luctus*
   Forearm 63-67. Lateral lappets at base of sella;   p. 192
   noseleaf and fur dark; large.

2. LESSER WOOLLY HORSESHOE BAT *Rhinolophus sedulus*
   a) head, b) hanging from branch (x ½). Forearm 40-44.   p. 191
   Lateral lappets at base of sella; small and dark.

3. TREFOIL HORSESHOE BAT *Rhinolophus trifoliatus*   p. 191
   Forearm 47-52. Lateral lappets at base of sella; fur pale;
   noseleaf and ears yellowish.

4. HOLLOW-FACED BAT *Nycteris javanica*   p. 185
   a) head, b) interfemoral membrane and tail.
   Forearm 46-51. Ears large and separate; deep groove in
   centre of face; tail very long with T-shaped tip.

5. LESSER FALSE VAMPIRE *Megaderma spasma*   p. 185
   a) head, b) interfemoral membrane. Forearm 54-61.
   Ears large, joined at base; tall noseleaf with convex sides;
   no tail.

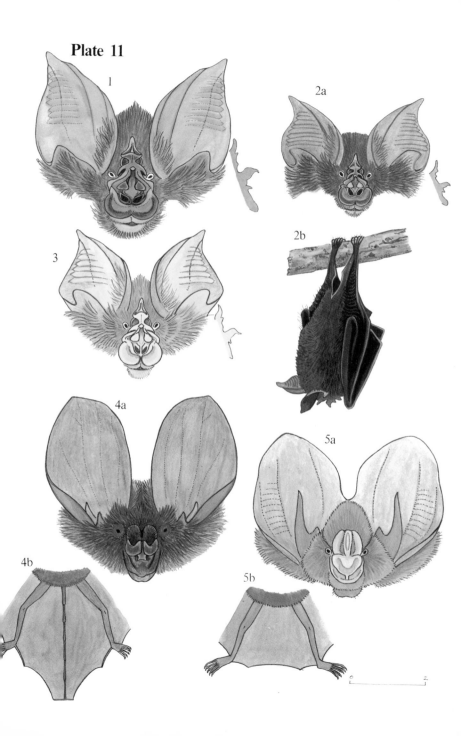

Plate 11

Plate 12

ROUNDLEAF BATS

1. DIADEM ROUNDLEAF BAT *Hipposideros diadema*   p. 197
   a) head, b) female roosting with young (x ½),
   c) male with wings spread (not to scale). Forearm 76-87.
   Very large; 3-4 lateral leaflets; pale spots on shoulder.

2. INTERMEDIATE ROUNDLEAF BAT *Hipposideros larvatus*
   Forearm 56-64. 3 lateral leaflets.   p. 196

3. DAYAK ROUNDLEAF BAT *Hipposideros dyacorum*   p. 194
   Forearm 38-42. No lateral leaflets; noseleaf dark; ears triangular.

4. DUSKY ROUNDLEAF BAT *Hipposideros ater*   p. 193
   Forearm 39-43. No lateral leaflets; noseleaf pinkish;
   internarial septum slightly swollen at base, narrow in middle;
   ears small, rounded.

5. ASHY ROUNDLEAF BAT *Hipposideros cineraceus*   p. 194
   Forearm 36-41. No lateral leaflets; internarial septum
   swollen in middle; ears large and rounded.

6. BICOLORED ROUNDLEAF BAT *Hipposideros bicolor*   p. 194
   Forearm 45-48. No lateral leaflets; internarial septum
   fairly uniform width; ears large; long forearm.

Plate 12

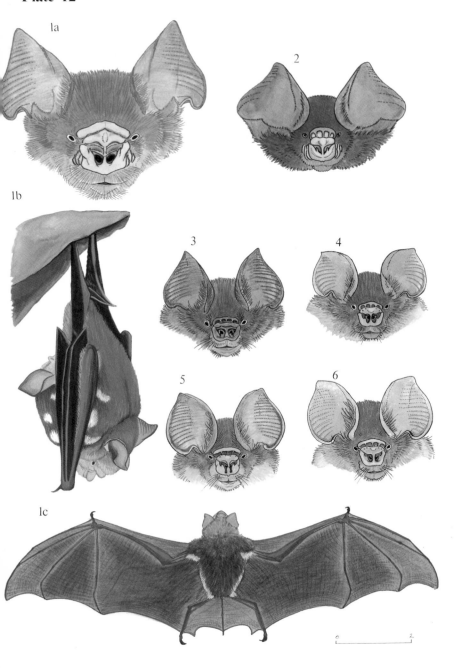

Plate 13

ROUNDLEAF BATS

1. COX'S ROUNDLEAF BAT *Hipposideros coxi*   p. 196
   Forearm 53-55. Two lateral leaflets; noseleaf very large.

2. RIDLEY'S ROUNDLEAF BAT *Hipposideros ridleyi*   p. 195
   Forearm 47-49. No lateral leaflets; noseleaf and ears large;
   disk-like internarial septum.

3. CANTOR'S ROUNDLEAF BAT *Hipposideros galeritus*   p. 196
   Forearm 47-51. Two lateral leaflets; intermediate noseleaf
   wider than posterior leaf; tail over 30.

4. FAWN ROUNDLEAF BAT *Hipposideros cervinus*   p. 195
   a) head, b) roosting in cave. Forearm 44-50.
   Two lateral leaflets; intermediate noseleaf narrower than
   posterior leaf; tail 21-28.

5. LEAST ROUNDLEAF BAT *Hipposideros sabanus*   p. 195
   Forearm 34-37. Very small; no lateral leaflets;
   no supporting septa on posterior leaf.
   (Note: colour based on old specimen — may have faded.)

6. LESSER TAILLESS ROUNDLEAF BAT *Coelops robinsoni*
   a) head, b) legs and interfemoral membrane.   p. 197
   Forearm 34-37. Anterior noseleaf forms two lobes;
   lateral leaflets expanded forwards; no tail.
   (Note: colour based on old specimen).

Plate 13

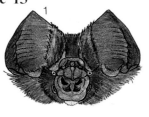

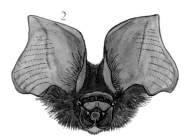

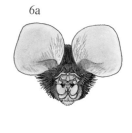

0 _____ 2

Plate 14

WOOLLY BATS

Woolly bats can all be readily recognized by the funnel-shaped ears with a long pointed tragus; long woolly fur; six upper and lower cheek teeth.

1. PAPILLOSE WOOLLY BAT *Kerivoula papillosa*   p. 215
    a) wings spread (not to scale), b) head,
    c) roosting (x ½). Forearm 38-49. Large.

2. SMALL WOOLLY BAT *Kerivoula intermedia*   p. 216
    a) head, b) roosting against tree trunk (x ½).
    Forearm 27-31. Small; uniform orange-brown; ears small;
    premolars rounded; weight 3-4g.

3. LEAST WOOLLY BAT *Kerivoula minuta*   p. 216
    Forearm 25-29. Like Small Woolly Bat,
    but smaller — weight 1.9-2.3g.

4. CLEAR-WINGED WOOLLY BAT *Kerivoula pellucida*   p. 215
    Forearm 29-32. Pale bases to fur; semi-translucent wings;
    ears very long.

5. HARDWICKE'S WOOLLY BAT *Kerivoula hardwickii*   p. 215
    Forearm 32-34. Dark bases to greyish fur;
    ears moderately long.

6, WHITEHEAD'S WOOLLY BAT *Kerivoula whiteheadi*   p. 216
    Forearm 28-29. Small; whitish below; premolars elongate.

7. GILDED GROOVE-TOOTHED BAT *Phoniscus atrox*   p. 217
    a) head, b) resting on tree (x ½). Forearm 31-33.
    Tragus white; canine grooved; hairs banded,
    with black centres and golden tips.

8. FROSTED GROOVED-TOOTHED BAT *Phoniscus jagorii* p. 217
    Forearm 37-39. Tragus white; hairs banded black and white
    (colour based on type description).

Plate 14

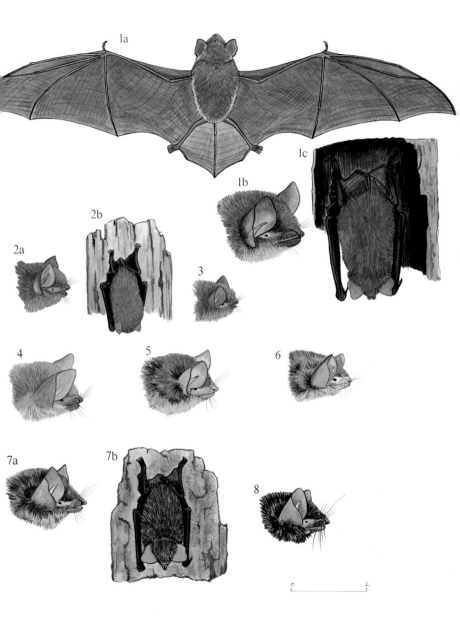

Plate 15

TUBE-NOSED AND BENT-WINGED BATS

Tube-nosed bats have elongate nostrils, rounded ears and a long pointed tragus.

1. HAIRY-WINGED BAT *Harpiocephalus harpia*   p. 214
    a) roosting (x ½), b) head. Forearm about 48. Large;
    bright orange; wing and tail membranes covered in
    short hairs. May be two species — see text.

2. BRONZED TUBE-NOSED BAT *Murina aenea*   p. 213
    a) roosting (x ½), b) head. Forearm 35-38.
    Fur with orange-brown tips; belly dark.

3. LESSER TUBE-NOSED BAT *Murina suilla*   p. 214
    a) roosting (x ½), b) head. Forearm 28-31.
    Small; fur without shiny tips.

4. GILDED TUBE-NOSED BAT *Murina rozendaali*   p. 213
    Forearm 31-34. Fur with golden tips; belly whitish.

5. ORANGE TUBE-NOSED BAT *Murina cyclotis*   p. 213
    Forearm 34-41. Pale orange and grey; moderately large;
    membranes not especially hairy.

Bent-winged bats have a distinctive wing shape (8c) with a very long last digit on
the third finger. The species are distinguished mainly by measurements (see text
for further details).

6. SMALL BENT-WINGED BAT *Miniopterus pusillus*   p. 219
    Forearm 40-43, skull (cbl) 12.8-13.3.
    Relatively short skull and long forearm.

7. MEDIUM BENT-WINGED BAT *Miniopterus medius*   p. 219
    Forearm 41-42, skull (cbl) 13.8-14.5.

8. LESSER BENT-WINGED BAT *Miniopterus australis*   p. 220
    a) head, b) roosting in a cave (x ½),
    c) wing (not to scale). Forearm 36-39, skull (cbl) 13.5-14.0.
    M. a. witkampi (illustrated). Forearm 35-37,
    skull (cbl) 11.8-12.6. *M. a. paululus* (not illustrated).

9. COMMON BENT-WINGED BAT *Miniopterus schriebersi* p. 219
    Forearm 44-49, skull (cbl) 15.1-16.0.

10. LARGE BENT-WINGED BAT *Miniopterus magnater*   p. 219
    a) head, b) roosting in cave (x ½). Forearm 47-52,
    skull (cbl) 15.8-16.8. Head wider than Common Bent-winged Bat.

Plate 15

Plate 16

MYOTIS BATS

Myotis can be recognized by their distinctive ear shapes with a tapered, bent tragus and, usually, 3 upper and lower cheek teeth, though the front one is often very small and inconspicuous. The hind foot and associated membrane is shown for each species as it is important for identification.

1. WHISKERED MYOTIS *Myotis muricola*   p. 201
   a) roosting in banana leaf (x ½), b) head, c) hind foot.
   Forearm 33-3737. Feet small; wing attached at base of toes;
   second premolar usually not especially reduced.

2. BLACK MYOTIS *Myotis ater*   p. 202
   a) head, b) hind foot. Forearm 40-43. Feet small;
   fur dark, often with golden belly; second premolar
   very small and displaced inwards.

3. LARGE BROWN MYOTIS *Myotis montivagus*   p. 202
   a) head, ¦b) hind foot. Forearm 42-45. Feet small;
   large skull.

4. RIDLEY'S MYOTIS *Myotis ridleyi*   p. 203
   a) head, b) hind foot. Forearm 27-32. Small,
   dark and heavy (4-6 g); only two premolars.

5. SMALL-TOOTHED MYOTIS *Myotis siligorensis*   p. 202
   a) head, b) hind foot. Forearm 30-33.
   Small and light (2-3g); three premolars.

6. PALLID LARGE-FOOTED MYOTIS *Myotis macrotarsus* p. 204
   a) roosting in cave (x ½), b) hind foot, c) head.
   Forearm 45-49. Feet very large; white and pale grey fur.

7. GREY LARGE-FOOTED MYOTIS *Myotis adversus*   p. 204
   a) head, b) hind foot. Forearm 39-40. Feet large;
   wing attached at ankle; second premolar not displaced inwards.

8. HASSELT'S LARGE-FOOTED MYOTIS *Myotis hasseltii*   p. 204
   a) head, b) hind foot. Forearm about 37. Feet large;
   wing attached at ankle; second upper premolar displaced
   inwards so first and third premolars are touching.

9. HORSFIELD'S MYOTIS *Myotis horsfieldii*   p. 203
   a) roosting in cave (x ½), b) hind foot, c) head.
   Forearm 35-38. Feet large; wing attached at side of foot.

Plate 16

Plate 17

PIPISTRELLES

All species have two upper and lower premolars, but anterior upper premolar is often quite reduced. Skull characters are often necessary to confirm identifications — see text.

1. JAVAN PIPISTRELLE *Pipistrellus javanicus*   p. 205
    Forearm 34-36. Tragus narrow but rounded at tip;
    anterior upper premolar not especially reduced.

2. LEAST PIPISTRELLE *Pipistrellus tenuis*   p. 205
    a) roosting (x ½), b) head. Forearm 29-32.
    Tragus narrow; small.

3. WOOLLY PIPISTRELLE *Pipistrellus petersi*   p. 206
    Forearm 40-42. Fur long and woolly; muzzle narrow.

4. NARROW-WINGED PIPISTRELLE *Pipistrellus stenopterus*
    Forearm 38-42. Fur short; muzzle broad; fifth finger short. p. 208

5. COPPERY PIPISTRELLE *Pipistrellus cuprosus*   p. 207
    a) roosting (x½), b) head
    Forearm 34-36. Fur with black bases and coppery tips;
    buff rims to ears.

6. DARK BROWN PIPISTRELLE *Pipistrellus ceylonicus*   p. 206
    a) roosting (x½), b) head
    Forearm about 38. Fur uniform dark brown; broad tragus;
    large skull.

7. RED-BROWN PIPISTRELLE *Pipistrellus kitcheneri*   p. 206
    a) roosting (x½) b) head
    Forearm 35-38. Fur red-brown with blackish bases
    broad tragus.

8. WHITE-WINGED PIPISTRELLE *Pipistrellus vordermanni* p. 209
    a) head, b) wings outstretched (x½)
    Forearm about 30. Ears large with broad tragus;
    wings whitish.

Plate 17

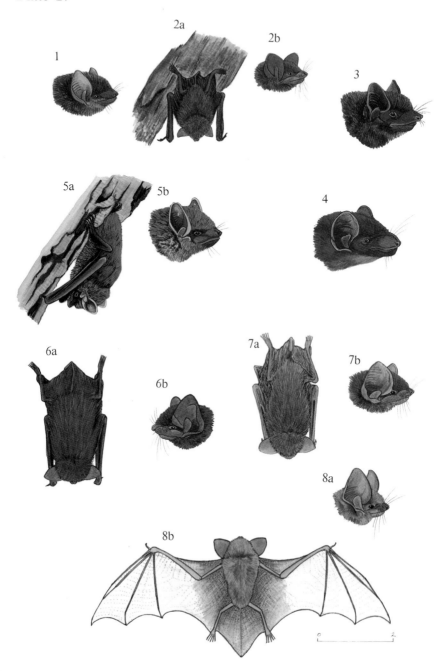

Plate 18

OTHER COMMON BATS

1. GREATER BAMBOO BAT *Tylonycteris robustula* p. 211
   a) emerging from bamboo (x ½), b) head, c) thumb pad,
   d) foot pad. Forearm 26-30. Head very flat;
   large round thumb and foot pads; fur shiny dark brown.

2. LESSER BAMBOO BAT *Tylonycteris pachypus* p. 211
   Forearm 24-28. As above species, but fur fluffier
   and redder.

3. THICK-THUMBED PIPISTRELLE *Glischropus tylopus* p. 209
   a) head, b) thumb pad, c) foot pad. Forearm 28-30.
   Small pink thumb and foot pads; head rounded; fur fluffy

4. NARROW-WINGED BROWN BAT *Philetor brachypterus* p. 209
   Forearm 30-36. Like a pipistrelle, but only one upper
   premolar; fifth finger short; upper incisor long and narrow.

5. YELLOW HOUSE BAT *Scotophilus kuhlii* p. 212
   a) head, b) roosting in attic. Forearm 47-52. Only one
   pair of upper incisors which are large and conical.

6. LEAST FALSE SEROTINE *Hesperoptenus blanfordi* p. 210
   a) head, b) thum pad, c) foot pad. Forearm 24-27.
   Small dark thumb and foot pads; second upper incisor
   behind first.

7. FALSE SEROTINE *Hesperoptenus doriae* p. 210
   Forearm 38-41. Only one upper premolar; first upper
   incisor large and conical.

8. TOMES' FALSE SEROTINE *Hesperoptenus tomesi* p. 211
   a) roosting (x ½), b) head. Forearm 50-53.
   Second upper incisor behind first, which is large and conical.

Plate 18

Plate 19

PANGOLIN, COLUGO, SLOW LORIS AND TARSIER

Plate 19

Plate 20

LANGURS (LEAF MONKEYS)

1. MAROON LANGUR or RED LEAF MONKEY p. 226
   Presbytis rubicunda
   Fur entirely reddish; tail long.

2. HOSE'S LANGUR or GREY LEAF MONKEY p. 226
   Presbytis hosei
   Upperparts grey, underparts white; face pinkish with
   prominent black bands across cheeks.
   a,b) *P. h. sabana*
   c)   *P. h. hosei*, male.
   d)   *P. h. hosei*, female.

3. WHITE-FRONTED LANGUR *Presbytis frontata* p. 227
   Pale spot in centre of forehead.

4. SILVERED LANGUR *Presbytis cristata* p. 227
   a) Adult: dark, silvery grey; dark face.
   b) Infant: orange.

5. BANDED LANGUR *Presbytis melalophos* p. 225
   a) *P. m. chrysomelas:* black; white around base of tail.
   b) *P. m. cruciger:* reddish with variable black and
      white markings.

74

Plate 20

1

2b

2a

2c ♂

2d ♀

3

4a

4b

5a

5b

KP

0   2.4

Plate 21

PROBOSCIS MONKEY AND MACAQUES

1. PROBOSCIS MONKEY *Nasalis larvatus*   p. 228
   Nose prominent; large.
   a) Adult male; tail normally hangs vertically.
   b) Adult female.

2. LONG-TAILED or CRAB-EATING MACAQUE   p. 228
   Macaca fascicularis
   Brownish coloration; facial whiskers often prominent.

3. PIG-TAILED MACAQUE *Macaca nemestrina*   p. 229
   Tail short.
   a) Small adult male.
   b) Small adult female.

Plate 21

Plate 22

GIBBONS AND ORANG-UTAN

1. BORNEAN GIBBON *Hylobates muelleri*   p. 229
   No tail; lives in small groups.
   a) *H. m. funereus:* grey-brown with chest and top of
   head blackish.
   b) *H. m. abbotti:* entirely pale grey.

   AGILE GIBBON *Hylobates agilis*   p. 230
   Not illustrated; similar to the Bornean Gibbon;
   calls different — see text.

2. ORANG-UTAN *Pongo pygmaeus*   p. 230
   No tail; hair entirely reddish, paler in juveniles,
   darker in old animals.
   a) Juvenile.
   b) Adult male on nest.

Plate 22

1a

1b

2a

2b

Karen Phillipps

Plate 23

GIANT SQUIRREL

(Note: 1b and 1c drawn to smaller scale to fit on page)

1.   GIANT SQUIRREL *Ratufa affinis*   p. 233
     Largest tree squirrel.
     a) *R. a. sandakanensis:* whitish underparts.
     b) *R. a. cothurnata:* orange tinge; pale thighs.
     c) Pale form.

Plate 23

Plate 24

KINABALU AND PREVOST'S SQUIRRELS

(Note: 2b - 2e drawn to smaller scale to fit on page)

1. KINABALU SQUIRREL *Callosciurus baluensis*   p. 236
   Upperparts grey-black with bright buffy-red speckling.

2. PREVOST'S SQUIRREL *Callosciurus prevostii*   p. 234
   Coloration varies between subspecies but all have
   reddish underparts.
   a) *C. p. pluto:* black; some individuals have a
   thin white line along side of body between limbs.
   b) *C. p. borneensis:* prominent white side-stripe.
   c) *C. p. caroli:* upperparts grizzled, varying from pale to
   dark grey.
   d) *C. p. sanggaus:* tail plain blackish.
   e) *C. p. atricapillus:* upperparts grizzled olive.

Plate 24

Plate 25

SMALLER *CALLOSCIURUS* SQUIRRELS

All species have black and white/buff stripes on the flanks.

1. BORNEAN BLACK-BANDED SQUIRREL   p. 238
    Callosciurus orestes
    Underparts grey; pale spot behind ear.

2. PLANTAIN SQUIRREL *Callosciurus notatus*   p. 236
    Underparts reddish; no pale spot.

3. EAR-SPOT SQUIRREL *Callosciurus adamsi*   p. 237
    Underparts reddish; pale spot behind ear.

Plate 25

1

2

3

Plate 26

SUNDASCIURUS SQUIRRELS OF LOWLANDS AND HILLS

1. HORSE-TAILED SQUIRREL *Sundasciurus hippurus*   p. 238
   Head grey; tail bushy.
   a) *S. h. pryeri:* underparts white.
   b) *S. h. borneensis:* underparts reddish; thighs grey.

2. LOW'S SQUIRREL *Sundasciurus lowi*   p. 239
   Tail bushy, short; underparts buffy white.

3. SLENDER SQUIRREL *Sundasciurus tenuis*   p. 239
   Tail long, thin; coloration dull.

Plate 26

1a

1b

2

3

Plate 27

SQUIRRELS OF HILLS AND MOUNTAINS

1. BROOKE'S SQUIRREL *Sundasciurus brookei*   p. 240
   Reddish patch between hind legs (not visible from side).

2. JENTINK'S SQUIRREL *Sundasciurus jentinki*   p. 240
   Creamy-white "moustache", eye-ring, ear margins
   and underparts; tail long, thin.

3. BORNEAN MOUNTAIN GROUND SQUIRREL   p. 241
   Dremomys everetti
   Tail short, bushy; muzzle slightly pointed.

Plate 27

Plate 28

GROUND SQUIRRELS

1. FOUR-STRIPED GROUND SQUIRREL *Lariscus hosei*   p. 241
   Pale and dark stripes on each side of midline of upperparts;
   underparts orange.

2. THREE-STRIPED GROUND SQUIRREL *Lariscus insignis* p. 241
   Three dark stripes along midline of upperparts;
   underparts whitish.

3. SHREW-FACED GROUND SQUIRREL   p. 242
   Rhinosciurus laticaudatus
   Narrow, pointed head (like a treeshrew); tail short, bushy;
   underparts whitish.

Plate 28

Plate 29

PIGMY AND SCULPTOR SQUIRRELS

1. WHITEHEAD'S PIGMY SQUIRREL *Exilisciurus whiteheadi*
   Very small; tufted ears.   p. 243

2. PLAIN PIGMY SQUIRREL *Exilisciurus exilis*   p. 243
   Very small; plain coloration.

3. BLACK-EARED PIGMY SQUIRREL *Nannosciurus melanotis*
   Very small; pale stripe across cheek.   p. 242

4. RED-BELLIED SCULPTOR SQUIRREL *Glyphotes simus* p. 240
   Small; coloration as Ear-spot Squirrel (Plate 25).

Plate 29

Plate 30

TUFTED GROUND SQUIRREL

TUFTED GROUND SQUIRREL *Rheithrosciurus macrotis* p. 243

Plate 30

Plate 31

SMALL FLYING SQUIRRELS

1. HOSE'S PIGMY FLYING SQUIRREL *Petaurillus hosei*   p. 245
   Very small; tail tip white.

2. LESSER PIGMY FLYING SQUIRREL *Petaurillus emiliae* p. 245
   Like Hose's, but smaller; cheeks entirely pale.

3. TEMMINCK'S FLYING SQUIRREL *Petinomys setosus*   p. 247
   Small; no orange tinge on any part of body.

4. VORDERMANN'S FLYING SQUIRREL *Petinomys vordermanni*
   Small; margin of gliding membrane buffy.   p. 247

Plate 31

Plate 32

MEDIUM-SIZED FLYING SQUIRRELS

1. HORSFIELD'S FLYING SQUIRREL *Iomys horsfieldi*   p. 245
   Plain coloration; dull orange tinge; traces of grey on
   hairs of back and cheeks.

2. RED-CHEEKED FLYING SQUIRREL *Hylopetes spadiceus*
   Margin of gliding membrane white; cheeks and base of   p. 248
   tail with distinct orange tinge.

3. GREY-CHEEKED FLYING SQUIRREL *Hylopetes lepidus*
   Margin of gliding membrane white; cheeks and base of   p. 247
   tail buffy-grey, sometimes with yellowish tinge,
   but never distinctly orange.

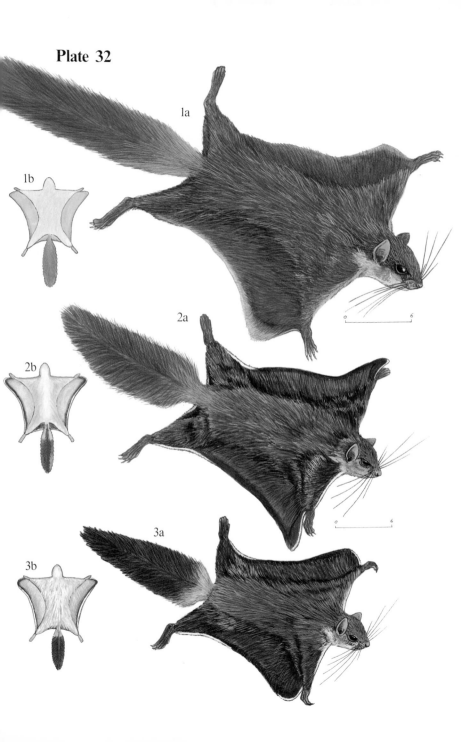

Plate 32

Plate 33

BLACK, SMOKY AND WHISKERED FLYING SQUIRRELS

1. BLACK FLYING SQUIRREL *Aeromys tephromelas*   p. 246
   Large; grey-black.

2. SMOKY FLYING SQUIRREL *Pteromyscus pulverulentus* p. 248
   Blackish with fine pale grey speckling; white underparts.

3. WHISKERED FLYING SQUIRREL *Petinomys genibarbis* p. 246
   Tuft of whiskers behind eye.

   HAGEN'S FLYING SQUIRREL *Petinomys hageni*   p. 246
   Not illustrated; a broad band of reddish-brown between
   and around eyes, extending to ears (in Sumatran form);
   see text.

Plate 33

Plate 34

LARGE FLYING SQUIRRELS

1. SPOTTED GIANT FLYING SQUIRREL *Petaurista elegans*
    Upperparts black with white flecking.   p. 249

2. RED GIANT FLYING SQUIRREL *Petaurista petaurista*   p. 249
    Tip of tail and nose black.

3. THOMAS'S FLYING SQUIRREL *Aeromys thomasi*   p. 246
    Entirely reddish.

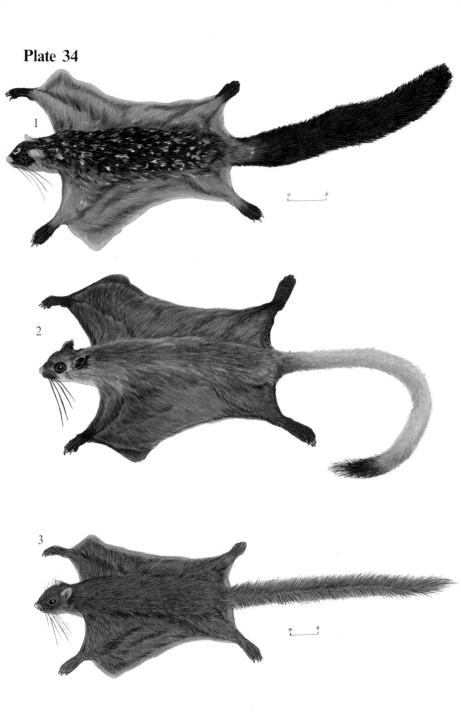

Plate 34

1

2

3

Plate 35

RATS AND MICE ASSOCIATED WITH MAN

Plate 35

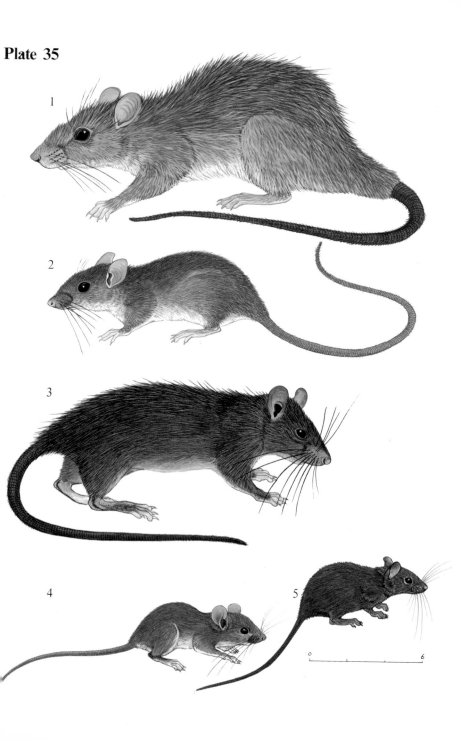

Plate 36

DARK-TAILED RATS

Plate 36

1

2

3

4

0   4

Plate 37

MOUNTAIN RATS

1. SUMMIT RAT *Rattus baluensis* p. 253
   Medium-size; fur long, fluffy.
2. MOUNTAIN GIANT RAT *Sundamys infraluteus* p. 254
   Very large; tail long.
3. MOUNTAIN SPINY RAT *Maxomys alticola* p. 256
   Very spiny; underparts whitish, without yellow tinge.

Plate 37

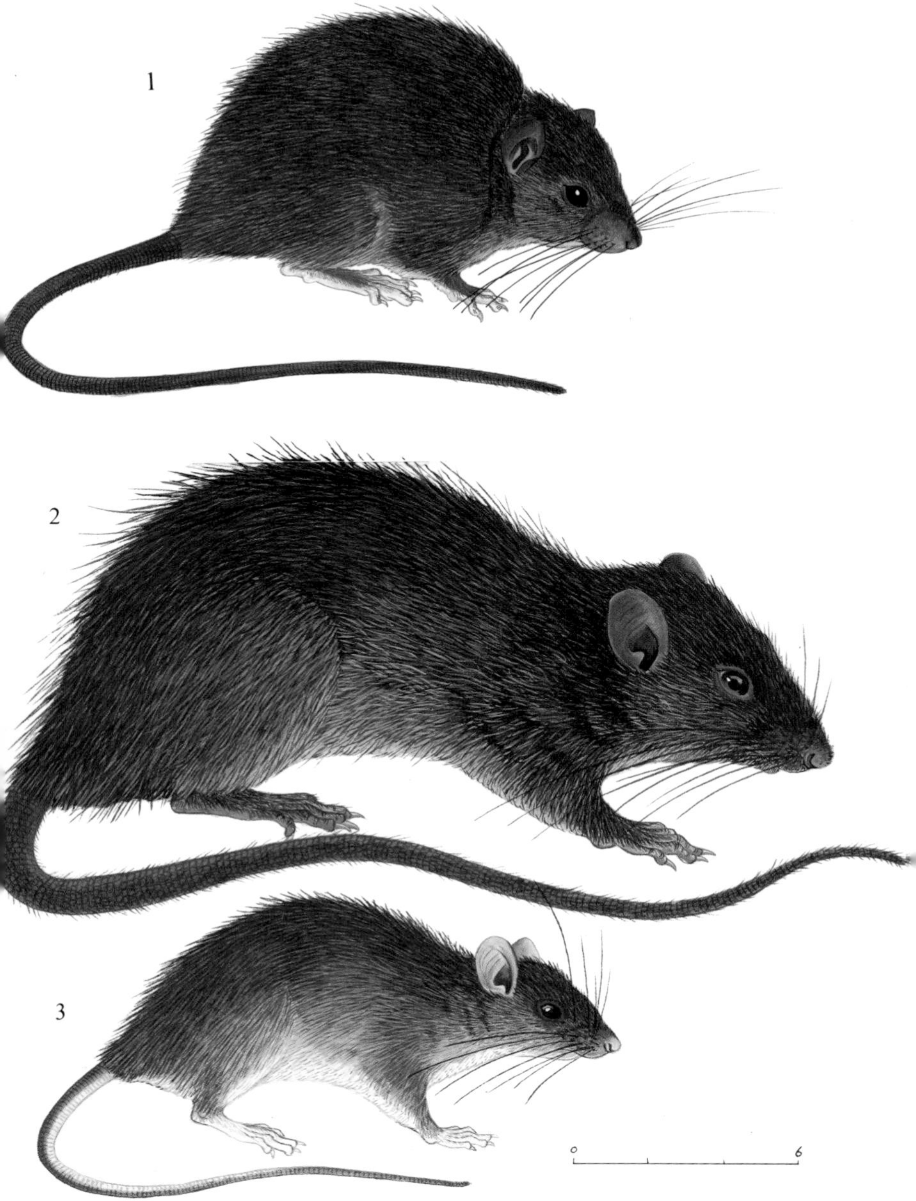

1

2

3

0   6

Plate 38

RATS

1. RED SPINY RAT *Maxomys surifer*   p. 256
    Upperparts bright orange-brown, spiny; adults usually with
    "collar"and inner sides of thighs same colour as upperparts.
    a) Young rat, adult coloration.
    b) Immature rat, before adult coloration; dark brown,
    soft fur; tail entirely pale at tip — similar to Brown
    Spiny Rat.

2. BROWN SPINY RAT *Maxomys rajah*   p. 255
    Upperparts brown or dull orange-brown, spiny; centre of
    underparts usually with a brown streak in adults.
    a) Adult rat.
    b) Immature very similar to Red Spiny Rat.

3. DARK-TAILED TREE RAT *Niviventer cremoriventer*   p. 255
    Tail long, with hairy tip; upperparts with long,
    black guard hairs.

Plate 38

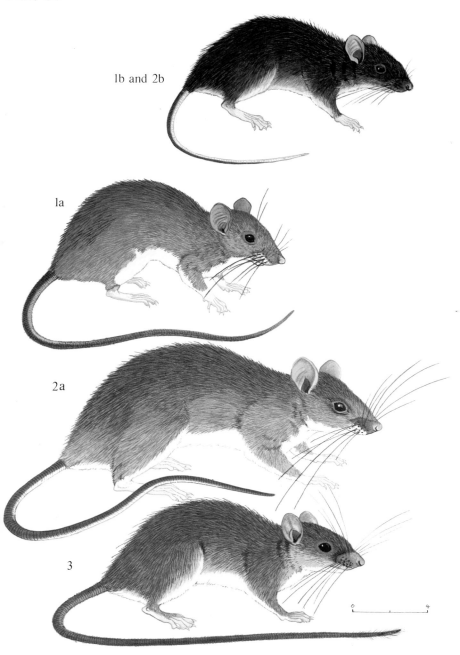

1b and 2b

1a

2a

3

Plate 39

RATS

1. LONG-TAILED MOUNTAIN RAT *Niviventer rapit*   p. 255
   Sides of body reddish-brown; tail long.

2. GREY TREE RAT *Lenothrix canus*   p. 258
   Bicoloured tail; fur grey, soft.

3. WHITEHEAD'S RAT *Maxomys whiteheadi*   p. 257
   Small; spiny; underparts pale orange or pink with grey
   underfur.

4. SMALL SPINY RAT *Maxomys baeodon*   p. 257
   Small; entire body very spiny; underparts buffy.

Plate 39

Plate 40

RATS

1. LONG-TAILED GIANT RAT *Leopoldamys sabanus*   p. 258
    Tail very long; underparts white.
    a) Mount Kinabalu form: brown with blackish face.
    b) Lowland form: reddish-brown.

2. CHESTNUT-BELLIED SPINY RAT *Maxomys ochraceiventer*
    Very spiny; underparts with distinct yellow-orange   p. 257
    tinge.

Plate 40

Plate 41

CLIMBING MICE

All these mice have an opposable inner toe (as in illustration 4b)

1. LARGE PENCIL-TAILED TREE-MOUSE   p. 260
    Chiropodomys major
    Underparts white; hind foot 21-28 mm.

2. COMMON PENCIL-TAILED TREE-MOUSE *Chiropodomys
    gliroides*   p. 259
    Underparts white; hind foot 16-18 mm.

3. GREY-BELLIED PENCIL-TAILED TREE-MOUSE   p. 260
    Chiropodomys muroides
    Underparts grey.

4. RANEE MOUSE *Haeromys margarettae*   p. 260
    Very long tail.
    a) Showing tail.
    b) Underside of foot.

5. LESSER RANEE MOUSE *Haeromys pusillus*   p. 260
    Smaller than Ranee Mouse (but see text).

Plate 41

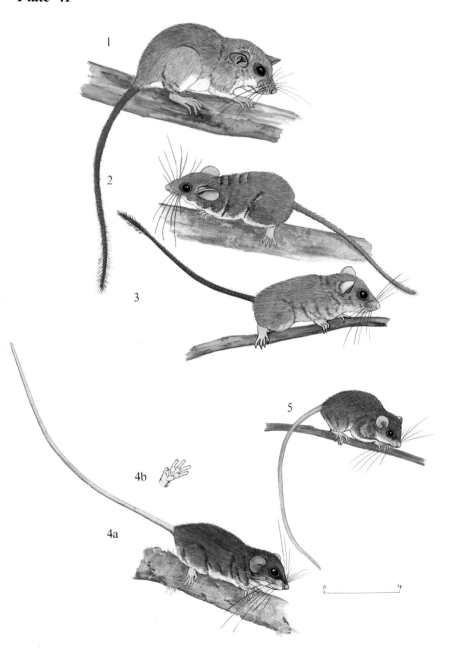

Plate 42

PORCUPINES

1. COMMON PORCUPINE *Hystrix brachyura*   p. 261
   Long spines white with narrow black bands;
   short spines on front of body mostly black.

2. LONG-TAILED PORCUPINE *Trichys fasciculata*   p. 261
   Appearance of a large, spiny rat; tail missing in some
   individuals.

3. THICK-SPINED PORCUPINE *Thecurus crassispinis*   p. 262
   Long spines dark brown with white tips; short spines on
   front of body grey-brown with white tips.

Plate 42

Karen Phillipps

Plate 43

SUN BEAR AND DUGONG

Plate 43

1

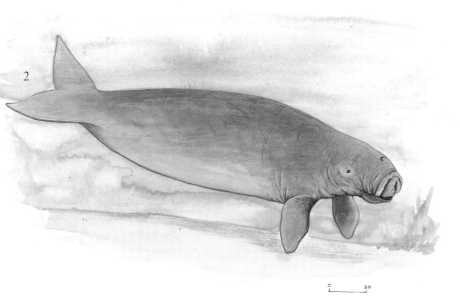

2

Plate 44

MUSTELIDS

Plate 44

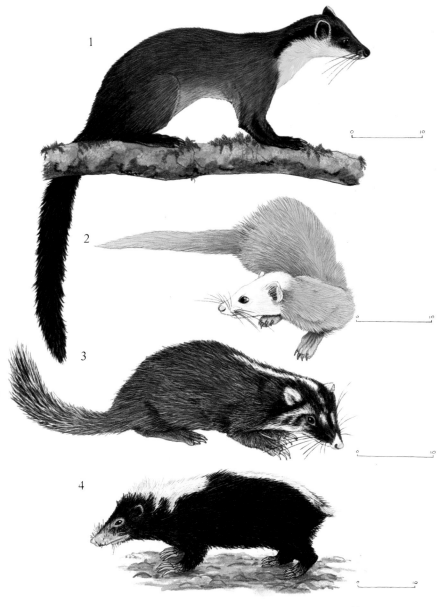

Karen Phillipps .

Plate 45

OTTERS

1. HAIRY-NOSED OTTER *Lutra sumatrana*   p. 278
   Nose entirely hairy; fur rough; tail oval in cross-section.

2. SMOOTH OTTER *Lutra (Lutrogale) perspicillata*   p. 280
   Nose bare; fur sleek; tail flattened underneath.

3. ORIENTAL SMALL-CLAWED OTTER   p. 280
   Aonyx (Amblonyx) cinerea
   Small; chin, cheeks and neck buffy coloured;
   claws very small.

   EURASIAN OTTER *Lutra lutra*   p. 280
   Not illustrated; nose bare, fur contains short and long hairs;
   see text.

Plate 45

1

2

3

Plate 46

CIVETS

Plate 46

1

2

3

0   10

Plate 47

CIVETS

Plate 47

Plate 48

CIVETS

Plate 48

1a

1b

2

3

Plate 49

MONGOOSES

Plate 49

Plate 50

WILD CATS

134

Plate 50

1a

1b

1c

2

3

4

5a

5b

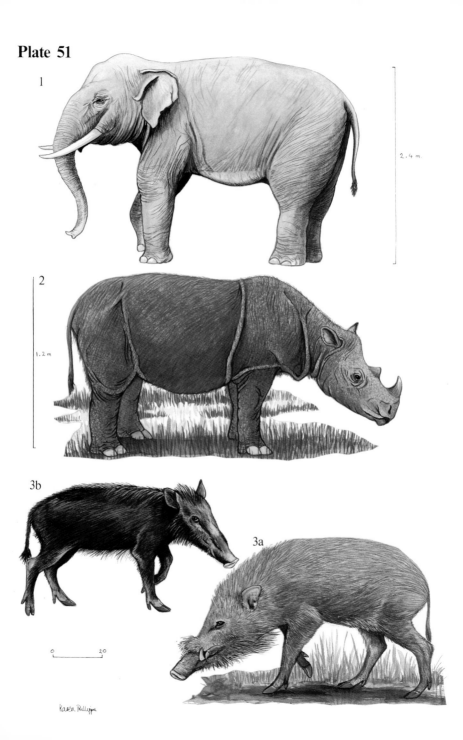

Plate 51

1

2.4 m.

2

1.2 m

3b

3a

0   20

Karen Phillipps

Plate 52

MOUSE-DEER

Plate 52

1

2

0   20

Plate 53

MUNTJAC (BARKING DEER)

1. BORNEAN RED MUNTJAC   p. 298
   (COMMON BARKING DEER) *Muntiacus muntjac*
   a) Antlers with two spikes each, the larger curving
      sharply towards the tip; burr present at base of antler;
      pedicel (bone below antler) thick and straight.
   b) Body coloration dark reddish.

2. BORNEAN YELLOW MUNTJAC   p. 299
   Muntiacus atherodes
   a) Antlers with one spike each, slender, slightly curved;
      no burr; pedicel thin and curved.
   b) Body coloration yellowish-red, dark along midline of
      upperparts.

Plate 53

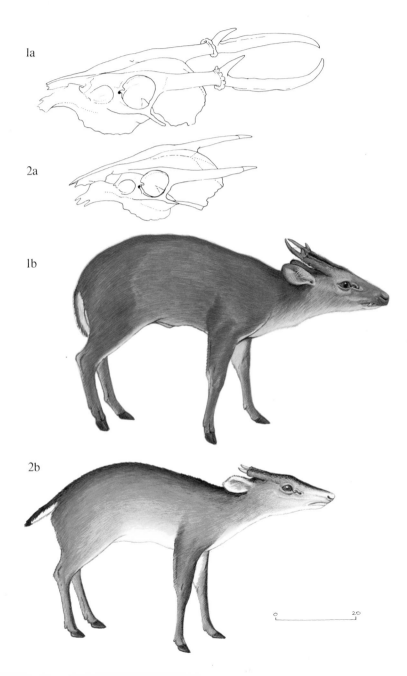

1a

2a

1b

2b

Plate 54

SAMBAR DEER, RUSA AND TEMBADAU (BANTENG)

1. SAMBAR DEER *Cervus unicolor*   p. 299
   Upperparts reddish-brown to dark grey-brown;
   tail dark, bushy. Antlers have inner branch of terminal fork
   shorter than outer.
   a) Male.
   b) Female.

   JAVAN RUSA *Cervus timorensis*   p. 300
   Body not illustrated; antlers have inner branch of
   terminal fork longer than outer; see text.

2. TEMBADAU (BANTENG) *Bos javanicus*   p. 300
   White rump and "stockings".
   a) Mature male: black.
   b) Mature female: reddish-brown.

Antlers of mature Sambar Deer   Antlers of mature Javan Rusa

 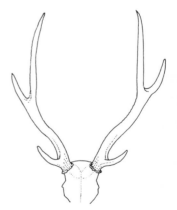

Plate 54

1a

1b

1.1 m

2b

2a

1.5 m

Plate 55

GREAT WHALES

1. BLUE WHALE *Balaenoptera musculus*   p. 263
   Huge; mottled coloration; small dorsal fin very far back;
   U-shaped head (from above).

2. FIN WHALE *Balaenoptera physalus*   p. 264
   Dark and unmottled; V-shaped rostrum; asymmetric
   head colour—white on right lower lip, dark on left;
   shallowly angled dorsal fin visible just after blow.

3. SEI WHALE *Balaenoptera borealis*   p. 264
   Steeply angled dorsal fin, usually visible at same
   time as blow; mainly dark; only one ridge on top of head.

4. BRYDE'S (TROPICAL) WHALE *Balaenoptera edeni*   p. 265
   Three prominent ridges on top of head; similar to Sei Whale.

5. MINKE (PIKED) WHALE *Balaenoptera acutorostrata*   p. 265
   Relatively small; narrow V-shaped head; white marks on
   fins may sometimes be lacking.

6. HUMPBACK WHALE *Megaptera novaeangliae*   p. 265
   Very large flippers, white underneath; dorsal fin variable
   in shape; tail usually raised high in air before
   diving — distinctive white marks on underside.

7. (GREAT) SPERM WHALE *Physeter macrocephalus*   p. 266
   Blow angled forwards; low hump instead of dorsal fin;
   tail often raised before a deep dive—all dark with
   a level edge.

Plate 55

1

2

3

4

5

6

7

Karen Phillipps

Plate 56

MEDIUM WHALES

Plate 56

Plate 57

SMALL WHALES AND DOLPHINS

1. PIGMY SPERM WHALE *Kogia breviceps*   p. 266
    "Shark-like" head pattern; low dorsal fin.

2. DWARF SPERM WHALE *Kogia simus*   p. 266
    Similar to Pigmy Sperm, but slightly smaller,
    dorsal fin larger and further forwards.

3. PIGMY KILLER WHALE *Feresa attenuata*   p. 268
    Rounded head; indistinct cape; flippers rounded at tip.

4. MELON-HEADED WHALE *Peponocephala electra*   p.268
    Head triangular from above; slim pointed flippers.

5. GREY (RISSO'S) DOLPHIN *Grampus griseus*   p. 272
    Body dark grey when young, turning whiter with age;
    high domed forehead with a crease in the middle.

6. BOTTLENOSE DOLPHIN *Tursiops truncatus*   p. 271
    Uniform dark brown to grey; thick beak; tall curved
    dorsal fin.

Plate 57

Plate 58

DOLPHINS AND PORPOISE

Plate 58

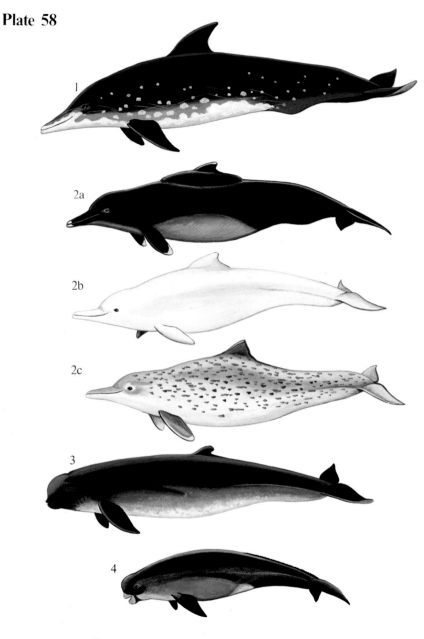

Karen Phillips

Plate 59

DOLPHINS

1. FRASER'S (SHORTSNOUT) DOLPHIN *Lagenodelphis hosei*
   Short beak; relatively small flippers and dorsal fin;   p. 271
   dark stripe through eye to anus.

2. LONG-SNOUTED SPINNER DOLPHIN   p. 273
   Stenella longirostra
   Long dark beak; tall dorsal fin; colour variable —
   can be all dark grey.

3. STRIPED DOLPHIN *Stenella coeruleoalba*   p. 273
   Long black stripes from eye to anus and flipper.

4. SPOTTED (BRIDLED) DOLPHIN *Stenella attenuata*   p. 272
   Spotting variable, but pattern distinctive.

5. COMMON DOLPHIN *Delphinus delphis*   p. 271
   Criss-crossing pattern of pale and dark stripes;
   dark V-shaped saddle below dorsal fin.

Plate 59

Plate 60

SOME DOMESTIC MAMMALS

1. WATER BUFFALO *Bubalus bubalis*   p. 301
   Dark grey; pale, broad V shaped mark on upper chest.

2. DOMESTIC PIG *Sus scrofa*   p. 296
   Short, plump, mainly blackish.

3. DOMESTIC CATTLE *Bos indicus*   p. 301
   Hump between shoulders; coloration variable.

4. DOMESTIC GOAT *Capra aegagrus*   p. 301
   Coat pattern usually uneven and asymmetrical.

Plate 60

Order INSECTIVORA   Moonrats and shrews

Insectivores are small mammals which resemble and may be confused with rodents. The muzzle of insectivores is relatively longer and more pointed.Their front feet each have five long digits with sharp claws, while in rodents the inner digit on each front foot is short, with a flat nail instead of a sharp claw. All the teeth in insectivores are generally rounded or conical with sharp points, while the front (incisor) teeth of rodents have a cutting edge like a chisel and are separated from the relatively broad cheek teeth by a large gap (diastema).

Treeshrews (family Tupaiidae) were formerly included in the Insectivora, but are now placed in their own order, Scandentia, by most zoologists.

Family ERINACEIDAE   Moonrat and Lesser Gymnure

Two representatives occur in Borneo, each with a distinctive shape and coloration. Both have 44 teeth (3 incisors, 1 canine, 4 premolars and 3 molars on each side of both the upper and lower jaw), more than any other small mammal in Borneo.

MOONRAT *Echinosorex gymnurus*   Plate 1

Measurements: HB 320-396, T 207-292, HF 65-75 (11 specimens). Wt 870-1100.

Identification. Fur generally white, with a sparse scattering of black hairs; appears to be totally white from a distance, unlike any other wild mammal. Has a distinct, pungent odour with a strong ammonia content, different from the musky smell of carnivores. Moonrats from western Borneo *(E. g. candidus)* tend to have a greater proportion of black hairs than those from the east *(E. g. albus)*, but animals from Brunei appear intermediate.

Ecology and Habitat. Nocturnal and terrestrial. Stays in burrows during the daytime.In Borneo, occurs mainly in forests, but in Peninsular Malaysia, also found in gardens and plantations. Prefers damp situations. Feeds on earthworms and various small animals, mostly arthropods.

Distribution: Burmam, Peninsular Thailand and Malaysia, Sumatra. **Borneo:** known from many sites throughout the lowlands and up to 900 m in the Kelabit uplands. Apparently absent or rare in some localities, possibly due to a shortage of suitable food. Two subspecies have been described: *E. g. albus* in the eastern and southern regions of Borneo and in the Kelabit uplands; *E. g. candidus* on the western side of Borneo from P. Labuan south at least to Kuching.

LESSER GYMNURE *Hylomys suillus*   Plate 1

Measurements. HB 116-145, T 20-24, HF 20-26 (5 Sabah specimens). Wt 50-70.
Identification. Upperparts brownish; underparts paler. Resembles a large shrew (family Soricidae), but with a distinctive short, naked tail.

Ecology and Habitat. Diurnal and probably also nocturnal. Terrestrial. Feeds on arthropods and earthworms. Shelters in nests of dead leaves made in hollows in the ground or under rocks. Occurs only in montane forests.

Distribution. South-western China through South-east Asia, Sumatra, Java. **Borneo:** *H. s. dorsalis.* Occurs on G. Kinabalu (1200-3400 m), G.Trus Madi, G. Mulu and in the Kelabit uplands (above 1190 m).

Figure 8. Skull of a House Shrew, *Suncus Murinus*.

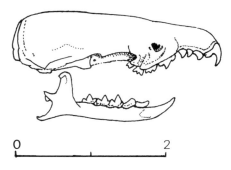

Family SORICIDAE   Shrews

Shrews include the smallest mammals other than bats. They have rather short legs, a sparsely-haired tail, short fur and small eyes. The smaller species in Borneo are all very similar. They can be identified tentatively from body and tail measurements, but for confirmation it is often necessary to examine the teeth or measure the skull. *Suncus* shrews have 9 teeth in each side of the upper jaw, of which the 2nd, 3rd, 4th and 5th (counting from the front) have only one cusp. The 5th tooth is much smaller than the other teeth and may be overlooked if examined without a magnifying glass (Figure 9b). *Crocidura* shrews lack this extra tooth, and thus have a total of only 8 teeth on each side of the upper jaw (Figure 9a).

HOUSE SHREW *Suncus murinus*   Plate 1

Measurements. HB 92-146, T 46-86 (50-64% of HB), HF 17-23 (6 specimens). Skull: cbl 33.1-33.4, io 5.9-6.0, mt 13.7-14.4 (3 specimens).

Identification. Entire body and tail uniform mid-grey to brownish grey. Tail thick, especially at base — narrower at tip. Has a musk gland, sometimes visible, on the middle of each side of the body. **Similar species:** the South-east Asian White-toothed Shrew, *Crocidura fuliginosa*, and the Himalayan Water Shrew, *Chimarrogale himalayica*, differ in habitat, tail shape and number of teeth.

Ecology and Habitat. Usually found in or near houses.

Distribution. Africa, Madagascar, most of Asia, Philippines, Indonesia. **Borneo:** *S. m. murinus.* Known from scattered localities in Sabah and West, South and East Kalimantan. Probably also occurs in other areas.

Figure 9. Upper right toothrow of shrews: a) *Crocidura* **b)** *Suncus.*

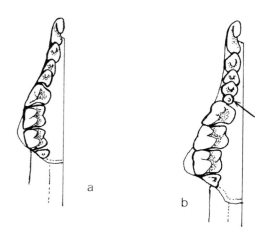

BLACK SHREW *Suncus ater*   Plate 1

Measurements. HB 75, T 57 (76% of HB), HF 12. Skull: cbl 21.3, mt 9.2 (1 specimen).

Identification. Upperparts dark blackish brown; underparts scarcely paler. Tail with scattered long, dark hairs on basal 1 cm. Illustration based on description of the only known specimen. **Similar species:** the House Shrew, *S. murinus*, is larger, paler and lives near houses; the South-east Asian White-toothed Shrew, *Crocidura fuliginosa*, lacks the small extra tooth (Figure 9a).

Ecology and Habitat. The only known specimen was trapped in montane forest.

Distribution. Known only from a site called "Lumu-lumu" on G. Kinabalu (1700 m).

SAVI'S PIGMY SHREW *Suncus etruscus* Plate 1

Measurements. HB 50-56, T 24-32 (48-56% of HB), HF 9.0-9.5 (4 specimens). Skull: cbl 14.5, io 4.1, mt 6.4 (type specimen).

Identification. Upperparts dark grey with fine whitish grizzling; underparts somewhat paler. Ears and feet dark brown. Tail brownish with very short hairs and a few long hairs on the basal two thirds. **Similar species:** the Black Shrew, *S. ater*, is larger; the Sunda Shrew, *Crocidura monticola*, lacks the extra tooth (Figure 9a).

Ecology and Habitat. Terrestrial in tall dipterocarp forest.

Distribution. Southern Europe, northern Africa, Madagascar, most of Asia. **Borneo:** *S. e. hosei.* Recorded only from Sepilok in Sabah; Bakong and G. Mulu National Park in northern Sarawak. Probably widespread.

SUNDA SHREW *Crocidura monticola* Plate 1

Measurements. HB 62, T 37 (1 specimen). Skull: cbl 15.2-17.4, mt 6.6-7.3 (15 Bornean and non-Bornean specimens).

Identification. Body uniform dull grey-brown. Tail paler, with sparse, long, pale hairs on basal 1 cm. Illustration based on an old specimen which may have changed colour slightly. **Similar species:** Savi's Pigmy Shrew, *Suncus etruscus*, has an extra small tooth (as in Figure 9b).

Ecology and Habitat. Unknown.

Distribution. Peninsular Malaysia, Java to Flores. **Borneo:** known from G. Kinabalu (1500 m) in Sabah; G. Mulu and the Kelabit uplands in northern Sarawak; Karangan in East Kalimantan. Probably widespread in upland forests.

SOUTH-EAST ASIAN WHITE-TOOTHED SHREW Plate 1
Crocidura fuliginosa

Measurements. *C. f. foetida* and *C. f. baluensis:* HB 52-112, T 57-97 (54-90% of HB), HF 14-18.5 (8 Sabah and Sarawak specimens). *C. f. kelabit:* HB 65-78, T 70-83 (100-110% of HB), HF 15-16 (4 specimens). Skull: cbl 21.3-25.0, mt 9.4-11.5 (217 non-Bornean and Bornean specimens).

Identification. Upperparts dark brownish grey; underparts slightly paler. Tail brownish, with few or no long hairs. Three subspecies can be distinguished: *C. f. foetida* has body hair 3-4 mm long, tail shorter than HB; *C. f. kelabit* has body hair 5-6 mm long, tail longer than HB; *C. f. baluensis* has body hair 8 mm or more long, tail shorter than HB.

Note: the *baluensis* form may represent a separate species, further research is required.

Similar species: the Black Shrew, *Suncus ater*, has an extra tooth (Figure 9b).

Ecology and Habitat. *C. f. foetida:* generally in lightly wooded or open areas. *C. f. baluensis:* in grass, rocky areas and moss forest. *C. f. kelabit:* in grassland.

Distribution. North-eastern India, southern China, South-east Asia, Sumatra, Java, Sulawesi. **Borneo:** *C. f. foetida.* Reported from scattered lowland sites including the lower slopes of G. Kinabalu, Sandakan, upper Kinabatangan and Tawau in Sabah; Lawas, S. Rajang, G. Dulit (up to 1500 m) and Kuching in Sarawak; Bengkayang in West Kalimantan. *C. f. baluensis.* Occurs on the upper slopes of G. Kinabalu (about 1500-3700 m). *C. f. kelabit.* Found above 1000 m in the Kelabit uplands, northern Sarawak.

HIMALAYAN WATER SHREW *Chimarrogale himalayica*   Plate 1

Measurements. HB 91-110, T 75-90 (about 82% of HB), HF 19-22 (6 specimens). Skull: cbl 23.0-26.0, mt 11.5-11.9 (4 specimens).

Identification. Very dark grey-brown with conspicuous silvery guard hairs on the hind quarters. Feet fringed with short, rather stiff hairs, a feature unique to this shrew.

Ecology and Habitat. Lives in or near small forest streams.

Distribution. Himalayas through southern China, Japan, Taiwan, Southeast Asia, Sumatra. **Borneo:** *C. h. phaeura.* Known only from G. Kinabalu (460-1700 m) and G. Trus Madi in Sabah.

Figure 10. Skull of a Common Treeshrew, *Tupaia glis.*

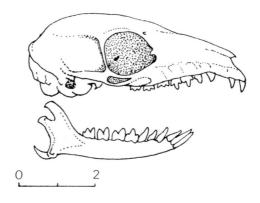

0   2

Order SCANDENTIA

Family TUPAIIDAE   Treeshrews

Superficially, treeshrews resemble small tree squirrels but differ in many details of anatomy and behaviour. They have a very long muzzle with a total of 38 teeth, pointed rather than chisel-like incisors (Figure 10; compare Figures 30-32), and five clawed digits on each foot.

Treeshrews have been variously classified as primates or insectivores, but are now thought to be distinct from both, and are placed in their own order, Scandentia, by most zoologists.

The 8 species of *Tupaia* treeshrews which occur in Borneo closely resemble each other, but can usually be distinguished by careful observation of coloration and size. The Shrew-faced Ground Squirrel, *Rhinosciurus laticaudatus*, sometimes resembles a treeshrew at a distance, but can be distinguished by its shorter tail, pale underparts and, if captured, the modified digits on the front feet and the different dentition. Also belonging to the family Tupaiidae, but superficially different from *Tupaia* treeshrews, are the Pentail Treeshrew, the only nocturnal member of the family, and the Smooth-tailed Treeshrew, a montane form with a long, thin tail.

PENTAIL TREESHREW *Ptilocercus lowii*   Plate 2

Measurements. HB 134-150, T 160-202, HF 24-30 (4 specimens).

Identification. Upperparts grey-brown; underparts yellowish-grey. Eyes and ears relatively large. Tail long and naked except for a diagnostic feather-like tip.

Ecology and Habitat. Nocturnal. Usually arboreal. Diet mainly insects and other arthropods. Occurs mainly in forests, but elsewhere has been recorded in gardens.

Distribution. Peninsular Thailand and Malaysia, Sumatra and adjacent islands. **Borneo:** *p. l. lowii*. Known only from the lowlands of Sabah and Sarawak, from Sandakan in the north-east to Kuching in the south-west, as well as P. Labuan.

COMMON TREESHREW *Tupaia glis*   Plates 2 and 5

Measurements. HB 170-235, T 170-242, HF 45-56 (21 specimens). Skull: cbl 48.0-51.0, mt 19.1-21.0 (11 specimens).

Identification. Hairs on upperparts banded dark and pale, appearing finely speckled brown or reddish-brown. Usually has a pale stripe on each shoulder. *T. g. longipes* is somewhat duller in coloration than *T. g. salatana*, although both forms usually have a reddish tinge. In *longipes*, the underparts are dull buff to reddish buff and the underside of the tail is normally greyish. In *salatana*, the underparts and underside of the tail are dark reddish. Intermediate coloration has been recorded. **Similar species:** the Ruddy Treeshrew, *T. splendidula*, has the tail hairs uniformly reddish, not barred; the Mountain Treeshrew, *T. montana*, has a shorter hindfoot and occurs at higher altitudes.

Ecology and Habitat. Diurnal. Most often seen active around fallen trees and branches, in low woody vegetation or on the ground. Diet mainly insects and other arthropods, and sweet or oily fruits. Occurs in forests as well as in gardens and plantations where these habitats border on forest.

Distribution. Nepal, southern China, South-east Asia, Sumatra, Java and smaller Indonesian islands. **Borneo:** probably present throughout the lowlands and hills with records up to 1100 m in the Kelabit uplands. *T. g. longipes.* Occurs north of approximately S. Rajang in Sarawak and S. Kayan in East Kalimantan, including all of Sabah. *T. g. salatana.* Occurs south of S. Rajang and S. Kayan.

RUDDY TREESHREW *Tupaia splendidula*   Plates 4 and 5

Measurements. HB 173-185, T 130-158 (72-87% of HB), HF 40-44 (5 Kalimantan specimens). Skull: cbl 42.2-48.8, io 13.2-13.8, mt 17.0-20.2 (6 Kalimantan specimens).

Identification. A plain reddish treeshrew, with shoulder stripe (if present) pale orange. Upperparts tend to be darker in the midline and brighter on the sides; underparts dark reddish with an orange throat. Hairs on tail pure dark red above, orange below. *T. s. splendidula* coloration is dull, but *T. s. carimatae* (illustrated) is brighter and has a proportionately shorter tail and hindfeet. **Similar species:** the Common Treeshrew, *T. glis*, is slightly larger and more uniformly coloured above, with banded hairs on the tail.

Ecology and Habitat. Diurnal. Otherwise unknown.

Distribution. Confined to Borneo and small adjacent islands. *T. s. splendidula.* Known from only a few specimens, all from southern Borneo, with records as far north as G. Liang Kubung in West Kalimantan and Kutai in East Kalimantan. *T. s. carimatae.* On P. Karimata.

MOUNTAIN TREESHREW *Tupaia montana*   Plates 3 and 5

Measurements. HB 156-227, T 135-190 (usually more than 75% of HB), HF 37-45 (54 specimens, both subspecies). Wt 95-219. Skull: cbl 43.1-46.1, io 12.7-15.3, mt 16.2-18.0 (4 specimens).

Identification. General coloration varies from dark brown to reddish or olive-brown, but always with a fine reddish speckling. Underparts buffy red on grey underfur. A pale shoulder stripe present in some individuals. Usually appears entirely dark brown when glimpsed in the field. *T. m. montana* has a black stripe on the underparts, narrow between the shoulders and broadening out between the hind limbs. This black colouring is absent in *T. m. baluensis* (illustrated). **Similar species:** the Common Treeshrew, *T. glis*, has a larger hind foot and usually occurs at lower altitudes; the Bornean Mountain Ground Squirrel, *Dremomys everetti*, and the Shrew-faced Ground Squirrel, *Rhinosciurus laticaudatus*, have proportionately shorter tails; the former has a shorter muzzle and the latter appears not to overlap in distribution.

Ecology and Habitat. Active throughout the daylight hours but mainly early morning and late afternoon. Travels and feeds on the ground and among fallen trees, rarely in the canopy of small trees. Diet a mixture of plant and animal material. One of the commonest mammals in primary montane forests in Sabah.

Distribution. Confined to Borneo in the hill ranges and mountains of the north-west. *T. m. baluensis.* Recorded from G. Kinabalu (about 900-3170 m), G. Trus Madi (1530-2380 m) and the Crocker Range (above 1200 m) in Sabah; the Sabah-Sarawak border mountains (above 1070 m); G. Murud (up to 2140 m), the Kelabit uplands (above 1130 m), G. Mulu (above 1220 m), upper S. Rajang (above 900 m), G. Penrisen (1160 m), G. Pueh and G. Sidong (370 m) in Sarawak. *T. m. montana.* Recorded from the more isolated mountain areas of northern Sarawak, including Batu Song (900 m), G. Kalulung, G. Dulit (above 600 m) and Usun Apau.

LESSER TREESHREW *Tupaia minor*   Plates 2 and 5

Measurements. HB 116-135, T 131-172 (always longer than HB, usually 115-125%), HF 29-34 (41 specimens). Wt 30-71.'Skull: cbl 31.9-34.9, io 10.5-12.1, mt 11.4-12.7 (21 specimens).

Identification. Hairs on upperparts banded light and dark giving an overall speckled olive-brown appearance. Underparts buffy, often with a reddish tinge towards the rear. Upper side of tail darker than body. Small size and long, thin tail are distinctive features. *T. m. minor* is reported to differ only slightly from *T. m. caedis* (illustrated) in having a wider, whiter shoulder stripe and browner uppperparts. **Similar species:** the Slender Treeshrew, *T. gracilis,* usually has no reddish tinge, and tends to have a bushier tail, but can be distinguished positively only by hindfoot or skull measurements.

Ecology and Habitat. Diurnal and mainly arboreal. Often seen at 3-8 m above the ground, sometimes to 20 m, travelling along lianas or branches of small trees. Diet includes insects and fruits. Occurs in forests, gardens and plantations.

Distribution. Peninsular Thailand and Malaysia, Sumatra. **Borneo:** Most common below 1000 m but also known from higher altitudes. *T. m. minor.* Found throughout the lowlands and hills except in the north-east. *T. m. caedis.* Recorded in eastern Sabah from Kudat to at least Kalabakan, as well as P. Banggi and P. Balembangan.

SLENDER TREESHREW *Tupaia gracilis*   Plates 2 and 5

Measurements. HB 135-165, T 162-190 (115-135% of HB), HF 37-43 (17 specimens). Wt 60-98. Skull: cbl 34.6-36.6, io 11.6-12.7, mt 13.3-14.3 (5 specimens).

Identification. Upperparts speckled olive-brown; underparts buffy white usually with no reddish tinge. Tail long, darker above than the body. **Similar species:** the Lesser Treeshrew, *T. minor,* tends to have a less bushy tail and often has a reddish tinge, but can be distinguished positively only by hind foot or skull measurements.

Ecology and Habitat. Apparently similar to the Lesser Treeshrew, *T. minor* — differences unknown.

Distribution. Confined to Borneo and adjacent small islands. *T. g. gracilis.* Recorded from the lowlands and hills in most areas except the south-east between Riam in Central Kalimantan and S. Mahakam in East Kalimantan. Up to 1200 m in the Kelabit uplands, but usually at lower altitudes. Also on P. Banggi. *T. g. edarata.* On P. Karimata.

163

PAINTED TREESHREW *Tupaia picta*   Plates 4 and 5

Measurements. HB 168-240, T 140-170 (64-90% of HB), HF 40-46 (17 specimens of both subspecies). Skull: cbl 43.6-48.5, io 13.7-14.5, mt 17.4-19.0 (7 specimens of both subspecies).

Identification. *T. p. picta:* upperparts generally brown, with heavy buff flecking and a black central stripe on the front half of the body. Pale buff shoulder stripe usually present. Underparts dull orange with pale grey bases to the fur. Underside and distal end of tail with a strong orange or reddish tinge. *T. p. fuscior:* smaller and duller in coloration than *picta* with the tail entirely grizzled reddish on black. A specimen of the Painted Treeshrew from Balingian on the Sarawak coast is very dark, like *fuscior.* Centre of eye to tip of muzzle less than 37 mm in both subspecies. **Similar species:** some forms of the Large Treeshrew, *T. tana*, are similarly coloured but are larger with a relatively longer muzzle.

Ecology and Habitat. Diurnal. Otherwise unknown.

Distribution. Confined to Borneo. All records below 1000 m. *T. p. picta.* Recorded from the north-west between Balingian in Sarawak and Tasek Merimbun in Brunei, encompassing Usun Apau, G. Batu Song, the Kelabit uplands and G. Mulu. *T. p. fuscior.* Known only from three localities near the coast of East Kalimantan all between Samarinda and Labuhan Kelambu.

STRIPED TREESHREW *Tupaia dorsails*   Plates 3 and 5

Measurements. HB 160-220, T 140-162 (68-83% of HB), HF 40-46 (11 specimens). Skull: cbl 43.6-48.0, io 11.9-14.3, mt 16.8-18.2 (16 specimens).

Identification. Hairs on the upperparts banded dark and pale, giving an overall finely speckled olive-brown appearance. Uniform, thin, black line running from the neck almost to the base of the tail diagnostic, but often not obvious when glimpsed from a distance. Underparts grey-buff. Shoulder stripe whitish, thin but usually distinct.

Ecology and Habitat. Diurnal and apparently mainly terrestrial. Occurs in tall and secondary forests.

Distribution. Confined to Borneo. Found in the lowlands and hills of most areas except the south-east between Riam in Central Kalimantan and S. Mahakam in East Kalimantan. Up to 1000 m on G. Dulit, but usually recorded at lower altitudes. Rarely caught compared to other treeshrews with a similarly wide distribution.

LARGE TREESHREW *Tupaia tana*   Plates 4 and 5

Measurements. HB 165-321, T 130-220, HF 43-57 (54 specimens of five subspecies). Wt 154-305. Skull: cbl 50.8-57.5, io 13.3-14.9, mt 18.5-21.0 (9 specimens). Slight size differences between subspecies, with *besara* the largest and *kretami* the smallest.

Identification. All subspecies have a basically similar colour pattern (Plates 4 and 5): upperparts paler towards the front of the body, but with a darker midline, and blacker towards the rump. Underparts reddish-buff. Centre of eye to tip of muzzle more than 37 mm in adults. The subspecies differ as follows: *T. t. speciosa* generally dark, dull coloration. *T. t. besara* very dark, dull coloration, with entirely black rump; large. *T. t. nitida* reddish tinge on entire body, especially the tail. *T. t. utara* generally bright coloration with black rump; pale area on each side of the dorsal dark stripe with a grey tinge. *T. t. kelabit* darker, duller coloration than in the other northern subspecies. *T. t. chrysura* buffy tail; *T. t. paitana* generally bright and dark reddish coloration, pale area on each side of the dorsal dark stripe yellowish-grey; *T. t. kretami* similar to *paitana*, but without a strong reddish tinge. **Similar species:** the Painted Treeshrew, *T. picta*, is smaller with a relatively shorter muzzle.

Ecology and Habitat. Diurnal and mainly terrestrial. Feeds on arthropods and earthworms with some fruit. Rarely found outside of tall forest or dense, shaded areas in secondary forests.

Distribution. Sumatra and adjacent small islands. **Borneo:** widely distributed, probably throughout the lowlands and hills, mainly below 1000 m, although sometimes up to 1500 m. Eight subspecies are recognised on the main island of Borneo (Map 2): 1. *T. t. speciosa*, 2. *T. t. besara*, 3. *T. t. nitida*, 4. *T. t. utara*, 5. *T. t. kelabit*, 6. *T. t. chrysura*, 7. *T. t. paitana*, 8. *T. t. kretami*. Also *T. t. banguei* from P. Banggi.

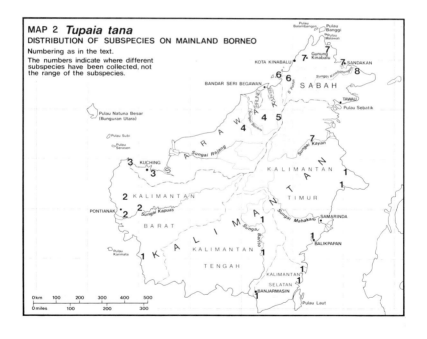

MAP 2 *Tupaia tana*
DISTRIBUTION OF SUBSPECIES ON MAINLAND BORNEO
Numbering as in the text.
The numbers indicate where different subspecies have been collected, not the range of the subspecies.

SMOOTH-TAILED TREESHREW *Dendrogale melanura*   Plate 3

Measurements. HB 103-137, T 135-149 (109-122% of HB), HF 28-30 (9 specimens).

Identification. Upperparts dark brown; underparts fur orange-buff with grey bases. Tail thin, with short hairs; shiny black with reddish streaking along the sides. *D. m. melanura* is darker above and more reddish below than *D. m. baluensis*.

Ecology and Habitat. Diurnal. Active in mossy trees and on rocky boulders in montane forests.

Distribution. Confined to Borneo in the mountains of the north-west above 900 m. *D. m. melanura.* Recorded from G. Dulit, G. Mulu and the Kelabit uplands in northern Sarawak and from the Sabah-Sarawak border. *D. m. baluensis.* Recorded from G. Kinabalu and G. Trus Madi in Sabah.

Order DERMOPTERA

Family CYNOCEPHALIDAE   Colugo

There are only two colugos or flying lemurs, one confined to the southern Philippines and the other to Borneo and elsewhere in South-east Asia. They cannot fly, but glide with the aid of membranes between the legs. The teeth are highly specialised and unlike those of any other mammal. There are no teeth at the front of the upper jaw and the two pairs of lower front teeth look like finely-toothed combs (Figure 11).

Figure 11. Skull with lower incisor (enlarged 3x) of a Colugo, *Cynocephalus variegatus*

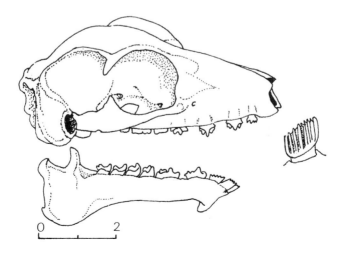

COLUGO or FLYING LEMUR *Cynocephalus variegatus*   Plate 19

Measurements. HB 344-375, T 241-245, HF 65-73, Wt 925-1300 (2 specimens).

Identification. Most Colugos are grey with heavy black and white markings, but some individuals are tinged reddish-brown or are totally reddish-brown with few markings. In the field, the most distinctive feature is the gliding membrane, which extends between the front and hind legs, and encloses the tail. Often carries small young, sometimes wrapped in the gliding membrane. **Similar species:** large flying squirrels have a relatively long tail completely free of an enclosing membrane.

Ecology and Habitat. Nocturnal but sometimes active in the morning and late afternoon. Usually noticed when clinging to the side of a tree trunk or gliding between tall trees. Rests both in tree holes and in the crowns of trees. The form of the teeth suggests a diet including sap from plants. At Poring (eastern foothills of G. Kinabalu) a Colugo was observed licking fluid oozing from a cut in the trunk of a coconut tree during heavy rain. Published literature states that the Colugo feeds on leaves, leaf shoots and flower buds. Occurs in tall and secondary forests, gardens and (in Peninsular Malaysia) plantations.

Distribution. Burma, southern Indochina, peninsular Thailand and Malaysia, Sumatra, Java and smaller Indonesian islands. **Borneo:** *C. v. natunae.* Known from throughout the lowlands and hills up to 900 m. Occurs on P. Banggi.

Bats are distinguished from all other mammals by their wings and their ability to fly. Two other groups of Bornean mammals — the colugo and the flying squirrels — have developed the ability to glide long distances, but they are not capable of true flight. They have gliding membranes between their legs, quite different from the wings of bats which are formed from elongate fingers on the hands (Figure 12). Flying bats are often confused with birds but can be easily distinguished with practice by the shape of their wings and the pattern of flight.

Bats are difficult to identify unless they can be captured and examined closely. In the hand, most species can be distinguished based on easily visible characters and measurements, but some features such as coloration are rather variable and it is sometimes necessary to examine the skull or dentition for confirmation. With care the teeth can usually be examined in a live bat by gently opening the mouth with a toothpick or similar tool. A small magnifying glass is helpful to see the details. The skull can only be properly examined in a museum specimen, but many features of skull shape are reflected in the outward appearance of the head.

Figure 12. Parts of a bat.

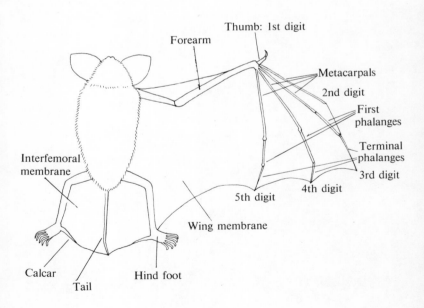

Bats have been very little studied in Borneo, and it is likely that additional species occur in the area. For the benefit of scientists who wish to confirm their identifications or who may have caught species not in this book, technical descriptions of each genus are provided, together with diagrams of most of the skull types. To make the species descriptions as readable as possible, these technical characters are mainly confined to separate sections at the start of each genus.

Care must be taken when identifying bats not to confuse immatures with adults. Immatures are generally much duller in colour, grey or grey-brown. If held against a bright light, the wing joints of immatures appear banded where the cartilage has not yet turned to bone (the adult joint looks like a solid lump).

The Bornean species of bats are classified into 8 families, which can be distinguished based on ear shape, muzzle shape, the presence or absence of a noseleaf and the tail pattern.

Family PTEROPODIDAE   Fruit Bats

Fruit bats have large, conspicuous eyes which produce a dull red eyeshine in torchlight at night. The ears are relatively small and simple with a complete unbroken margin. The muzzle appears rather dog-like, without modifications or leaflets although the nostrils are well developed and sometimes slightly tubular. The tail is short or lacking and the interfemoral membrane is narrow. The second finger is well developed, independent of the third finger and usually with a claw at the tip (except *Eonycteris*). The teeth have simple cusps, quite unlike the sharp W-shaped cusps of other bats.

Many of these features are reflections of their behaviour. Fruit bats lack echolocation (except *Rousettus*) and rely instead on eyesight and smell to find their way. They feed mainly on nectar and fruit and often climb through trees using their wings as well as their feet to grip branches.

Eleven genera of fruit bats are currently recognized from Borneo. They fall into two main groups — the macroglossine bats such as *Macroglossus* and *Eonycteris* which have a long narrow muzzle, weak jaws and reduced teeth for nectar feeding, and the cynopterine bats such as *Cynopterus* and *Dyacopterus* which have shorter, more powerful jaws with smaller numbers of larger heavily cusped teeth for feeding on fruit (Figure 13). *Pteropus* and *Rousettus* are somewhat intermediate, and may represent a primitive condition from which the others evolved. Dental characters are important for distinguishing the genera but must be examined carefully, as some teeth, particularly the smaller cheek teeth, are sometimes missing or shed in older individuals.

Genus *Rousettus*: large with a fairly long muzzle, a claw on the second digit and a well developed tail. Produces a distinctive clicking call with the tongue for echolocation. Skull moderately long with slightly decurved rostrum (Figure 13e). Cheek teeth unspecialized with poorly developed cusps. Dental formula $\frac{2}{2}\frac{1}{1}\frac{3}{3}\frac{2}{3}$.

Figure 13. Fruit bat skulls (x1)
  a) *Pteropus vampyrus,*
  b) *Cynopterus brachyotis,*
  c) *Megaerops ecaudatus,*
  d) *Dyacopterus spadiceus,*
  e) *Rousettus spinalatus,*
  f) *Eonycteris major,*
  g) *Macroglossus minimus.*

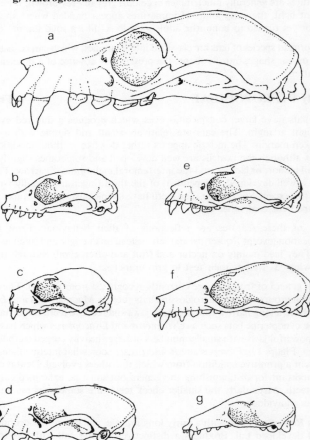

GEOFFROY'S ROUSETTE *Rousettus amplexicaudatus*   Plate 6

Measurements. FA 78-87, T 21, E 16.5-18.5, Wt 60-80 (5 specimens). Males average slightly larger than females.

Identification. Upperparts grey-brown to brown, darker on top of head; underparts paler grey-brown. Fur short and sparse except for long pale hairs on chin and neck. Adults, especially males, sometimes have pale yellow tufts of hair on the sides of the neck. Wings attached to sides of back, separated by a broad band of fur. Produces a distinctive, audible clicking call when flying or disturbed (used for echolocation). **Similar species:** the Bare-backed Rousette, *Rousettus spinalatus*, has the wings joined along the middle of the back; nectar bats, *Eonycteris* spp., lack a claw on the second digit; short-nosed fruit bats, *Cynopterus* spp., and the Dayak Fruit Bat, *Dyacopterus spadiceus*, have thicker shorter muzzles and fewer, larger cheek teeth.

Ecology and Habitat. Roosts in caves, sometimes in complete darkness, often in association with Cave Nectar Bats, *Eonycteris spelaea*. Feeds on fruit as well as nectar and pollen.

Distribution. Southern Burma, Thailand, Peninsular Malaysia, Philippines, Indonesia through New Guinea and the Solomon Islands. **Borneo:** *R. a. amplexicaudatus.* Recorded from P. Balembangan, Sukau, Madai Caves and Tawau in Sabah; Tasek Merimbun in Brunei; S. Baram and Niah Caves in Sarawak; S. Landak in West Kalimantan.

BARE-BACKED ROUSETTE *Rousettus spinalatus*   Plate 6

Measurements. FA 83-89, T 12-18, E 15.5-18 (13 Sabah specimens). Wt. 66-80 (3 females), 88-94 (3 males).

Identification. Fur generally pale grey-brown, short and sparse except for shaggy long hairs on the neck and chin. Adult males have yellow tufts of fur on the sides of the neck. Males larger and heavier than females. Wing membranes joined along middle of back and merging with tail membrane over legs. Produces an audible clicking call. **Similar species:** Geoffroy's Rousette, *R. amplexicaudatus,* has the wing membranes separate and inserted at the sides of the back.

Ecology and Habitat. Roosts in dark caves. One colony of 300 individuals contained both adult males and pregnant females. May occasionally associate with Geoffroy's Rousette, *R. amplexicaudatus,* in caves. Regular food presumably nectar and fruit, but has been reported to damage and possibly eat edible bird's nests (made by the swiftlet *Collocalia fuciphaga).*

Distribution. Sumatra. **Borneo:** known from caves at Sukau and the upper S. Kuamut in Sabah; Niah and the Bintulu area in Sarawak.

171

Genus *Pteropus:* very large bats including the largest in the world. First finger very long; second finger has a well developed claw. Skull large and elongate with an almost tubular braincase (Figure 13a). Three upper premolars, but anterior very small and often shed in older individuals. Remaining teeth relatively simple and unspecialized. Dental formula $\frac{2}{2}\,\frac{1}{1}\,\frac{3}{3}\,\frac{2}{3}$.

LARGE FLYING FOX *Pteropus vampyrus*   Plate 8

Measurements. FA 185-200, T none, Wt 645-1100 (5 Malayan specimens).

Identification. Largest Bornean bat. Back black with grey streaking; back of head and neck orange-brown; rest of head and underparts blackish brown. Immatures uniform dull grey-brown. **Similar species:** the Island Flying Fox, *P. hypomelanus*, is much smaller, with different coloration.

Ecology and Habitat. Roosts in large established colonies on open branches of trees, often in mangrove or nipah palm. Sometimes flies long distances to feed in flowering or fruiting trees. Eats both nectar and fruit including some orchard species such as rambutans and mangoes. Pollinates the flowers of many forest trees including durians.

Distribution. Southern Burma, Thailand, Indochina, Peninsular Malaysia, Philippines, Java, Lesser Sundas and adjacent islands. **Borneo:** *P. v. natunae.* Found throughout lowland coastal areas, occasionally invading the interior during the fruiting season. Also occurs on P. Balembangan and P. Banggi.

ISLAND FLYING FOX *Pteropus hypomelanus*   Plate 8

Measurements. FA 121, T none, E 25, Wt 213 (1 specimen).

Identification. Lower back dark grey-brown; upper back, neck, back of head and underparts pale golden brown; underside of head and flanks dark brown. **Similar species:** the Large Flying Fox, *P. vampyrus* is larger, while other Bornean bats are much smaller.

Ecology and Habitat. Roosts on islands in the fronds of coconut palms or amongst the branches of small trees. Sometimes flies to the mainland to feed.

Distribution. Small islands off coastal Southeast Asia through Indonesia to New Guinea and the Solomons. **Borneo:** *P. h. tomesi.* Recorded from many of the islands off the coasts of Sabah and East Kalimantan.

Genus Cynopterus: medium to large bats with a short stout muzzle. Most species have brown fur with a yellowish or reddish tinge and contrasting whitish wing bones and rims to the ears, although some old individuals have dark rims to the ears. Skull compact with a short rostrum (Figure 13b). Anterior upper premolar very small. Upper canines have a slight posterior secondary cusp; cheek teeth fairly stout, generally unspecialized. Dental formula $\frac{2}{2} \frac{1}{1} \frac{3}{3} \frac{1}{2}$.

Figure 14. Lower front incisors of: a) *Cynopterus*
b) *Penthetor*.

SHORT-NOSED FRUIT BAT *Cynopterus brachyotis*   Plate 6

Measurements. FA 55-65, T 8-10, E 14-16, Wt 21-32. Skull: cbl 26.4-28.5.

Identification. Generally brown to yellowish brown with a brighter collar which is dark orange in adult males, yellowish in females. Immature greyer with indistinct collar. Ears and wing bones are usually edged in white. Two pairs of lower incisors (Figure 14a). Specimens from tall forest are significantly smaller than the typical form found in forest edge and gardens, but there is some overlap and the taxonomic situation is unresolved. **Similar species:** the Greater Short-nosed Fruit Bat, *C. sphinx*, is very similar but has a generally longer forearm, longer ears and a much longer skull; Horsfield's Fruit Bat, *C. horsfieldi*, is larger and has squarer, heavily cusped molars (Figure 15a,b); the Dusky Fruit Bat, *Penthetor lucasi*, has only one pair of lower incisors (Figure 14b), lacks white edges to the ears and is usually greyer; the Tailless Fruit Bat, *Megaerops ecaudatus*, has a more upturned nose, lacks a bright collar, has no tail and only one pair of lower incisors.

Ecology and Habitat. Occurs in most habitats in Borneo including lower montane forest, dipterocarp forest, gardens, mangrove and strand vegetation. Roosts in small groups in trees, under leaves, or in the brighter areas of caves. Feeds mainly on small fruit, sucking out the juices and soft pulp, but nectar and pollen are also eaten.

Distribution. Sri Lanka, Southeast Asia, Philippines, Indonesia. **Borneo:** *C. b. brachyotis.* One of the commonest and most widespread fruit bats, found in all areas from sea level up to 1600 m in the mountains. Also reported from several off-shore islands including P. Balembangan.

Figure 15. Right lower jaw of fruit bats (x3):
a, b) *Cynopterus horsfieldi*
c) *C. sphinx,*
d) *Dyacopterus spadiceus.*

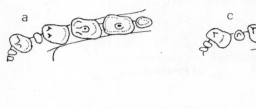

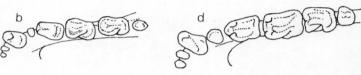

GREATER SHORT-NOSED FRUIT BAT *Cynopterus sphinx* Plate 6

Measurements. FA 65-76, T 18-22 (15 Malayan specimens). Skull: cbl 30.1-32.0.

Identification. Upperparts brown to grey-brown; underparts paler. Collar rich red-brown in males, yellow in females. Ears and wing bones edged in white. Lower cheek teeth rounded without accessory cusps (Figure 15c). **Similar species:** the Short-nosed Fruit Bat, *C. brachyotis*, is smaller with shorter ears; Horsfield's Fruit Bat, *C. horsfieldi*, has squarer cheek teeth with extra cusps or ridges (Figure 15a,b). *C. titthaecheileus*, which might occur in Borneo, is similar but even larger: FA 73-81, cbl 33.0-34.8 (in Sumatra).

Ecology and Habitat. In Thailand roosts in trees, under palm fronds or occasionally under roofs of houses. Feeds on nectar and fruit.

Distribution. Sri Lanka, India through southern China and Southeast Asia, Sumatra, Java, Timor and adjacent islands. **Borneo:** *C. s. angulatus*. The only Bornean record is from Central Kalimantan.

HORSFIELD'S FRUIT BAT *Cynopterus horsfieldi* Plate 6

Measurements. FA 68-76, T 14, E 17-20, Wt 50-70 (9 specimens). Skull: cbl 31.0-31.7.

Identification. Upperparts grey-brown; underparts slightly yellowish brown; collar dark reddish brown in adult males, paler in females. Ears and wingbones edged in white. Cheek teeth broader and squarer than other *Cynopterus* with distinct cusps or ridges on the last lower premolar and first lower molar (Figure 15a,b). **Similar species:** the Greater Short-nosed Fruit Bat, *C. sphinx*, has smaller, more rounded cheek teeth (Figure 15c); the Dayak Fruit Bat, *Dyacopterus spadiceus*, is larger, lacks the small anterior upper premolar and has massive teeth (Figure 15d).

Ecology and Habitat. Often roosts in rock shelters or caves, usually near the entrance. Occasionally found in trees or palms. Feeds mainly on fruit.

Distribution. Thailand, Peninsular Malaysia, Sumatra, Java, and adjacent islands. **Borneo:** *C. h. persimilis.* Reported from scattered localities in all districts except East Kalimantan with cave roosts known from G. Kinabalu at 1400 m and Gomantong in Sabah; near Kuching in Sarawak.

Genus *Penthetor:* medium sized bats, very similar to *Cynopterus*, but coloration generally dark grey-brown; cheek teeth slightly wider and flatter; only one pair of lower incisors (Figure 14b); outer upper incisors about half the length of the inner pair. Dental formula $\frac{2}{2}\ \frac{1}{1}\ \frac{3}{3}\ \frac{1}{2}$.

DUSKY FRUIT BAT *Penthetor lucasi*   Plate 6

Measurements. FA 57-62, T 8-13, E 14-16.5, Wt 30-44 (14 specimens).

Identification. Upperparts dark grey-brown; underparts pale buffy grey. Top of head often distinctly darker down the centre and paler near the eyes. Ears have dark edges. Only one pair of lower incisors (Figure 14b); outer upper incisors shorter than inner pair. **Similar species:** the Short-nosed Fruit Bat, *Cynopterus brachyotis*, has two pairs of lower incisors (Figure 14a); the Tailless Fruit Bat, *Megaerops ecaudatus*, lacks a tail, has broader nostrils and small, even, upper incisors.

Ecology and Habitat. Roosts mainly in rock shelters or caves, sometimes in near total darkness. Eats fruit which it carries back to the cave to eat. Roosts can sometimes be recognized by sprouting seeds.

Distribution. Peninsular Malaysia, Riau archipelago. **Borneo:** Recorded throughout the lowlands, up to 600 m on G. Mulu. Cave roosts known from Gomantong, upper S. Kuamut, and Sapulut in Sabah; Niah, S. Baram, and the mouth of S. Sarawak in Sarawak.

Genus *Megaerops:* small to medium bats, similar to *Cynopterus*, but with a slightly shorter nose; no visible tail; only one pair of lower incisors. Skull similar to *Cynopterus*, but with a higher rostrum, slightly concave on top (Figure 13c). Canines lack secondary cusps. Upper incisors small and roughly equal, evenly spaced between the canines. Dental formula $\frac{2}{2}\ \frac{1}{1}\ \frac{3}{3}\ \frac{1}{2}$.

TAILLESS FRUIT BAT *Megaerops ecaudatus*   Plate 7

Measurements. FA 51-58, T none, Wt 20-38 (12 Malayan specimens). Skull: cbl 24.0-26.2.

Identification. Upperparts yellowish brown to reddish brown with grey bases to fur; underparts paler and greyer. Ears not edged in white. Muzzle short with broad slightly tubular nostrils. One pair of lower incisors. Interfemoral membrane narrow and thinly haired. **Similar species:** the White-collared Fruit Bat, *M. wetmorei,* is smaller with white shoulder tufts; the Short-nosed Fruit Bat, *Cynopterus brachyotis,* has white edges to the ears (usually), a short tail and two pairs of lower incisors; the Dusky Fruit Bat, *Penthetor lucasi,* has a short tail and greyer fur; the Grey Fruit Bat, *Aethalops alecto,* has a more pointed muzzle and a thickly furred interfemoral membrane.

Ecology and Habitat. Has been netted mainly in tall forest.

Distribution. Thailand, Vietnam, Peninsular Malaysia, Sumatra. **Borneo:** Recorded from G. Kinabalu (up to 1500 m), Danum, Tawau, and Tenom in Sabah; upper S. Temburong and Tasik Merimbun in Brunei; the Kelabit uplands in Sarawak; S. Kapuas in West Kalimantan; the Kutai district in East Kalimantan.

WHITE-COLLARED FRUIT BAT *Megaerops wetmorei*   Plate 7

Measurements. FA 46, T none, E 12, Wt 14 (1 Brunei specimen). FA 46-51 in the Philippines. Skull: cbl 21.2-23.2.

Identification. Body fur pale grey brown, lower back darker. Large white tufts on side of neck extending onto back to form a broken collar — may be lacking in some individuals (Note: colour based on specimens in formalin). Interfemoral membrane narrow and sparsely covered with hairs. Tail very short or lacking. Muzzle short and thick. One pair of lower incisors. Rostrum of skull less upturned than in the Tailless Fruit Bat, *M. ecaudatus.* **Similar species:** the Tailless Fruit Bat, *M. ecaudatus,* is larger, lacks white neck tufts, and has a slightly thicker muzzle; the Black-capped Fruit Bat, *Chironax melanocephalus,* has two pairs of lower incisors; the Grey Fruit Bat, *Aethalops alecto,* has a more pointed muzzle and a thickly furred interfemoral membrane.

Ecology and Habitat. Unknown.

Distribution. Philippines. **Borneo:** Recorded only from Tasek Merimbun, Brunei.

Genus *Dyacopterus:* similar to *Cynopterus,* with a distinct tail, short muzzle and thick jaws (Figure 13d), but cheek teeth greatly enlarged, squarish in outline with large cusps and ridges (Figure 15d). Only three upper cheek teeth. Dental formula $\frac{2}{2}\frac{1}{1}\frac{2}{3}\frac{1}{2}$.

DAYAK FRUIT BAT *Dyacopterus spadiceus*   Plate 6

Measurements. FA 77-81, T 19-24, E 17.5-21 (7 Sabah specimens). Wt 75-100.

Identification. Upperparts dark grey-brown; underparts paler. Fur short. Some adults have dull orange tufts on each side of the neck. Very thick jaw and stout muzzle with massive square cheek teeth (Figure 15d) distinguishes from all other Bornean fruit bats.

Ecology and Habitat. Has been caught near caves, but roosting sites unknown. In Peninsular Malaysia has been found roosting in a tree trunk. One flock was feeding in a fig tree with Horsfield's Fruit Bat, *Cynopterus horsfieldi.*

Distribution. Peninsular Malaysia, Sumatra. **Borneo:** *D. s. spadiceus.* Recorded from Sepilok and Baturong Caves in Sabah; Baram district, Niah and near Sibu in Sarawak.

Genus *Chironax:* small bat very similar to *Cynopterus*, but lacking a tail; canines lack an inner cusp; premaxillaries fused (in contact but not fused in *Cynopterus).* Dental formula $\frac{2}{2}\frac{1}{1}\frac{3}{3}\frac{1}{2}$.

BLACK-CAPPED FRUIT BAT *Chironax melanocephalus*   Plate 7

Measurements. FA 42.8-45.6, T none, E 13, Wt 15.7 (2 specimens).

Identification. Upperparts dark grey or brown; head darker, sometimes black; underparts pale brownish grey; chin yellowish. Most adults have yellow-orange tufts on the sides of the neck. Two pairs of lower incisors. **Similar species:** all other small tailless fruit bats have only one pair of lower incisors (as in Figure 14b).

Ecology and Habitat. Sabah specimen was netted in the understorey of dipterocarp forest. In Peninsular Malaysia has been found roosting in small groups in tree ferns and in a shallow cave.

Distribution. Thailand, Peninsular Malaysia, Sumatra, Java, Sulawesi. **Borneo:** Only two records, from Sepilok in Sabah and the upper S. Temburong in Brunei.

Genus *Balionycteris:* a small dark fruit bat easily recognized by pale spots on the wings. Skull similar to *Cynopterus*, but slightly more elongate with an extra very small upper molar and only one pair of lower incisors. Upper incisors close together and angled inwards. Canine lacks a supplementary cusp. Dental formula $\frac{2}{1}\frac{1}{1}\frac{3}{3}\frac{2}{2}$.

SPOTTED-WINGED FRUIT BAT *Balionycteris maculata*   Plate 7

Measurements. FA 40-45, T none, E 10-12, Wt 10-15.

Identification. Upperparts dark blackish brown, darkest on the head; underparts pale grey-brown. Wing membranes dark brown sparsely spotted with buff, especially on the joints. Pale spots on the edge of the ear and in front of the eye. One pair of lower incisors. **Similar species:** other fruit bats lack spots on the wings; the Black-capped Fruit Bat, *Chironax melanocephalus,* has two pairs of lower incisors.

Ecology and Habitat. Frequently netted in lowland dipterocarp forest. In Peninsular Malaysia has been found roosting in small groups in crowns of palms and clumps of epiphytic ferns, rarely in caves.

Distribution. Southern Thailand, Peninsular Malaysia, Riau archipelago. **Borneo:** scattered records throughout the north and west including Kota Kinabalu, Sepilok, Madai and Tawau in Sabah; the upper S. Temburung and Tasek Merimbun in Brunei; Mulu, Niah, G. Dulit and Kuching in Sarawak; G. Kenepai in West Kalimantan.

Genus *Aethalops:* small tailless bat similar to *Balionycteris*, but without the second upper molar. Rostrum slightly lower and more sloping than *Cynopterus*. Upper incisors about equal in length. Interfemoral membrane narrow but thickly furred. Dental formula $\frac{2}{1} \frac{1}{1} \frac{3}{3} \frac{1}{2}$.

GREY FRUIT BAT *Aethalops alecto*   Plate 7

Measurements. FA 42-46, T none, E 10-13, Wt 14-18 (4 specimens).

Identification. Upperparts dark grey-brown to reddish brown; underparts slightly paler. Fur thick and long. Interfemoral membrane covered in thick fluffy fur. Muzzle narrow and pointed. One pair of lower incisors. **Similar species:** tailless fruit bats, *Megaerops* spp., have thicker shorter muzzles; the Black-capped Fruit Bat, *Chironax melanocephalus,* has two pairs of lower incisors; the Spotted-winged Fruit Bat, *Balionycteris maculata,* has distinct pale spots all over the wings.

Ecology and Habitat. Apparently confined to montane forest above 1000 m.

Distribution. Peninsular Malaysia, Sumatra, Java. **Borneo:** *A. a. aequalis.* All records are from mountains in the northwest including G. Kinabalu (up to 2700 m) and the Crocker Range in Sabah; G. Mulu and the Kelabit uplands in Sarawak.

Genus *Eonycteris:* medium to large fruit bats with a long narrow muzzle and a very long sticky tongue. Distinguished from all other Bornean fruit bats by the absence of a claw on the second finger. Tail well developed. Skull similar to *Rousettus,* but rostrum longer and lower; braincase more heavily deflected downwards (especially in *E. major* — Figure 13f). Cheek teeth narrow and elongate with reduced cusps. Lower canines small and simple, heavily curved outwards. Dental formula $\frac{2}{2} \frac{1}{1} \frac{3}{3} \frac{2}{3}$.

CAVE NECTAR BAT *Eonycteris spelaea*   Plate 6

Measurements. FA 62-70, T 15-18, E 17-20, Wt 45-60 (16 specimens).

Identification. Upperparts grey-brown; underparts slightly paler, sometimes tinged with yellow or orange around the neck. Fur short. Muzzle elongate, teeth rather small. Lacks a claw on the second digit. **Similar species:** the Greater Nectar Bat, *E. major,* is larger with a longer more decurved muzzle and darker fur; rousettes, *Rousettus* spp., have a claw on the second digit.

Ecology and Habitat. Roosts in large noisy colonies in caves often in almost total darkness. Flies long distances daily in search of flowering trees to feed on pollen and nectar. Important pollinator of many forest trees including durians, *Durio* spp.

Distribution. Northern India through southern China, Southeast Asia, Philippines, Sumatra, Java and other Indonesian islands. **Borneo:** subspecies uncertain. Cave roosts have been found at Gomantong, Sukau, S. Segama and Madai in Sabah; Niah, S. Tinjar, and near Kuching in Sarawak. Also recorded from the upper S. Tengah in South Kalimantan and Kutai in East Kalimantan.

GREATER NECTAR BAT *Eonycteris major*   Plate 7

Measurements. FA 71-80, T 18, E 21 (2 specimens). Wt 91.

Identification. Fur uniform dark blackish brown. Muzzle elongate and slightly decurved. Teeth reduced in size. No claw on second digit of wing. **Similar species:** the Cave Nectar Bat, *Eonycteris spelaea*, is smaller, paler in colour with a shorter muzzle; rousettes, *Rousettus* spp., have shorter muzzles and a claw on the second digit.

Ecology and Habitat. Has been recorded at roost in caves and hollow trees.

Distribution. Philippines. **Borneo:** Scattered records from most areas except Central and West Kalimantan including Kota Kinabalu and Ranau in Sabah; G. Dulit and Kuching in Sarawak; Kutai in East Kalimantan and upper S. Tengah in South Kalimantan. Cave roosts have been found in Sarawak along the S. Tinjar and in the Bintulu district.

Genus *Macroglossus*: small bats with a long narrow muzzle and a very long tongue. Tail minute or lacking. Skull has a very narrow rostrum with the braincase strongly deflected downwards (Figure 13g). Lower jaw thin and weak. Cheek teeth small with a large diastema (gap) between the first two upper premolars. Canines long and needlelike, strongly curved outwards on the lower jaw. Upper incisors tiny, projecting slightly forwards and separated from each other and the canines by small gaps. Dental formula $\frac{2}{2} \frac{1}{1} \frac{3}{3} \frac{2}{3}$.

LONG-TONGUED NECTAR BAT *Macroglossus minimus*   Plate 7
(formerly called *Macroglossus lagochilus*)

Measurements. FA 38-42, T none, E 13-15.5, Wt 11-16 (8 specimens).

Identification. Upperparts buffy brown with pale bases; underparts paler and greyer. Wing membranes light brown. Long, narrow muzzle with very small teeth except for needle-like canines. **Similar species:** small size and long muzzle distinguishes them from all known Bornean fruit bats. The Greater Long-tongued Nectar Bat, *Macroglossus sobrinus*, known from S.E. Asia, Java and Sumatra might occur in Borneo — it is larger (FA 42-48.5) with a longer head, jutting chin, more outward pointing nostrils and no median groove on the upper lip. Blossom bats, *Syconyteris* spp., known from Sulawesi and nearby islands, have long upper incisors (instead of tiny separated ones as found in *Macroglossus*).

Ecology and Habitat. Found in most habitats including coastal mangrove, dipterocarp forest and lower montane forest (up to 1000 m). Feeds on nectar and pollen from many sources including mangrove and banana flowers.

Distribution. Coastal Thailand, Peninsular Malaysia, southern Philippines, Java through to New Guinea, the Solomon islands and northern Australia. **Borneo:** *M. m. lagochilus.* Recorded from most areas including Kota Kinabalu, the Witti Range, Sepilok, Sukau and Tawau in Sabah; near Bandar Seri Begawan in Brunei; the Kelabit uplands, Niah and Bako in Sarawak; G. Kenepai in West Kalimantan; near Kutai in East Kalimantan; upper S. Tengah in South Kalimantan.

Small to medium sized bats with a distinctive tail which emerges from the middle of the interfemoral membrane (Figure 16a). When the legs are out-stretched the membrane completely encloses the tail. The muzzle is simple with no noseleaf. The ears are short to moderate with a short rounded tragus and the eyes are relatively large. These bats often roost in fairly bright areas, suggesting vision may be important, but they can echolocate as well. The wings are long and narrow.

The skull has a high full braincase and a moderately short rostrum. The postorbital processes are long and slender and the premaxillaries (where the upper incisors attach) are small and delicate.

Genus *Emballonura:* small and dark brown. Two distinct pairs of upper incisors; anterior upper premolar very small. Skull has a very shallow depression between the eyes (Figure 17g). Dental formula $\frac{2}{3}\,\frac{1}{1}\,\frac{2}{2}\,\frac{3}{3}$.

Figure 16. Tail and hind legs of
      a. Sheath-tailed bats — Emballonuridae
      b. Free-tailed bats — Molossidae

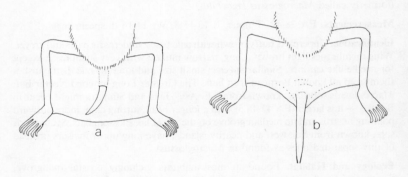

Figure 17. Mixed bat skulls:
    a, b) *Nycteris javanica,*
    c) *Megaderma spasma,*
    d) *Cheiromeles torquatus,*
    e) *Tadarida plicata,*
    f) *Taphozous melanopogon,*
    g) *Emballonura sp,*

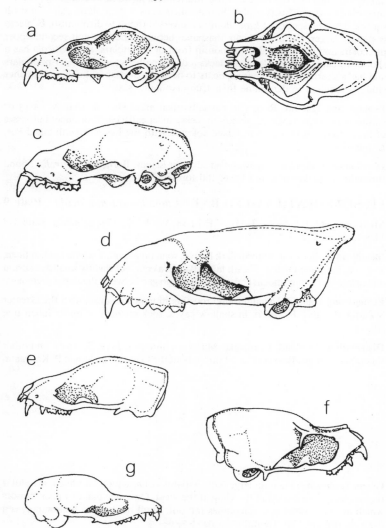

GREATER SHEATH-TAILED BAT   *Emballonura alecto*   Plate 9

Measurements. FA 45-48, T 14-15, E 12-13, Wt 4.5-7 (9 specimens). Skull: ccl 12.7-13.8.

Identification. Uniformly dark brown to reddish-brown. This and the next species are distinguished from all other bats by their small size, dark coloration and short tail protruding from the middle of the interfemoral membrane. Roosting posture, supported by the wrists (see Plate 9) is distinctive, as is their alarm call — a shrill squeak. The two species of *Emballonura* are very difficult to distinguish. *E. alecto* is slightly larger, has a short gap (diastema) between the first and second upper premolars and a longer palatal region in front of the molars. *E. monticola* has a shorter forearm and smaller skull, lacks a diastema between the upper premolars and has a shorter palate. There appears to be slight overlap, though, and further study is required to determine their true taxonomic status.

Ecology and Habitat. Roosts in partially open areas such as shallow caves or entrances of deeper caves, in crevices in rocks, under earth banks or under buttresses of fallen tree trunks. Often in mixed colonies with the Lesser Sheath-tailed Bat, *E. monticola*.

Distribution. Philippines, Sulawesi and adjacent islands. **Borneo:** *E. a. rivalis.* Found throughout the lowland and lower hill forests.

LESSER SHEATH-TAILED BAT   *Emballonura monticola*   Plate 9

Measurements. FA 43-45, T 11-14, E 12-13, Wt 4.5-5.5 (5 specimens). Skull: ccl 11.8-12.8.

Identification. Body fur uniform dark brown, sometimes with a strong reddish tinge. Very similar to the Greater Sheath-tailed Bat, *E. alecto*, but slightly smaller; rostrum and palate (in front of molars) relatively short; no gap between the upper premolars.

Ecology and Habitat. Usually found roosting in mixed colonies with the Greater Sheath-tailed Bat, *E. alecto*, in shallow caves, rock crevices or under fallen tree trunks.

Distribution. Thailand, Peninsular Malaysia, Sumatra, Java, Sulawesi and other Indonesian islands. **Borneo:** Found throughout the lowlands including P. Karimata.

Genus *Taphozous*: medium large bats, variably coloured. Often have a glandular throat pouch or a pocket in the wing at the wrist. Only one pair of upper incisors which are very small and sometimes fall out. Skull has a deep hollow between the eyes (Figure 17f). Dental formula $\frac{1}{3}\frac{1}{1}\frac{2}{2}\frac{3}{3}$.

POUCHED TOMB BAT   *Taphozous saccolaimus*   Plate 9

Measurements. FA 71-78, T 33-34, E 19-21, Wt 40-50 (5 specimens).

Identification. Upperparts blackish brown variably marked with white. Underparts usually white, but in one colour phase, dark brown. Metacarpal pouch (at the wrist) poorly developed (Figure 18a). Has a distinct glandular pouch under the chin. Legs and feet hairless. All tomb bats, *Tapohozous* spp., can be recognized in flight by their long, narrow, translucent whitish wings and the audible clicks of their echolocation calls. This is the largest species with the whitest wings. **Similar Species:** other tomb bats, *Taphozous* spp., are smaller, have a well developed metacarpal pouch (Figure 18b), and fur on the legs.

Ecology and Habitat. Sometimes found in houses in colonies varying from a few individuals to a few hundred. Also roosts in hollow trees and rock crevices.

Distribution. India, Sri Lanka, Burma, Thailand, Peninsular Malaysia, Sumatra, Java through to New Guinea and Australia. **Borneo:** *T. s. saccolaimus.* Recorded from Kota Kinabalu, Keningau and Tenom in western Sabah; near Bandar Seri Begawan in Brunei; Samunsam, Kuching and environs in Sarawak; Kutai in East Kalimantan; S. Martapura and upper S. Tengah in South Kalimantan.

Figure 18. Wings of tomb bats showing radio-metacarpal pouch:
    a) *Taphozous saccolaimus,*
    b) *T. melanopogon.*

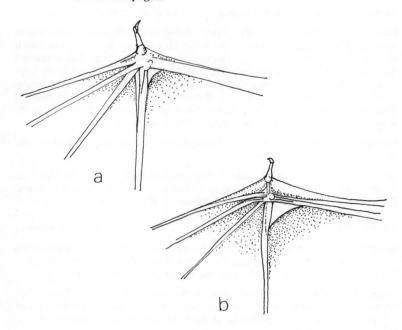

BLACK-BEARDED TOMB BAT *Taphozous melanopogon* Plate 9

Measurements. FA 60-63, T 25-28, E 19-22, Wt 23-26 (8 specimens).

Identification. Upperparts vary from grey-brown to buffy-brown; underparts usually paler, sometimes almost white. Chin covered with fur, lacking a throat pouch — most adult males have a black "beard". Legs and feet covered in short fur. Well developed wing pouch (Figure 18b). Tail slightly swollen at tip. Wing membrane attaches above ankle. Wings pale, appearing whitish in flight. **Similar Species:** the Pouched Tomb Bat, *T. saccolaimus,* has a reduced wing pouch and a distinct throat pouch; the Long-winged Tomb Bat, *T. longimanus,* has a naked chin with a throat pouch in males, tail tapers evenly to the tip and wing membrane attaches at the ankle.

Ecology and Habitat. Roosts in caves and large crevices in rocks, often in fairly well-lit areas.

Distribution. Sri Lanka, India through southern China and Southeast Asia, Sumatra, Java and smaller islands. **Borneo:** *T. m. fretensis.* Recorded from scattered locations over most of the mainland from northern Sabah to S. Martapura in South Kalimantan. Roosts have been found in sea caves near Kudat and Sandakan in Sabah and Samunsam in Sarawak; in limestone caves at Baturong, Tepadong, and at Niah.

LONG-WINGED TOMB BAT *Taphozous longimanus* Plate 9

Measurements. FA 54-58 (6 Peninsular Malaysian specimens).

Identification. Colour variable, dark brown to blackish occasionally speckled with white. In Thailand females greyer and males brown. Chin naked; throat pouch in males. Wings long and narrow, whitish and attached at ankle. Well developed wing (radio-metacarpal) pouch (as in Figure 18b). Tail tapers narrowly to tip. Legs covered with short fur. **Similar Species:** the Pouched Tomb Bat, *T. saccolaimus* is larger, lacks a wing pouch (Figure 18a) and has bare legs; the Black-bearded Tomb bats, *T. melanopogon* has a furred chin in both sexes with no throat pouch, wing membrane attached above ankle, tail thickened near tip.

Ecology and Habitat. In Peninsular Malaysia roosts under the eaves of houses, in hollow trees and under rocks.

Distribution. Sri Lanka, India, Burma, Thailand, Cambodia, Peninsular Malaysia, Sumatra, Java, Flores, Bali. **Borneo:** *T. l. albipinnis.* Reported from Ranau and P. Labuan in Sabah; G. Penrisen in Sarawak; S. Kapuas in West Kalimantan.

Family MEGADERMATIDAE False Vampires

Medium to large bats with a large erect noseleaf and large ears joined across the top of the head. The tragus is long and forked. The tail is very short, not visible externally, although the interfemoral membrane is well developed.

Genus *Megaderma:* interorbital region of skull not especially concave (Figure 17c). Premaxillaries minute with no upper incisors; canines project well forward with a distinct secondary cusp; anterior upper premolars minute and displaced inwards. Dental formula: $\frac{0}{2} \frac{1}{1} \frac{2}{2} \frac{3}{3}$.

184

LESSER FALSE VAMPIRE   *Megaderma spasma*   Plate 11

Measurements. FA 54-61, E 35-40, Wt 23-28 (Peninsular Malaysian and Bornean specimens).

Identification. Fur pale grey to grey-brown. Noseleaf has long dorsal lobe with stiffened central ridge and broad convex flaps on the sides. Ears very large, joined at bases. Tragus long and forked (bifid). No visible tail, although interfemoral membrane is well developed. *M. s. kinabalu* is reported to have a larger skull than *M. s. trifolium* (gsl 27-27.3), but few specimens are available to determine individual variation. **Similar Species:** the Hollow-faced Bat, *Nycteris javanica,* has a differently shaped noseleaf, short tragus and very long tail with a T-shaped tip.

Ecology and Habitat. In Peninsular Malaysia roosts in small groups in caves, tunnels or hollow trees. Eats mainly large insects but sometimes small vertebrates including other bats. Despite the name it does not drink blood and is unrelated to South American vampire bats.

Distribution. Sri Lanka, India through Southeast Asia, Philippines, Sumatra, Java, Sulawesi, Moluccas and other Indonesian islands. **Borneo:** *M. s. trifolium.* Found in most areas except central and western Sabah. Records include Sepilok, P. Berhala and the Darvel Bay area in Sabah; Niah and Kuching in Sarawak; the upper S. Kapuas in West Kalimantan; upper S. Tengah in South Kalimantan. *M. s. kinabalu.* Known from G. Kinabalu (at 1000 m) and the Crocker Range in Sabah (the subspecies of specimens collected on the coast at Marudu Bay in Sabah was not determined). *M. s. carimatae.* Found only on P. Karimata.

Family NYCTERIDAE   Hollow-faced Bats

Medium large bats with very long ears separated at the base, and a short rounded tragus. The tail is long with a T-shaped tip and fully enclosed in the interfemoral membrane. The face has a deep groove in the middle bordered by leaf-like flaps of skin.

The skull is distinguished by the deep frontal depression with broad ridges on either side (Figure 17a,b). The premaxillaries are broadly attached to the palate. Dental formula $\frac{2}{3}\ \frac{1}{1}\ \frac{1}{2}\ \frac{3}{3}$.

The family contains only the genus *Nycteris.*

HOLLOW-FACED BAT   *Nycteris javanica*   Plate 11

Measurements. FA 46-51, T 65-72, E 29-31, Wt 12-17 (5 Peninsular Malaysian specimens).

Identification. Fur long and fluffy, pale red-brown to greyish. Noseleaf and ears grey-brown with irregular pale patches. Deep hollow groove in middle of face fringed with large flaps which form a type of noseleaf. Ears long and rounded, not joined at bases. Tragus short and bent. Very long tail with T-shaped tip, totally enclosed in interfemoral membrane. **Similar Species:** the Lesser False Vampire, *Megaderma spasma,* has a different shaped noseleaf, ears joined at base, long forked tragus, no tail.

185

Ecology and Habitat. Roosts in small groups in hollow trees or caves.

Distribution. Burma, Thailand, Peninsular Malaysia, Sumatra, Java, Bali. **Borneo:** *N. j. tragata*. Recorded from Sepilok, Sukau and Tawau in Sabah; most parts of Sarawak including Niah and the Kuching area; upper S. Tengah in South Kalimantan.

Figure 19. a. Noseleaf of horseshoe bat *(Rhinolophus),* showing naming of parts.
b. side view.

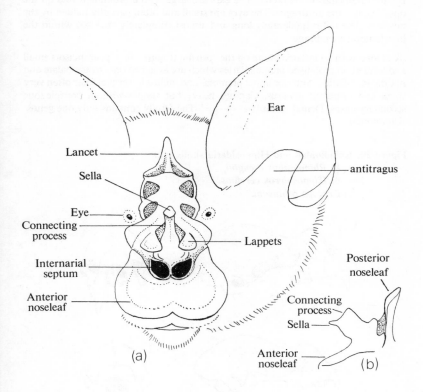

Family RHINOLOPHIDAE Horseshoe Bats

Horseshoe bats are small to medium sized bats with an elaborate noseleaf (Figure 19). The anterior section is rounded and roughly horseshoe-shaped. In the middle behind the nostrils is a raised portion called the sella. Behind this is the posterior noseleaf which rises to a long lancet-shaped point. The shape of the sella and the connecting process which joins it to the posterior leaf varies between species and is a useful diagnostic character. The ears are large with a prominent fold on the outside edge, the antitragus. The eyes are small and often partially hidden by the noseleaf. The tail is moderately long and almost completely enclosed within the interfemoral membrane.

Skull long with an inflated bump on the rostrum (Figure 20). Upper incisors small and located on prolonged premaxillaries which are attached only to the palate and not the maxillaries. Anterior upper premolar and middle lower premolar often very small and displaced inwards. Canines heavy but simple without conspicuous secondary cusps. Dental formula $\frac{1}{2}$ $\frac{1}{1}$ $\frac{2}{3}$ $\frac{3}{3}$. The family contains only one genus: *Rhinolophus*.

Figure 20. Rhinolophid and Hipposiderid skulls (x2).
  a, b) *Rhinolophus creaghii,*
  c, d) *Hipposideros cervinus,*
  e) *Ceolops robinsoni.*

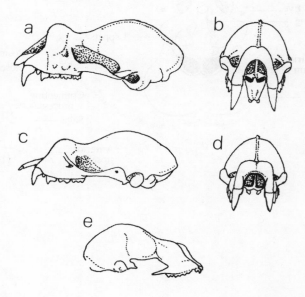

BORNEAN HORSESHOE BAT   *Rhinolophus borneensis*   Plate 10

Measurements. FA 40-44, T 21-26, E 17-19, Wt 7-8.5.

Identification. Overall colour varies from grey-brown to reddish. Ears relatively small. Noseleaf simple without extra lappets or flaps; connecting process varies from slightly rounded to bluntly pointed. **Similar species:** the Least Horseshoe Bat, *R. pusillus* is smaller with a slightly shorter forearm and very small noseleaf; other horseshoe bats are larger with a longer forearm and bigger ears.

Ecology and Habitat. Roosts in caves, sometimes in colonies of several hundred individuals.

Distribution. Con Son island (off Indochina), Java and smaller islands. **Borneo:** *R. b. borneensis.* Commonly found in most cave systems in Sabah including Gomantong, Sukau, Madai, Sapulut area and G. Kinabalu. Also reported from Niah, Hose Mts (at 1000 m), and near Kuching in Sarawak; Peleben and Kutai in East Kalimantan; upper S. Tengah in South Kalimantan. *R. b. spadix.* Only known from P. Karimata and P. Serutu off West Kalimantan.

LEAST HORSESHOE BAT   *Rhinolophus pusillus*   Plate 10

Measurements. FA 37-40, T 13, E 12.5 (1 Bornean and 5 Peninsular Malaysian specimens). Skull: ccl 13.8, io 2.1.

Identification. Upperparts light brown; underparts slightly paler. Smallest Bornean horseshoe bat, but with relatively large ears. Noseleaf simple and small; connecting process triangular and slightly pointed; sella parallel sided. **Similar species:** the Bornean Horseshoe Bat, *R. borneensis,* has a much larger noseleaf.

Ecology and Habitat. Unknown.

Distribution. India, southern China, Thailand, Peninsular Malaysia, Java and small adjacent islands. **Borneo:** *R. p. pusillus.* Only Bornean record is from near S. Karangan in East Kalimantan.

ARCUATE HORSESHOE BAT   *Rhinolophus arcuatus*   Plate 10

Measurements. FA 46-48 (2 specimens).

Identification. Uniformly dark brown. Ears large. Noseleaf broad, covering muzzle, lacking lateral lappets; connecting process broadly rounded, originating from tip of sella; sella broad and slightly expanded at base. **Similar species:** the Intermediate Horseshoe Bat, *R. affinis,* has the connecting process originating from below the tip of the sella (forming a slight notch), and sella narrower with a less expanded base; the Acuminate Horseshoe Bat, *R. acuminatus,* has a smaller noseleaf, not quite covering the muzzle, with a pointed connecting process.

Ecology and Habitat. The only known specimens were caught roosting in a cave.

Distribution. Philippines, Sumatra, Flores islands. **Borneo:** *R. a. proconsulis.* Known only from Bungoh Cave near Bau in Sarawak.

189

ACUMINATE HORSESHOE BAT *Rhinolophus acuminatus* Plate 10

Measurements. FA 48-50, T 21-31, E 20-21, Wt 11.5-13.5 (5 specimens).

Identification. Upperparts dark grey-brown; underparts paler. Noseleaf and ears dark grey. Ears moderately large. Noseleaf simple without lateral lappets on sella; connecting process sharply pointed. **Similar species:** the Borneo Horseshoe Bat, *R, borneensis* is smaller; the Intermediate Horseshoe Bat, *R. affinis* has a rounded connecting process.

Ecology and Habitat. Has been caught in the understorey of lowland dipterocarp forest.

Distribution. Laos, Cambodia, Thailand, Peninsular Malaysia, Philippines, Sumatra, Java and smaller Indonesian islands. **Borneo:** *R. a. sumatranus.* Recorded only from Sabah, at Betotan, G. Kinabalu (up to 1600 m), Tabin, upper S. Kuamut and Tawau.

INTERMEDIATE HORSESHOE BAT *Rhinolophus affinis* Plate 10

Measurements. FA 49-54, T 22-26, E 21-25 (24 Peninsular Malaysian specimens). Wt 12.5.

Identification. Upperparts dark brown to reddish brown; underparts slightly paler. Ears moderately large. Noseleaf simple without extra lappets on sella; connecting process broadly rounded, orginating from below tip of sella, forming a slight notch. **Smaller species:** the Bornean Horseshoe Bat, *R. borneensis,* has a shorter forearm and smaller ears; the Acuminate Horseshoe Rat, *R. acuminatus,* has a pointed connecting process; the Arcuate Horseshoe Rat, *R. arcuatus,* has a broader sella, slightly expanded at the base, and connecting process originating from tip of sella.

Ecology and Habitat. Has been found roosting in caves. Forages in understorey of forest.

Distribution. India through China, Southeast Asia, Sumatra, Java. **Borneo:** *R. a. nesites.* Recorded only from the south and west at Samunsam and near Kuching in Sarawak, S. Pangkalahan in West Kalimantan and S. Pasir in South Kalimantan.

CREAGH'S HORSESHOE BAT   Plate 10
Rhinolophus creaghi

Measurements. FA 46-51, E 19, Wt 10.5-13.5.

Identification. Fur colour variable, ranging from grey-brown to yellowish-brown to reddish. Ears and noseleaf moderately large. A distinctive conical tuft of stiff hairs on posterior noseleaf replaces connecting process. **Similar species:** all other Rhinolophus have a well developed connecting process.

Ecology and Habitat. Roosts in large colonies in caves, sometimes numbering over 100,000.

Distribution. Madura Is, Java, Timor. **Borneo:** *R. c. creaghi.* Common in nearly every cave system studied in Sabah. Also recorded from caves in the Baram district in Sarawak and near Kutai in East Kalimantan.

190

PHILIPPINE HORSESHOE BAT
Rhinolophus philippinensis
Plate 10

Measurements. FA 48-53, T 25-33, E 27-31, Wt 8.5-11.5.

Identification. Fur usually uniformly dark grey-brown. Noseleaf and ears dark grey. Ears very large. Posterior noseleaf long and triangular; sella long and protruding, expanded at base into a cup-like structure between the nostrils. **Similar species:** other Bornean *Rhinolophus* have smaller ears (except *R. luctus* which is much larger), and a less protruding sella which lacks a cup-like base.

Ecology and Habitat. Roosts in loose colonies in caves.

Distribution. Philippines, Sulawesi, Timor, Australia. **Borneo:** *R. p. sanborni.* Recorded from caves throughout Sabah including Gomantong, Madai, Tepadong, and near Sapulut, as well as various caves in Sarawak along S. Baram, near Bintulu and at Niah.

TREFOIL HORSESHOE BAT
Rhinolophus trifoliatus
Plate 11

Measurements: FA 47-52, T 27-37, E 22-26, Wt 10.5-18.

Identification. Fur long and woolly, pale buffy brown to brownish grey. Noseleaf pale yellow; ears and wing membranes yellowish brown with yellow elbows and knees. Noseleaf has lateral lappets at base of sella (as in Figure 19a). One rather large specimen caught at 1800 m on Trus Madi had dark membranes and dark brown fur — it may represent an unrecognized montane form, but could just have been a melanistic individual. **Similar species:** Woolly Horseshoe Bats, *R. luctus* and *R. sedulus*, have dark brown fur, blackish noseleafs and differ in size.

Ecology and Habitat. Often caught in the understorey of primary forest where it sometimes roosts under large leaves.

Distribution. Northeast India, Burma, peninsular Thailand and Malaysia, Sumatra, Java and adjacent islands. **Borneo:** *R. t. trifoliatus.* Known from most areas, primarily in the lowlands but with records up to 1200 m near the Kelabit uplands and 1800 m on G. Trus Madi.

LESSER WOOLLY HORSESHOE BAT
Rhinolophus sedulus
Plate 11

Measurements. FA 40-44, T 20-25, E 22-23, Wt 8.4-11 (7 specimens).

Identification. Fur long and fluffy, uniformly dark brown to dark grey. Noseleaf and ears dark grey. Noseleaf has lateral lappets at base of sella (Figure 19a). **Similar species:** the Great Woolly Horseshoe Bat, *R. luctus,* is similarly coloured but much larger; the Trefoil Horseshoe Bat, *R. trifoliatus,* is larger, has pale grey fur and a yellowish noseleaf.

Ecology and Habitat. Roosts in bushes or hollow trees. Forages in the understorey of tall forest up to 1500 m.

Distribution. Peninsular Malaysia. **Borneo:** *R. s. sedulus.* Probably widespread, with records from Sepilok, Tabin, and Trus Madi in Sabah; Samunsam in Sarawak; S. Landak in West Kalimantan; S. Sampit and S. Riam in Central Kalimantan.

GREAT WOOLLY HORSESHOE BAT   Plate 11
Rhinolophus luctus

Measurements. FA 63-67, T 38-50, E 31-35, Wt 29-37 (6 specimens).

Identification. Largest Bornean horseshoe bat. Fur long and woolly. Upperparts brownish black; underparts slightly greyer. Noseleaf and ears dark grey-brown. Noseleaf has lateral lappets at base of sella (as in Figure 19a). **Similar species:** the Lesser Woolly Horseshoe Bat, *R. sedulus,* and the Trefoil Horseshoe Bat, *R. trifoliatus,* have a similar noseleaf but are smaller, and the latter has paler fur and a yellowish noseleaf.

Ecology and Habitat. Roosts in small groups in caves and rock crevices or under roots of trees. In hill forest observed feeding in the middle storey by hanging from a branch, flying out periodically to grab food, then returning to its branch.

Distribution. Sri Lanka, India through southern China, Taiwan, Southeast Asia, Sumatra, Java, Bali. **Borneo:** *R. l. foetidus.* Occurs from the lowlands up to 1600 m in the mountains. Recorded from Betotan, Madai, Kinabalu and Trus Madi in Sabah; throughout Sarawak from Lawas to Serabang including the upper S. Tutoh and the Hose mountains; S. Landak in West Kalimantan; upper S. Tengah in South Kalimantan.

Family HIPPOSIDERIDAE   Roundleaf Bats

The roundleaf bats vary in size from quite small to moderately large. Like the true horseshoe bats (Rhinolophidae) they have an elaborate noseleaf (Figure 21). The anterior noseleaf is rounded and somewhat horseshoe-shaped (except in *Coelops*). The median leaf is a low cushion-like structure expanded laterally without a sella, while the posterior leaf is low and rounded, usually divided by vertical septa into several pockets. The internarial septum varies from very narrow to broadly expanded. Some species have additional lateral leaflets below the anterior noseleaf. The ears vary from moderately small to large with a low antitragus. The eyes are very small.

Genus *Hipposideros:* typical horseshoe-shaped anterior noseleaf (as in Figure 21). Tail short to moderate, largely enclosed in interfemoral membrane. Skull generally similar to *Rhinolophus,* but rostrum with paired swellings on top (Figure 20c,d), although these are sometimes low. Anterior upper premolar variably reduced; upper canines heavy but simple, without prominent supplementary cusps. Dental formula $\frac{1}{2}\ \frac{1}{1}\ \frac{2}{2}\ \frac{3}{3}$.

Figure 21. Noseleaf of typical roundleaf bat *(Hipposideros)* showing naming of parts.

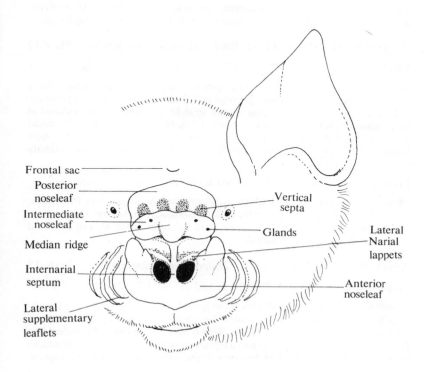

DUSKY ROUNDLEAF BAT   *Hipposideros ater*   Plate 12

Measurements. FA 39-43, T 22-26, E 15-17.5, Wt 5-7.5 (20 specimens). Skull: ccl 15.3.

Identification. Upperparts pale brown to grey-brown; underparts greyish white. Noseleaf pale pinkish. Ears broad and rounded but fairly small. Noseleaf simple, lacking lateral leaflets; three supporting septa divide posterior noseleaf into four pockets (as in Figure 21); internarial septum slightly swollen at base, very narrow in middle; anterior noseleaf unnotched. **Similar Species:** the Bicolored Roundleaf Bat, *H. bicolor*, has a longer forearm, larger ears and a straighter internarial septum; the Ashy Roundleaf Bat, *H. cineraceus*, has the internarial septum distinctly expanded in the middle and larger ears; the Dayak Roundleaf Bat, *H. dyacorum*, has dark brown noseleaf and fur and broadly triangular ears; the Least Roundleaf Bat, *H. sabanus*, has a very small noseleaf without supporting septa on the posterior leaf.

193

Ecology and Habitat. Roosts in caves in colonies of up to a few hundred individuals.

Distribution. Sri Lanka, India, Southeast Asia, Philippines, Indonesia through to Australia. **Borneo:** (subspecies uncertain). So far known only from limestone cave areas in eastern Sabah including Gomantong, Sukau, Madai and Segarong.

BICOLORED ROUNDLEAF BAT   *Hipposideros bicolor*   Plate 12

Measurements. FA 45-48, T 27-31, E 17.5-20, Wt 7-8.5 (5 specimens). Skull: ccl 16.4.

Identification. Upperparts brown to grey-brown; underparts paler, usually buffy white. Ears large and rounded. Noseleaf pale pinkish brown, simple and small, lacking lateral leaflets; internarial septum straight and only slightly widened at base. **Similar Species:** the Dusky Roundleaf Bat, *H. ater,* is smaller with smaller ears and internarial septum widened at base, narrower in middle; the Ashy Roundleaf Bat, *H. cineraceus,* is smaller with the internarial septum distinctly swollen in the middle.

Ecology and Habitat. In Peninsular Malaysia roosts in caves or tunnels.

Distribution. India to Southern China, Taiwan through Southeast Asia, Philippines, Sumatra, Java, Sulawesi and smaller islands. **Borneo:** *H. b. bicolor.* Known from only a few specimens from Gomantong and Sukau in Sabah as well as an old unconfirmed report from Sarawak.

ASHY ROUNDLEAF BAT   *Hipposideros cineraceus*   Plate 12

Measurements. FA 36-40.5, T 24-30, E 18.5-21, Wt 4-5.5. Skull: ccl 13.2-13.9.

Identification. Upperparts buffy brown to greyish-brown; underparts buffy-white to pale brown. Ears large and rounded. Noseleaf simple, lacking lateral leaflets; internarial septum expanded in middle. **Similar Species:** the Dusky Roundleaf Bat, *H. ater,* has smaller ears and internarial septum expanded at base, narrow in middle; the Bicolored Roundleaf Bat, *H. bicolor,* is larger with a straight internarial septum.

Ecology and Habitat. Roosts in caves in colonies of up to several hundred individuals, sometimes mixed with the Dusky Roundleaf Bat, *H. ater.*

Distribution. Pakistan, northern India, Burma, Thailand, Vietnam, Peninsular Malaysia. **Borneo:** *H. c. cineraceus.* Recorded only from Sabah in caves at Marudu Bay, Madai, Baturong, Segarong and on the upper S. Kuamut.

DAYAK ROUNDLEAF BAT   *Hipposideros dyacorum*   Plate 12

Measurements. FA 38-42, T 19-24, E 15-18, Wt 5-7.5.

Identification. Fur uniformly dark brown. Noseleaf, ears and wing membranes dark grey-brown. Ears broadly triangular and pointed. Noseleaf simple without lateral leaflets, closely resembling that of the Dusky Roundleaf Bat, *H. ater.* **Similar Species:** the Dusky Roundleaf Bat, *H. ater,* has a pale pinkish noseleaf, whitish underparts and rounded ears; the Fawn Roundleaf Bat, *H. cervinus,* is larger with a wider noseleaf and two lateral leaflets.

Ecology and Habitat. Has been found roosting in caves, under rocks or in hollow trees. Forages in the understorey of tall forest.

Distribution. Known only from Borneo. Recorded from scattered localities all over Sabah; G. Mulu and the Hose Mountains (up to 900 m) in Sarawak; Kg. Perbuah along S. Landak in West Kalimantan.

LEAST ROUNDLEAF BAT   *Hipposideros sabanus*   Plate 13

Measurements. FA 34-37, Wt 4.2 (Peninsular Malaysian specimens). Skull: ccl 12.9, mt 4.4-5.1.

Identification. Fur generally brown to buffy brown (based on an old specimen). Colour of noseleaf and ears not recorded in life. Ears broad and rounded. Noseleaf very small and simple with no lateral leaflets; anterior horseshoe has a small central notch; posterior noseleaf lacks supporting septa. **Similar Species:** the Dusky Roundleaf Bat, *H. ater,* and related species have larger noseleafs with distinct vertical ridges dividing the posterior noseleaf into four compartments.

Ecology and Habitat. unknown.

Distribution. Peninsular Malaysia, Sumatra. **Borneo:** Known only from Lawas in northern Sarawak.

RIDLEY'S ROUNDLEAF BAT   *Hipposideros ridleyi*   Plate 13

Measurements. FA 47-49, T 25-29, E 25-27, Wt 6.5-9.5 (6 specimens).

Identification. Fur uniformly dark brown. Ears, noseleaf and wing membranes dark grey. Ears very large and rounded. Noseleaf large, covering the whole muzzle; no lateral leaflets; internarial septum expanded into a large disk which nearly obscures the nostrils. **Similar Species:** Cox's Roundleaf Bat, *H. coxi,* also has a large noseleaf, but with a quite different structure and 2 lateral leaflets.

Ecology and Habitat. Occurs in lowland forest including kerangas. In Peninsular Malaysia has been found roosting in small groups in culverts and drainage pipes.

Distribution. Peninsular Malaysia. **Borneo:** Recorded only from Sabah at Sepilok, Tabin, and Menggalong.

FAWN ROUNDLEAF BAT   *Hipposideros cervinus*   Plate 13
(formerly confused with *Hipposideros galeritus*)

Measurements. FA 44-50, T 21-28, E 14-17, Wt 7-10.

Identification. Fur colour varies from grey-brown or yellowish-brown to bright red-brown or orange. Noseleaf greyish pink. Ears broadly triangular. Noseleaf simple with two lateral leaflets; median noseleaf narrower than posterior noseleaf. **Similar Species:** Cantor's Roundleaf Bat, *H. galeritus,* has median noseleaf broader than posterior noseleaf, ears broader and more rounded, tail longer; the Dayak Roundleaf Bat, *H. dyacorum,* lacks lateral leaflets on the nose.

Ecology and Habitat. Usually roosts in caves, sometimes in very large colonies (up to 300,000). Feeds in the forest understorey.

Distribution. Peninsular Malaysia, Philippines through Indonesia, New Guinea to Australia. **Borneo:** *H. c. labuanensis.* Found in virtually every cave system examined in Sabah and Sarawak, including offshore islands such as P. Balembangan, P. Mantanani and P. Labuan; G. Kenepai and S. Landak in West Kalimantan.

CANTOR'S ROUNDLEAF BAT   *Hipposideros galeritus*   Plate 13
(formerly included *Hipposideros cervinus)*

Measurements. FA 47-51, T 30-43, Wt 6.3-8.5.

Identification. Fur usually dark grey-brown, occasionally with a reddish tinge. Noseleaf pinkish grey. Ears broad, rounded at base, triangular at tip. Noseleaf with two lateral leaflets; median noseleaf broader than posterior noseleaf. **Similar Species:** the Fawn Roundleaf Bat, *H. cervinus,* has median noseleaf narrower than posterior noseleaf, shorter tail; Cox's Roundleaf Bat, *H. coxi,* has a very large noseleaf expanded posteriorly and completely covering the muzzle.

Ecology and Habitat. Roosts in caves, often in small groups with the Fawn Roundleaf Bat, *H. cervinus,* but sometimes in colonies of several hundred.

Distribution. India, Sri Lanka, Thailand, Peninsular Malaysia, Java. **Borneo:** *H. g. insolens.* Less common than the Fawn Roundleaf Bat, *H. cervinus,* but still widespread, with records from throughout Sabah and Sarawak; upper S. Pasir in South Kalimantan; East Kalimantan.

COX'S ROUNDLEAF BAT   *Hipposideros coxi*   Plate 13

Measurements. FA 53-55, (3 specimens). Wt 10.

Identification. Upperparts dark brown; underparts dull brown. Noseleaf, ears and wings very dark brown. 2 lateral leaflets. Noseleaf large (about 13 x 10 mm) completely covering muzzle; internarial septum ridged and swollen; median noseleaf with a raised central ridge; posterior noseleaf expanded upwards. **Similar Species:** the Fawn and Cantor's Roundleaf Bats, *H. cervinus* and *H. galeritus,* have much smaller noseleafs; Ridley's Roundleaf Bat, *H. ridleyi,* lacks lateral leaflets and differs in the structure of the noseleaf.

Ecology and Habitat. One found roosting in a cave at 1200 m. Has been netted in mangrove.

Distribution. Known only from southwest Sarawak from Bako and G. Penrisen.

INTERMEDIATE ROUNDLEAF BAT   Plate 12
Hipposideros larvatus

Measurements. FA 56-64, Wt 15.5-20 (5 specimens).

Identification. Upperparts dark grey-brown to reddish-brown; underparts slightly paler. Noseleaf, ears and wing membranes brown. Noseleaf has 3 lateral leaflets; slight notch in anterior noseleaf. **Similar Species:** the Diadem Roundleaf Bat, *H. diadema,* is larger with buff or white shoulder marks; other Bornean *Hipposideros* are smaller with at most 2 lateral leaflets.

Ecology and Habitat. Roosts in caves.

Distribution. Bangladesh to southern China, Southeast Asia, Sumatra, Java, Sumba and adjacent small islands. **Borneo:** *H.'l. neglectus.* Known from the south and west from near Kuching in Sarawak south to G. Kenepai in West Kalimantan, S. Pangkalahan and S. Pasir in South Kalimantan.

DIADEM ROUNDLEAF BAT   *Hipposideros diadema*   Plate 12

Measurements. FA 76-87, T 53, E 27-18.5, Wt 30-47.

Identification. Fur of upperparts dark brown with pale bases, white patches on the shoulders and sides; underparts greyish white. Adult females dark brown with orange-buff shoulders and sides. Juveniles dark grey and white. Noseleaf with 3 or 4 lateral leaflets; posterior noseleaf large and rounded. **Similar Species:** all other Bornean *Hipposideros* are smaller and lack pale shoulder tufts.

Ecology and Habitat. Usually roosts in large colonies in caves, often mixed with other species, but has been recorded in hollows in trees (in Peninsular Malaysia). Forms maternity colonies of females and young.

Distribution. Southeast Asia, Philippines, Indonesia through to the Solomon Islands and Australia. **Borneo:** *H. d. masoni.* Recorded from most parts of Sabah and Sarawak as well as Tasek Merimbun in Brunei; G. Liang Kubung in West Kalimantan; S. Ritan in East Kalimantan; upper S. Tengah in South Kalimantan.

Genus *Coelops:* Deep notch in anterior noseleaf which is expanded to the sides. Lateral leaflets large and expanded forwards. No visible tail, although interfemoral membrane is well developed. Skull and dentition as *Hipposideros,* but rostral swellings generally low; upper canines have a well developed secondary cusp (Figure 20e); lower incisors separated from canines by a distinct gap.

LESSER TAILLESS ROUNDLEAF BAT *Coelops robinsoni* Plate 13

Measurements. FA 34-37, T none, E 12-14 (2 Peninsular Malaysian specimens). Skull: mt 4.7.

Identification. Fur long and soft, brown to blackish with paler tips; underparts slightly greyer. Ears rounded and lacking supporting ridges — colour in life not recorded. Narrow interfemoral membrane with no visible tail. Anterior margin of noseleaf deeply notched, forming two lobes; one pair of lateral leaflets expanded forwards to form wide rounded lobes under the anterior noseleaf; posterior noseleaf low with a small median lobe. **Similar Species:** the Greater Tailless Roundleaf Bat, *C. frithi,* has not yet been recorded from Borneo, but might occur — it is larger (FA 43-47, mt 5.7) and has the lower lobes of the noseleaf elongated and narrow.

Ecology and Habitat. Only Bornean specimen was found dead in a large cave.

Distribution. Peninsular Thailand and Malaysia. **Borneo:** Only record is from G. Mulu in Sarawak.

197

Family: VESPERTILIONIDAE   Common Bats

The largest, most diverse and most widespread family of bats, occurring on every continent except Antarctica. The nose is simple without any noseleaf (in all Bornean species). The ears are small to large with a well-developed tragus. The tail is long, completely enclosed in the interfemoral membrane, although the terminal vertebra sometimes protrudes.

The skull and dentition are highly variable with a general trend towards shortening of the jaws and reduction in the number of teeth (Figure 23c-k). The premaxillary bones are separate, attached directly to the maxillaries, without contact with the palate.

The Bornean species are grouped into four subfamilies containing 11 genera (2 of which are further divided into subgenera). They can be distinguished by a combination of external features such as ear and wing shape as well as skull and dental characters.

Subfamily VESPERTILIONINAE

Genus *Myotis:* ears moderately long and triangular at the tip; tragus tapered, bluntly pointed and bent slightly forwards (Figure 24). **Subgenus *Selysius*** has small feet with the wing membrane attached at the base of the toes; **subgenus *Leuconoe*** has large feet with the wing attached at the ankle or the side of the foot. Skull relatively unspecialized with slightly elevated braincase, narrow rostrum (Figure 22a). Usually three upper and lower premolars, but middle premolar small and displaced inwards in many species, lacking in one species; however, the anterior premolar is always well developed and not displaced inwards (Figure 23c-e). Dental formula: $\frac{2}{3}$ $\frac{1}{1}$ $\frac{2\cdot3}{2\cdot3}$ $\frac{3}{3}$.

Figure 22. Skulls of common bats (x 2):
a) *Myotis muricola,*
b) *Pipistrellus javanicus,*
c) *Pipistrellus stenopterus,*
d) *Philetor brachypterus,*
e) *Scotophilus kuhlii,*
f) *Murina cyclotis,*
g) *Kerivoula intermedia,*
h) *Miniopterus australis,*
i) *Tylonycteris robustula.*

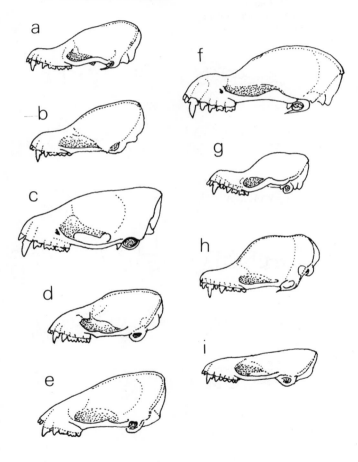

199

Figure 23. **Upper left toothrows of common bats:**
  a) *Kerivoula intermedia,*
  b) *K. whiteheadi,*
  c) *Myotis adversus,*
  d) *M. hasseltii,*
  e) *M. ridleyi,*
  f) *Pipistrellus javanicus,*
  g) *Glischropus tylopus,*
  h) *Philetor rohui,*
  i) *Hesperoptenus doriae,*
  j) *H. tomesi,*
  k) *Scotophilus kuhlii,*
  m) *Murina cyclotis.*

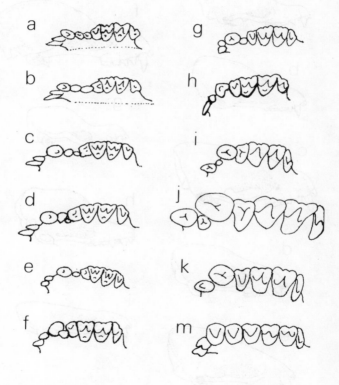

WHISKERED MYOTIS *Myotis (Selysius) muricola*   Plate 16

(formerly considered a subspecies of *Myotis mystacinus* from Europe)

Measurements. FA 33-37, T 37-42, E 13-14.5, HF 6-7, Wt 4-5.5 (11 Sabah specimens). Skull: ccl 12.0-12.5.

Identification. Upperparts brown to grey with dark bases; underparts with broad buffy-white to pale grey tips. Ears moderately long, tragus slender, bent forward and bluntly pointed (Figure 24a). Feet small with wing membrane attached at base of toes. Middle upper premolar small and slightly intruded from the tooth row (between Figure 23c and 23d). Upper canine much longer than posterior upper premolar. **Similar Species:** the Black Myotis, *M. ater,* is larger with a larger skull, and smaller second premolars; the Small-toothed Myotis, *M. siligorensis,* overlaps in forearm length, but is otherwise much smaller with more reddish brown fur; Ridley's Myotis, *M. ridleyi,* has a shorter forearm, darker fur and lacks the small second premolar; Horsfield's Myotis, *M. horsfieldii,* has larger feet with the wing membrane attached at the side of the foot; the Javan Pipistrelle, *Pipistrellus javanicus,* has a blunter, more rounded tragus (Figure 24b) and only two upper premolars, the anterior displaced inwards (Figure 23f); woolly bats, *Kerivoula* spp. have more funnel shaped ears with a long pointed tragus (Figure 24d) and longer fluffier hair.

Ecology and Habitat. Often roosts in the furled central leaves of banana plants, but occasionally found in caves (in Thailand).

Distribution. From eastern India through Burma, Thailand, Indochina, Peninsular Malaysia, Philippines, Indonesia through to New Guinea. **Borneo:** *M. m. muricola.* Found in most areas from the lowlands up to 1500 m on G. Kinabalu.

Figure 24. Ear shape of common bats:
      a) *Myotis,*
      b, c) *Pipistrellus,*
      d) *Kerivoula.*

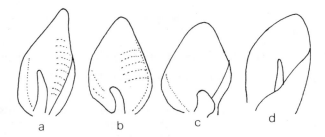

a   b   c   d

BLACK MYOTIS *Myotis (Selysius) ater* Plate 16

(formerly called *Myotis mystacinus nugax)*

Measurements. FA 40-43, T 37-41, E 13-15, HF 8-9, Wt 6.5-8 (11 Bornean specimens). Skull: cbl 14.5, mt 5.5-5.8, c-3 3.8-3.9, m-m 6.3-6.5.

Identification. Upperparts dark brown with black bases to the fur; underparts paler grey-brown, usually with a golden-brown patch in the centre of the belly. Feet small with wing membrane attached at base of toes. Ears and dentition similar to Whiskered Myotis, *M. muricola*, but posterior upper premolar as long as canine; second upper and lower premolars very small and displaced inwards so that the first and third premolars are touching or nearly so (as in Figure 23d). **Similar Species:** the Whiskered Myotis, *M. muricola*, is smaller with larger second premolars; the Large Brown Myotis, *M. montivagus*, has a slightly longer forearm and much larger body and skull; large-footed myotis, *M. (Leuconoe)* spp., have larger feet with the wing attached at the side of the foot or the ankle.

Ecology and Habitat. Roosts individually or in small colonies in caves.

Distribution. Philippines, Sulawesi and islands through to New Guinea. **Borneo:** *M. a. nugax*. Recorded from Gomantong, Baturong, and G. Kinabalu (up to 1500 m) in Sabah, as well as the Kelabit uplands in Sarawak.

LARGE BROWN MYOTIS *Myotis (Selysius) montivagus* Plate 16

Measurements. FA 42-45, T 43-48, E 15-16, HF 8-9, Wt 9-13.5 (12 Sabah specimens). Skull: cbl 16.4-16.9, mt 6.7-7.0, c-3 4.5-4.8, m-m 7.4-7.7.

Identification. Upperparts dark blackish brown with brown tips to the hairs; underparts similar with paler tips to the hairs. Feet small with wing membrane attached at base of toes. **Similar Species:** the Black Myotis, *M. ater*, has a slightly shorter forearm and much smaller body, skull and teeth; large-footed myotis, *M. (Leuconoe)* spp., have much larger feet.

Ecology and Habitat. Has been trapped flying along streams in tall forest.

Distribution. India through Burma, southern China, Thailand, Peninsular Malaysia, Sumatra. **Borneo:** *M. m. borneoensis*. So far known only from Sepilok and Madai in eastern Sabah.

SMALL-TOOTHED MYOTIS *Myotis (Selysius) siligorensis* Plate 16

Measurements. FA 30-33.5, Wt 2.3-2.6 (3 Peninsular Malaysian specimens). Skull: ccl 10.4, mt 4.4.

Identification. Upperparts brown with a reddish tinge and dark brown bases to the fur; underparts similar but slightly paler and buffier. Relatively long forearm, but otherwise very small and light. Feet small with wing membrane attached to base of toes. Ears reach past tip of nose when folded forwards. Second upper and lower premolars only slightly smaller than the corresponding first premolar and in line in the tooth row. Canines small—lower canine similar in height to posterior lower premolar. Skull has distinctly domed braincase. **Similar Species:** the Whiskered Myotis, *M. muricola,* is larger with longer canines and a flatter skull; Ridley's

Myotis, *M. ridleyi* has a shorter forearm but is otherwise much larger and heavier with dark fur and only two premolars (Figure 23e); Woolly Bats, Kerivoula spp., have more funnel-shaped ears.

Ecology and Habitat. In Peninsular Malaysia roosts in rock fissures in caves — the only Bornean specimen was in a crack in a rock near a stream.

Distribution. Nepal through southern China, Indochina, Thailand, Peninsular Malaysia. **Borneo:** reported only from near Ranau in Sabah.

RIDLEY'S MYOTIS *Myotis (Selysius) ridleyi*   Plate 16

Measurements. FA 27-32, T 30-36, Wt 4-6g (14 specimens).

Identification. A small dark bat with short wings but a relatively heavy body and a typical *Myotis* ear and tragus shape. Upperparts dark grey-brown; underparts paler and greyer. Feet small with wing membrane attached to side of foot. Differs from other *Myotis* in having only two upper and lower premolars (Figure 23e). **Similar Species:** the Whiskered Myotis, *M. muricola* is larger and paler, with three premolars, though the middle one is often small and hard to see; the Small-toothed Myotis, *M. siligorensis* is paler, with a lighter body, short canines and a conspicuous extra premolar; pipistrelles, *Pipistrellus* spp., have only 2 premolars, but anterior upper premolar is small and usually displaced inwards (eg. Figure 23f), ears have a blunter more rounded tragus (Figure 24b,c).

Ecology and Habitat. Netted in dipterocarp forest in lowlands up to 300 m. Has been found roosting in a small group under a house in the forest.

Distribution. Peninsular Malaysia. **Borneo:** recorded only from Sepilok and the Witti Range in Sabah.

HORSFIELD'S MYOTIS *Myotis (Leuconoe) horsfieldii*   Plate 16

Measurements. FA 35-38, T 37-39, HF 10-11, E 13.5-17, Wt 5-7.5. Skull: cbl 14.3-14.7, io 3.5-3.6, mt 5.8-6.0.

Identification. Upperparts grey-brown; underparts greyer. Ears large. Feet moderately large with wing membrane attached to side of foot at least 1 mm from base of toes. Second upper and lower premolars not displaced inwards (as in Figure 23c). **Similar Species:** Hasselt's and the Grey Large-footed Myotis, *M. hasseltii* and *M. adversus,* have wing membrane attached at ankle; the Whiskered Myotis, *M. muricola*, has smaller feet with wing attached at base of toes.

Ecology and Habitat. Roosts in crevices or bell-holes in caves, usually not far from large streams or rivers. Has been seen feeding low over open surfaces of water such as wide streams.

Distribution. India, Hainan, Thailand, Peninsular Malaysia, Java, Bali, Sulawesi and Sulawesi. **Borneo:** *M. h. horsfieldii.* Recorded from lowland localities in most areas including cave roosts at Sukau, Madai and Tepadong in Sabah; Niah in Sarawak.

HASSELT'S LARGE-FOOTED MYOTIS   Plate 16
Myotis (Leuconoe) hasseltii

Measurements. FA 37 (1 specimen). Skull: cbl 14.1-14.6, io 3.9-4.5, mt 5.6-5.8.Upperparts dark brown to dark grey with pale grey tips to the hairs; underparts greyish white with dark bases to some of the hairs. Fur short and velvety. Flight membranes pale grey-brown. Fur appears silvery when torchlit in flight at night. Feet large with wing membrane attached at ankle. Second upper premolar very small and displaced inwards so that the first and third premolars are in contact or nearly so (Figure 23d). **Similar Species:** the Grey Large-footed Myotis, *M. adversus*, has longer fur, second upper premolar larger and nearly in line in the tooth row (Figure 23c); the Pallid Large-footed Myotis, *M. macrotarsus* is much larger with pale grey and white fur; Horsfield's Myotis, *Myotis horsfieldii* has the wing membrane attached at the side of the foot.

Ecology and Habitat. In Peninsular Malaysia forages for food low over water in coastal areas, often near mangrove, frequently dipping its large feet into the water to grab food.

Distribution. Sri Lanka, Southeast Asia, Sumatra, Java and smaller islands. **Borneo:** *M. h. macellus.* Specimens are known from Sarawak, South Kalimantan and East Kalimantan. Bats seen feeding over an estuary near Sandakan in Sabah were probably this species.

GREY LARGE-FOOTED MYOTIS   Plate 16
Myotis (Leuconoe) adversus

Measurements. FA 39-40 (2 specimens). Skull: cbl 14.9-15.2, io 3.9-4.3, mt 5.9-6.0.

Identification. Upperparts blackish-brown to dark grey with narrow pale grey tips; underparts greyish white with black bases to the fur. Fur dense and woolly. Feet large with wing membrane inserted at ankle. Second (middle) upper and lower premolars not much smaller than first, and in line, or nearly in line with the other premolars (Figure 23c). **Similar Species:** Hasselt's Large-footed Myotis, *M. hasseltii* has shorter, more velvety fur, second upper premolar very small and displaced inwards (Figure 23d), second lower premolar reduced; Horsfield's Myotis, *M. horsfieldii*, has wing membrane attached near ankle.

Ecology and Habitat. In Australia, feeds by flying low over open water such as small lakes, scooping insects and other food off the water with its large feet. May occasionally catch small fish.

Distribution. Peninsular Malaysia, Java, Sulawesi and islands through to New Hebrides and Australia. **Borneo:** *M. a. carimatae.* Known only from a few specimens collected around Sandakan Bay in Sabah and on P. Karimata off West Kalimantan.

PALLID LARGE-FOOTED MYOTIS   Plate 16
Myotis (Leuconoe) macrotarsus

Measurements. FA 45-49, T 46-51, HF 12-14, E 18-20, Wt 12-16 (12 specimens).

Identification. Upperparts pale grey to white with dark grey bases; underparts white, often with a yellowish tinge. Wing membranes pale pinkish grey. Feet very large with wing attached at ankle. **Similar Species:** other large-footed myotis, *M. hasseltii* and *M. adversus*, are smaller and darker.

Ecology and Habitat. Roosts in singles, pairs or small groups in caves. Feeding unknown, but morphology suggests it could easily catch small fish.

Distribution. Philippines. **Borneo:** *M. m. saba.* Caught roosting in caves on P. Balembangan, at Madai, and near Semporna in Sabah; S. Baram in Sarawak.

Genus *Pipistrellus:* externally similar to *Myotis,* but ears generally more rounded, tragus shorter and not tapered — sometimes quite broad (Figure 24b,c). Skull variable, but with braincase generally low and rostrum slightly shortened (Figure 22b,c). Only two premolars, of which the anterior is usually displaced inwards, sometimes minute and hard to see (Figure 23f). Incisors variable, but usually fairly small. Dental formula: $\frac{2}{3}\,\frac{1}{1}\,\frac{2}{2}\,\frac{3}{3}$.

JAVAN PIPISTRELLE   *Pipistrellus javanicus*   Plate 17

Measurements. FA 34-36, T 34-41, E 11-12.5, Wt 3.8-4.7 (6 specimens). Skull: cbl 12.4, mt 4.6.

Identification. Upperparts dark brown with dark bases; underparts slightly paler. Ear moderately short and rounded, tragus long but not tapered with rounded tip (Figure 24b). Two upper and lower premolars, the first upper premolar small and slightly displaced inwards (Figure 23f). Braincase somewhat elevated anteriorly. **Similar Species:** the Least Pipistrelle, *P. tenuis,* is similar but smaller with a shorter, more sloping skull; the Red- Brown Pipistrelle, *P. kitcheneri* is larger with larger ears and a broad tragus (Figure 24c); the Whiskered Myotis, *Myotis muricola,* has a tapered, bluntly pointed tragus (Figure 24a) and three upper and lower premolars.

Ecology and Habitat. Commonly found in moss forest up to 1600 m. Elsewhere in Asia occurs in a wide variety of habitats including towns and lowland forest. In Sumatra recorded roosting in thatched roofs of village houses.

Distribution. Japan, eastern China through Southeast Asia, Philippines, Sumatra, Java. **Borneo:** *P. j. javanicus.* Definitely recorded only from 1200-1600 m on G. Kinabalu and the Crocker Range in Sabah.

LEAST PIPISTRELLE   Pipistrellus tenuis   Plate 17

Measurements. FA 29-32, T 32, E 8-11, Wt 4.2 (2 Sabah specimens). Skull: cbl 11.1, mt 4.0-4.2.

Identification. Upperparts uniformly dark brown; underparts similar or slightly paler. Ear and tragus similar to Javan Pipistrelle, *P. javanicus.* Second upper premolar slightly displaced inwards (as in Figure 23f). Rostrum of skull short with evenly sloping profile. **Similar Species:** the Javan Pipistrelle, *P. javanicus* is larger with a longer skull; the White-winged Pipistrelle, *P. vordermanni,* has large ears and distinctive coloration; Ridley's Myotis, *Myotis ridleyi,* has a typical Myotis ear shape and the first upper premolar in line in the tooth row (Figure 23e).

Ecology and Habitat. Has been caught in coastal areas near mangrove.

Distribution. Southern Thailand, Peninsular Malaysia, Philippines, Indonesia through to New Guinea various Pacific islands and Australia. **Borneo:** *P.t. nitidus.* Recorded from coastal areas in Sabah on P. Labuan and on the Darvel Bay as well as at 1500 m on G. Kinabalu.

DARK BROWN PIPISTRELLE   Plate 17
Pipistrellus ceylonicus

Measurements. FA 38 (one specimen). Skull: cbl 14.1-14.9, mt 5.4-5.9 (non-Bornean specimens).

Identification. Fur (of only known specimen) dark brown. Ears large, tragus broad (as in Figure 24c). Skull large and broad. Anterior upper premolar relatively large, but displaced inwards such that the canine and second premolar almost touch. **Similar Species:** the Red-brown Pipistrelle, *P. kitcheneri,* has reddish-brown fur with black bases and a smaller skull; the Narrow-winged Pipistrelle, *P. stenopterus,* has a shortened fifth finger; the Coppery Pipistrelle, *P. cuprosus,* has buff rims to the ears and brighter fur colours; the False Serotine, *Hesperoptenus doriae,* lacks a small anterior premolar and has large inner incisors.

Ecology and Habitat. Unknown.

Distribution. Sri Lanka, Pakistan, India, Burma, southern China, Vietnam. **Borneo:** *P. c. borneanus.* The only known specimen is from 1300 m on Trus Madi in Sabah.

RED-BROWN PIPISTRELLE   Pipistrellus kitcheneri   Plate 17
Measurements. FA 35-38 (11 specimens). Skull: cbl 13.1-13.6, mt 4.6-4.9.

Identification. Upperparts reddish-brown with black bases to the fur; underparts similar but paler. Ears moderate with a short, broad tragus (as in Figure 24c). Anterior upper premolar small and displaced inwards so that the canine and second premolar are touching. **Similar Species:** the Dark Brown Pipistrelle, *P. ceylonicus,* has dark brown fur and a larger skull; the Javan Pipistrelle, *P. javanicus,* has smaller ears and a narrow tragus (Figure 24b); the False Serotine, *Hesperoptenus doriae,* has only one upper premolar and large, conical inner incisors.

Ecology and Habitat. Unknown.

Distribution. Known only from Borneo. Recorded from Sandakan in Sabah; East Kalimantan; Buntuk, S. Barito in S. Kalimantan.

WOOLLY PIPISTRELLE   Pipistrellus petersi   Plate 17

Measurements. FA 40-42, T 39-41, E 13-15.5, Wt 6-7 (4 specimens). Skull: cbl 15.3, mt 5.6.

Identification. Fur very long and shaggy, dark blackish brown with pale grey-brown tips on the upperparts, shorter and browner on the head and underparts. Facial skin, ears and wings dark grey. Ears broad and rounded. Muzzle broad and narrow. First upper premolar not especially small. **Similar Species:** the Narrow-winged Pipistrelle, *P. stenopterus,* has short brown fur, a broad skull and a short fifth finger; other pipistrelles such as *P. kitcheneri* and *P. ceylonicus,* are smaller with shorter browner fur.

Ecology and Habitat. Colony found roosting under the eaves of an isolated house in lower montane forest.

Distribution. Sulawesi, Moluccas. **Borneo:** known only from the Crocker Range in Sabah at 1500 m.

COPPERY PIPISTRELLE   Pipistrellus cuprosus   Plate 17

Measurements. FA 34.5-36.5, T 38-39, E 12.5, Wt 5.3-5.6 (2 specimens). Skull: cbl 12.9-13.0, mt 4.8-4.9.

Identification. Fur of upperparts long and thick with black bases and red-orange tips; fur of underparts with dark brown bases and pale yellow or greyish-white tips. Ears and tragus dark brown with buff rims. Ear moderately large with distinct lobe at base near eye. Anterior upper premolar very tiny and displaced inwards (sometimes lacking) so the canine and second premolar are touching. **Similar Species:** distinctive coloration separates this from all other known Bornean pipistrelles. Two pipistrelles from Peninsular Malaysia are similar and might occur in Borneo — they differ mainly in larger size: *P. circumdatus* FA 40-44, mt 5.9-6.5; *P. societatus* FA 37.5-39.5, mt 5.2-5.5.

Ecology and Habitat. Trapped in understorey of tall forest.

Distribution. Known only from Sepilok in Sabah.

Figure 25. Wing shape of pipistrelles:
a) *Pipistrellus stenopterus,*
b) *P. petersi.*

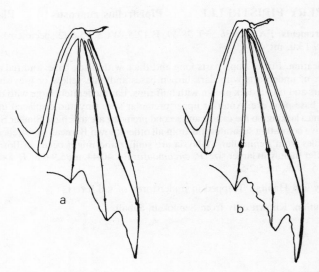

Plate 17

NARROW-WINGED PIPISTRELLE   Pipistrellus stenopterus

Measurements. FA 38-42 (19 Peninsular Malaysian specimens).

Identification. Fur short; upperparts uniform reddish brown to brown; underparts slightly paler and greyer. Muzzle broad and fairly heavy. Wing narrow — fifth finger very short, not much longer than metacarpal of fourth finger (Figure 25a). **Similar Species:** other known Bornean pipistrelles have longer fifth fingers (as in Figure 25b); the Woolly Pipistrelle, *P. petersi,* has a narrow muzzle and longer hair; the Narrow-winged Brown Bat, *Philetor brachypterus,* also has a narrow wing, but is much smaller and has only one upper premolar; the False Serotine, *Hesperoptenus doriae,* has large conical inner upper incisors.

Ecology and Habitat. Sometimes roosts in houses. Has been collected while feeding over open fields.

Distribution. Peninsular Malaysia, Philippines, Sumatra. **Borneo:** recorded from Sandakan, Poring, Kota Kinabalu and G. Trus Madi (at 600 m) in Sabah; the Kelabit uplands (at 1200 m) and Kuching in Sarawak.

WHITE-WINGED PIPISTRELLE Pipistrellus vordermanni Plate 17

Measurements. FA 30.5, T 15.1 (1 specimen). Skull: cbl 11.1, ccl 10.8, io 3.5, mt 3.8.

Identification. Fur pale reddish brown with darker bases. Wings translucent white, greyer near body. Ears large, tragus slightly hatchet-shaped. Anterior upper premolar tiny and displaced inwards so the canine and second premolar are touching. **Similar Species:** other Bornean pipistrelles have dark wings; the Least Pipistrelle, *P. tenuis*, has a narrow tragus (as in Figure 24b).

Ecology and Habitat. Has been caught in coastal areas near mangrove.

Distribution. Belitung Island in Indonesia. **Borneo:** recorded only from Samunsam in Sarawak.

Genus Glischropus: very similar to *Pipistrellus*, but sole of foot and base of thumb bear thickened unpigmented pads; second (outer) upper incisor displaced outwards from tooth row (Figure 23g). Dental formula $\frac{2}{3} \frac{1}{1} \frac{2}{2} \frac{3}{3}$.

THICK-THUMBED PIPISTRELLE   Glischropus tylopus   Plate 18

Measurements. FA 28-30, T 32-38, E 9-11, Wt 3.5-4.5 (5 specimens).

Identification. upperparts dark brown; underparts paler buffy brown. Fur rather long and shaggy. Short broad face with rounded head. Base of thumb and sole of foot have thickened unpigmented whitish or pink pads. Second upper incisor is displaced outwards while the anterior upper premolar is small but in line in the tooth row (Figure 23g). **Similar Species:** the Least False Serotine, *Hesperoptenus blanfordi*, has dark thumbpads, short smooth fur, and the second upper incisor displaced inwards (as in Figure 24j); bamboo bats, *Tylonycteris* spp. have very flat skulls and large rounded, dark thumb pads.

Ecology and Habitat. In Peninsular Malaysia often roosts in dead or damaged bamboo stems as well as rock crevices or new banana leaves.

Distribution. Burma, Thailand, Peninsular Malaysia, Philippines, Sumatra. **Borneo:** *G. t. tylopus,* Recorded from scattered localities in Sabah, Sarawak, West and Central Kalimantan.

Genus *Philetor:* externally similar to *Pipistrellus* with short fifth finger (as in *P. stenopterus*, Figure 25a). External genitalia quite elaborate. Skull slopes evenly in profile; rostrum thickened (Figure 22d). Only one upper premolar; inner upper incisors long and narrow with two cusps (Figure 23h). Dental formula $\frac{2}{3} \frac{1}{1} \frac{1}{2} \frac{3}{3}$.

NARROW-WINGED BROWN BAT Philetor brachypterus Plate 18

Measurements. FA 30-36, T 30-38, E 13-16, Wt 8-13 (12 specimens).

Identification. Upperparts dark brown; underparts paler and greyer. Fur short and dense. Head somewhat flattened, ears large, rounded and prominent. Wings narrow with fifth digit shortened (as in Figure 25a). Only one, shortened, upper premolar. First upper incisor long and narrow with two cusps, second incisor small and conical. **Similar Species:** the Narrow-winged Pipistrelle, *Pipstrellus stenopterus*, also has a narrow wing, but is larger and has an extra upper premolar; Bamboo Bats, *Tylonycteris* spp. have large thumb pads and are extremely flattened; the False Serotine, *Hesperoptenus doriae*, is larger with a conical inner incisor.

Ecology and Habitat. Roosts in hollow trees. Feeds in understorey of forest.

Distribution. Peninsular Malaysia, Philippines, Sumatra, Java, New Guinea. **Borneo:** *P. b. verecundus.* Recorded from Sepilok and near Ranau in Sabah; Niah and G. Mulu in Sarawak.

Genus Hesperoptenus: ears fairly short and rounded, tragus slightly hatchet-shaped. One species has a small thickened thumb pad. Only one upper premolar; distinctive upper incisors: first (inner) incisor very large and conical about half the size of the canine; second incisor small, in subgenus *Milithronycteris* displaced inwards so that canine and first incisor are in contact (Figure 23i), in subgenus *Hesperoptenus* separating canine and first incisor (Figure 23j). Dental formula $\frac{2}{3} \frac{1}{1} \frac{1}{2} \frac{3}{3}$.

FALSE SEROTINE Hesperoptenus doriae Plate 18

Measurements. FA 38-41 (1 Sarawak and 1 Peninsular Malaysian specimen). Skull: cbl 13.3-13.6, mt 4.9-5.0.

Identification. Fur generally dark brown. Only one upper premolar; first upper incisor large and conical, second incisor slightly displaced inwards (Figure 23i). **Similar Species:** the Tomes' False Serotine, *H. tomesi*, is larger and blacker with the second upper incisor displaced inwards; the Narrow-winged Brown Bat, *Philetos rohui*, is smaller with the upper incisors low and multi-cusped; the Narrow-winged Pipistrelle, *Pipistrellus stenopterus*, has small upper incisors and an extra upper premolar.

Ecology and Habitat. Unknown.

Distribution. Peninsular Malaysia. **Borneo:** known from only one specimen collected somewhere in Sarawak.

LEAST FALSE SEROTINE Hesperoptenus blanfordi Plate 18

Measurements. FA 24-26.5, T 27-30, E 11, Wt 6.1-6.4 (8 specimens).

Identification. Very small with upperparts dark reddish brown to brown; underparts similar. Base of thumb and sole of foot have thickened dark brown pads. Thumb pad small and slightly triangular in shape. Second upper incisor small and displaced inwards (as in Figure 23j). Head rather flattened. **Similar Species:** bamboo bats, *Tyloncyteris* spp., are much flatter with large round thumb pads, first incisors small with two cusps and separated from canine by second incisor; the Thick-thumbed Pipistrelle, *Glischropus tylopus*, has longer fur, more rounded head, white or pink thumb pads and second upper incisor displaced outwards (Figure 23g).

Ecology and Habitat. Has been caught in understorey of tall dipterocarp forest.

Distribution. Southern Burma, Thailand, Peninsular Malaysia. **Borneo:** recorded only from the Witti Range and Sepilok in Sabah.

TOMES' FALSE SEROTINE   Hesperoptenus tomesi   Plate 18

Measurements. FA 50-53, T 49-53, E 17-18, Wt 30-32g (3 Peninsular Malaysian and 2 Bornean specimens). Skull: cbl 20.4, io 5.8, mt 8.5.

Identification. Upperparts uniform dark blackish brown; underparts similar. Head rounded, forehead sloping. Teeth large with well developed cusps. First upper incisor large and conical, touching the canine; second incisor small and displaced inwards (Figure 23j); only one upper premolar. **Similar Species:** the False Serotine, *H. doriae*, is smaller with the second upper incisor separating the canine from the first (Figure 23i); the Yellow House Bat, *Scotophilus kuhlii*, is paler, with only one pair of upper incisors.

Ecology and Habitat. One pair was netted flying along a stream in lowland dipterocarp forest.

Distribution. Peninsular Malaysia. **Borneo:** recorded only in eastern Sabah from the Sandakan Bay area and Tabin.

Genus *Tylonycteris:* body and skull extremely flattened (Figure 22i); base of thumb and foot bear large dark brown disk-shaped pads. Dental formula $\frac{2}{3}\frac{1}{1}\frac{1}{2}\frac{3}{3}$.

GREATER BAMBOO BAT   Tylonycteris robustula   Plate 18

Measurements. FA 26-30, T 29-36, E 11, Wt 6.5-8.5 (11 specimens). Skull: ccl 12.3-12.7, mt 4.3-4.5 (5 Peninsular Malaysian specimens).

Identification. Upperparts dark brown to dark greyish brown; underparts slightly paler. Fur very smooth and sleek. Large dark brown, flattened disk-like pads at base of thumb and on sole of foot. Head (skull) and body extremely flattened — can fit through a slot less than 5mm wide. **Similar Species:** the Lesser Bamboo Bat, *T. pachypus*, overlaps in forearm length but is otherwise much smaller with more reddish, fluffy fur; the Thick-thumbed Pipistrelle, *Glischropus tylopus*, is larger with a more rounded head, smaller and pale pink thumb and foot pads; the Least False Serotine, *Hesperopytenus blanfordi*, is less flattened, has thumb pad much smaller and triangular, and distinctive upper incisors.

Ecology and Habitat. Roosts in the internodes of bamboos, entering through narrow slits created by beetles.

Distribution. Southern China through Southeast Asia, Sumatra, Java, 'Sulawesi and smaller islands. **Borneo:** occurs throughout the northwest from G. Kinabalu (up to 1000 m) south through the Crocker Range intermittently as far as Kuching.

LESSER BAMBOO BAT   Tylonycteris pachypus   Plate 18

Measurements. FA 24-28, T 27-29, E 8-9, Wt 3.5-5 (4 Bornean and many Peninsular Malaysian specimens). Skull: ccl 10.4-10.6, mt 3.1-3.5.

Identification. Upperparts brown to reddish brown; underparts slightly paler and strongly tinged orange. Fur rather short and fluffy. Body and skull extremely flattened with enlarged disk-shaped pads on the thumb and feet. **Similar Species:** the Greater Bamboo Bat, *T. robustula*, overlaps slightly in forearm length, but is otherwise much larger with sleek dark brown fur.

211

Ecology and Habitat. Roosts in small groups in the internodes of bamboos, entering through small slits created by beetles. Frequently chooses small live bamboos, while the Greater Bamboo Bat, *T. robustula*, prefers larger often dead stems, although both species may sometimes use the same roost at different times.

Distribution. India through southern China, Southeast Asia, Philippines, Sumatra, Java and smaller islands. **Similar Species:** *T. p. pachypus.* Recorded from near Kota Kinabalu in Sabah; near Bandar Seri Begawan in Brunei; the Kuching area in Sarawak; West Kalimantan; East Kalimantan.

Genus Scotophilus: ears moderate, tragus very long and curved forwards. Skull thick and heavy (Figure 22e) with reduced dentition; only one pair of upper incisors which are large and well developed (Figure 23k). Dental formula $\frac{1}{3} \frac{1}{1} \frac{1}{2} \frac{3}{3}$.

YELLOW HOUSE BAT Scotophilus kuhlii Plate 18

Measurements. FA 47-52, T 45-52, E 14-15, Wt 18-23 (4 specimens).

Identification. Upperparts brown; underparts paler yellowish-brown. Ear with long narrow tragus bent forwards. One upper premolar. Only one pair of large conical upper incisors (Figure 23k). **Similar Species:** other Bornean bats have two pairs of upper incisors; false serotines, *Hesperoptenus* spp., have a short, broad, hatchet-shaped tragus.

Ecology and Habitat. Often roosts in the attics of houses.

Distribution. Sri Lanka, Pakistan, India to Taiwan, Southeast Asia, Philippines, Sumatra, Java, Bali. **Borneo:** *S. k. castaneus.* Recorded from towns in western Sabah including Kota Kinabalu and Kota Belud as well as upper S. Tengah in South Kalimantan.

212

Subfamily MURININAE

Genus *Murina:* nostrils expanded into short tubes which protrude either side of the' muzzle. Ears rounded, not funnel shaped, tragus long and pointed. Skull has a long palate and large rostrum. Anterior upper premolar large, similar in size to the second premolar. Upper molars with well developed W-shaped cusps (Figure 23m). Dental formula $\frac{2}{3} \frac{1}{1} \frac{2}{2} \frac{3}{3}$.

ORANGE TUBE-NOSED BAT   *Murina cyclotis*   Plate 15

Measurements. FA 34-41, T 38-50, E 13-16, Wt 6.5-10 (8 specimens). Skull: cbl 16.8-16.9, mt 5.9, c-c 4.7.

Identification. Upperparts pale orange mixed with grey or grey-brown; underparts paler and greyer. Tail membrane thinly covered in long reddish hairs. Ear rounded, tragus long, pointed and white. Nostrils large and tubular. **Similar Species:** other tube-nosed bats, *Murina spp.,* differ in coloration and have smaller skulls; the Hairy-winged Bat, *Harpiocephalus harpia,* is larger and brighter orange with heavier teeth and a reduced third upper molar.

Ecology and Habitat. Found in the understorey of lowland dipterocarp forest.

Distribution. Sri Lanka, east India through southern China, Southeast Asia and Philippines. **Borneo:** *M. c. peninsularis.* Recorded from Sepilok, Tabin and Gomantong in eastern Sabah; Tasek Merimbun in Brunei; G. Mulu in Sarawak.

BRONZED TUBE-NOSED BAT   *Murina aenea*   Plate 15

Measurements. FA 35-38, T 35-41, E 13.5-15.5, Wt 6-8.5 (5 specimens). Skull: cbl 15.3-16.1, mt 5.7-6.0, c-c 4.7-4.8.

Identification. Fur of upperparts with dark bases and orange-brown tips; underparts with dark brown bases and pale buff-brown tips. Nostrils long and tubular. **Similar Species:** the Gilded Tube-nosed Bat, *M. rozendaali,* has yellower tips to the back fur, white underparts and is slightly smaller; the Orange Tube-nosed Bat, *M. cyclotis,* has grey and orange upperparts and a larger skull.

Ecology and Habitat. Has been caught in lowland dipterocarp forest and hill moss forest.

Distribution. Peninsular Malaysia. **Borneo:** Found at Sepilok, Segarong, and in the Crocker Range (1200 m) in Sabah.

GILDED TUBE-NOSED BAT   *Murina rozendaali*   Plate 15

Measurements. FA 31.5-33.5, T 35-41, E 13-15, Wt 4.3-4.8 (5 specimens). Skull: cbl 14.4-14.6, mt 5.2-5.6, c-c 3.8-4.1.

Identification. Upperpart fur with dark brown bases and shining yellow or golden brown tips; underparts white with a slight buffy tinge. Nostrils tubular. **Similar Species:** the Bronzed Tube-nosed Bat, *M. aenea,* has dark bases to the belly fur and is larger; the Lesser Tube-nosed Bat, *M. suilla,* is smaller without golden tips to the back fur.

213

Ecology and Habitat. Caught flying low over streams in disturbed lowland dipterocarp forest.

Distribution. Known only from Poring, Gomantong and Tepadong in Sabah.

LESSER TUBE-NOSED BAT   *Murina suilla*   Plate 15

Measurements. FA 28-31, T 26-35, E 10.5-13, Wt 3.2—b5- (15 specimens). Skull: cbl 12.6-13.3, mt 4.7-4.9, c-c 3.6-3.7.

Identification. Upperparts buffy brown to grey brown; underparts greyish white. Tubular nostrils. **Similar Species:** the Gilded Tube-nosed Bat, *M. rozendaali*, has pale yellowish tips to the back fur and is slightly larger; Whitehead's Woolly Bat, *Kerivoula whiteheadi*, has small nostrils and large funnel shaped ears.

Ecology and Habitat. Occurs in lowland dipterocarp forest.

Distribution. Peninsular Malaysia, Sumatra, Java. **Borneo:** Recorded from all over Sabah; Samunsam in Sarawak; Peleben and S. Mahakan in East Kalimantan.

Genus *Harpiocephalus:* similar to *Murina* with tubular nostrils and the same dental formula, but posterior upper molar reduced to a tiny flake, sometimes lacking; anterior upper molars with reduced cusps except the central one, thus resembling the premolars; canines low and massive; rostrum slightly shortened.

HAIRY-WINGED BAT   *Harpiocephalus harpia*   Plate 15
(including *Harpiocephalus mordax)*

Measurements. FA 48 (1 specimen). Skull: gl 22.1, mt 6.6, c-c 6.0, m-m 7.1.

Identification. Upperparts bright orange with dark bases; underparts similar but slightly greyer. Nostrils elongate and tubular. Ear rounded with long-pointed tragus. Forearm, much of wing membrane and interfemoral membrane covered in short orange hairs. Third upper molar tiny, sometimes lacking. One specimen has a much broader skull (gl 22.3, mt 6.9, c-c 7.8, m-m 8.0) and has been tentatively identified as *H. mordax*. However, since insufficient specimens are available to determine the extent of individual variation, the 2 species are treated together here. **Similar Species:** all Bornean tube-nosed bats, *Murina* spp., are smaller with a well developed third upper molar (Figure 23m).

Ecology and Habitat. Sepilok specimen was trapped in the understorey of lowland dipterocarp forest.

Distribution. India, Burma, Thailand, Indochina, Taiwan, Sumatra, Java, Moluccas. **Borneo:** *H. h. harpia*. One specimen has been collected near Tawau, and a second, possibly *H. mordax* at Sepilok, both in Sabah.

Subfamily KERIVOULINAE

Genus *Kerivoula:* ears funnel-like with a large flap on the outside (Figure 24d); tragus long, narrow and pointed. Fur long and woolly, often covering much of the face. Nostrils small. Skull has a high domed braincase and a long rostrum (Figure 22g). Teeth relatively unspecialized with no reduction in any of the cheek teeth (Figure 23a,b). Dental formula $\frac{2}{3} \frac{1}{1} \frac{3}{3} \frac{3}{3}$.

PAPILLOSE WOOLLY BAT   *Kerivoula papillosa*   Plate 14

Measurements. FA 38-49, T 49-56, E 14-17, Wt 6-13 (20 specimens).

Identification. Upperparts brown to buffy-brown, sometimes with buff near the wings; underparts paler. Ears funnel-shaped with a long pointed tragus. Three upper and lower premolars, all well developed. There is a great deal of size variation and further study may show that more than one species is included. **Similar Species:** Hardwicke's Woolly Bat, *K. hardwickei*, is smaller and greyer; *Myotis* spp., have different shaped ears with a shorter, bluntly pointed tragus (Figure 24a), and a shorter rostrum and a reduced second premolar.

Ecology and Habitat. Flies slowly through the forest understorey. Has been found roosting in hollow trees and (in Peninsular Malaysia) in bamboo.

Distribution. Northeast India, Indochina, Peninsular Malaysia, Sumatra, Java and Sulawesi. **Borneo:** *K. p. malayana.* Known from scattered localities throughout Sabah and Sarawak.

HARDWICKE'S WOOLLY BAT   *Kerivoula hardwickii*   Plate 14

Measurements. FA 32-34, T 44-47, E 12-14, Wt 3.5-4.2 (4 specimens).

Identification. Upperparts grey-brown with dark grey bases to the fur; underparts paler and greyer. Ears moderately large. A specimen from 1500 m on G. Kinabalu was quite large (FA 36.5, Wt 5.2) with dark grey fur, and might represent a distinct montane form. **Similar Species:** the Clear-winged Woolly Bat, *K. pellucida*, has pale bases to the fur and longer ears; the Small Woolly Bat, *K. intermedia*, is more orange-brown with smaller ears; the Papillose Woolly Bat, *K. papillosa*, is larger with browner fur; groove-toothed bats, *Phoniscus* spp., have tricoloured fur, a notched white tragus and a groove in the side of the canine.

Ecology and Habitat. Frequents the understorey of tall forest. Roosts in hollow trees, and once found roosting in a dead *Nepenthes* pitcher.

Distribution. Sri Lanka and India through southern China, South-east Asia, Philippines, Sumatra, Java, Sulawesi, and other Indonesian islands. **Borneo:** *K. h. hardwickii.* Recorded at scattered localities from Sabah and Sarawak south to Peleben in East Kalimantan and S. Kapuas in West Kalimantan.

CLEAR-WINGED WOOLLY BAT   *Kerivoula pellucida*   Plate 14

Measurements. FA 29.5-32, T 39-53, E 14.5-17, Wt 3.5-4.8 (8 specimens).

Identification. Upperparts pale orange-brown with paler grey bases; underparts greyish white. Wing membranes and ears pale brown — almost translucent. Ears very long. **Similar Species:** Hardwicke's Woolly Bat, *K. hardwickii*, has shorter ears with dark bases to the fur; the Small Woolly Bat, *K. intermedia*, has darker fur and very small ears.

Ecology and Habitat. Has been found roosting in dead curled banana leaves. Forages in the understorey of tall forest.

Distribution. Peninsular Malaysia, Philippines, Sumatra, Java. **Borneo:** Recorded from scattered localities throughout Sabah and Sarawak as well as northern East Kalimantan; Riam in Central Kalimantan and near S. Pasaguan in West Kalimantan.

SMALL WOOLLY BAT   *Kerivoula intermedia*   Plate 14

Measurements. FA 26.5-31, T 37-41, E 9-11.5, Wt 2.9-4.2 (18 specimens). Skull: cbl 11.1-11.8, mt 4.6-5.0.

Upperparts orange-brown with dark bases; underparts paler. Ears relatively small. Premolars small and rounded (Figure 23a). **Similar Species:** the Least Woolly Bat, *K. minuta*, is very similar and overlaps in forearm length, but is lighter with a smaller skull; Whitehead's Woolly Bat, *K. whiteheadi*, has different coloration — pale brown above, white below — longer ears and very narrow premolars (Figure 23b); Hardwicke's Woolly Bat, *K. hardwickii*, is slightly larger with larger ears and greyer fur with dark grey bases; the Clear-winged Woolly Bat, *K. pellucida*, has pale fur with whitish bases and very long ears.

Ecology and Habitat. Occurs in tall and secondary forest, often in similar habitat to *K. intermedia*.

Distribution. Peninsular Malaysia. **Borneo:** Recorded from Sepilok, Tabin and the Witti Range in Sabah; East Kalimantan.

LEAST WOOLLY BAT   *Kerivoula minuta*   Plate 14

Measurements. FA 25-29.5, T 8-10, Wt 1.9-2.3 (23 specimens). Skull: cbl 10.0-11.1, mt 4.1-4.6.

Identification. Smallest Bornean bat. Upperparts orange-brown with brown bases to the fur; underparts slightly paler. Ear small and rounded. Very similar to the Small Woolly Bat, *K. intermedia*, but skull smaller and body lighter. **Similar Species:** Whitehead's Woolly Bat, *K. whiteheadi*, differs in colour and has narrow premolars (Figure 23b).

Ecology and Habitat. Lives in the understorey of dipterocarp forest. Flight slow and fluttering.

Distribution. Peninsular Thailand and Malaysia. **Borneo:** reported from localities through Sabah including P. Balembangan, Gomantong, Tabin, Madai, Tawau and the Witti Range.

WHITEHEAD'S WOOLLY BAT   *Kerivoula whiteheadi*   Plate 14

Measurements. FA 28-29 (2 Thai specimens).

Identification. Upperparts brown with dark grey bases; underparts greyish white. Ears moderately large. Anterior two upper and lower premolars elongate and oval in cross-section (Figure 23b). **Similar Species:** the Small Woolly Bat, *K. intermedia*, has smaller ears, browner underparts and rounded premolars (Figure 23a).

Ecology and Habitat. A group of 20-30 bats were found roosting in a hanging cluster of large dead leaves by a river.

Distribution: Peninsular Thailand, Philippines. **Borneo:** *K. w. pusilla*. Recorded from the lower S. Kinabatangan in Sabah; G. Mulu and below Usun Apau in Sarawak.

Genus *Phoniscus:* very similar to *Kerivoula*, but tragus unpigmented (white) with a distinct notch in its posterior margin near the base; fur banded, often with pale tips; upper canines have longitudinal grooves on the outer faces.

FROSTED GROOVE-TOOTHED BAT   *Phoniscus jagorii*   Plate 14

Measurements. FA 37-39 (2 Javan specimens). Skull: cbl 15.3-15.9, mt 6.7-7.1.

Identification. Fur greyish black-hairs banded with black then white then black, sometimes with a shiny white tip; short shiny yellow hairs along the forearm and fingers (colour based on type description of Javan specimens). Tragus white and notched. Canine grooved. **Similar Species:** the Gilded Groove-toothed Bat, *P. atrox*, is smaller and browner.

Ecology and Habitat. Unknown.

Distribution. Philippines (Samar Is.), Java, Bali, Sulawesi. **Borneo:** *P. j. javanus.* One specimen was collected near Riam in Central Kalimantan.

GILDED GROOVE-TOOTHED BAT   *Phoniscus atrox*   Plate 14

Measurements. FA 31-33, T 39, E 12.5-14, Wt 3.5-3.8 (4 specimens). Skull: cbl 12.9-13.2, mt 5.6-5.7.

Identification. Upperparts overall golden brown and black—hairs banded with grey and brown bases, black centres and orange-brown or buff tips; underparts paler and greyer. Tragus white with a deep notch in the posterior edge. Dentition similar to *Kerivoula*, but canines have a longitudinal groove on the outside. **Similar Species:** the Frosted Groove-toothed Bat, *Phoniscus jagorii*, is larger, with grey and black fur; tube-nosed bats, *Murina* spp., have long, tubular nostrils and only 2 upper premolars (Figure 23m).

Ecology and Habitat. Has been trapped in the understorey of lowland dipterocarp forest.

Distribution. Southern Thailand, Peninsular Malaysia, Sumatra. **Borneo:** all known specimens are from eastern Sabah, at Sepilok, Tabin and Madai.

217

Subfamily MINIOPTERINAE

Genus *Miniopterus:* the bent-winged bats have a distinctive wing shape, especially the third finger which has a short first phalanx and very long terminal phalanx (Figure 26). The ear is short and rounded with a moderate posterior fold and a short blunt tragus curved slightly forwards. The fur is generally dark blackish or brownish, occasionally with reddish patches or even completely reddish.

The species are all very similar, and difficult to distinguish. Forearm length and weight separate most specimens, but since there is some overlap, skull measurements are sometimes necessary for confirmation. Identification is easier if other species are available for size comparison.

Owing to the similarities, the taxonomy is very unsettled—various scientists disagree about which forms in different areas belong to which species. The names used here are based on Hill (1983), and the world ranges correspond to his interpretation; but further research may require many changes.

Skull with large high braincase, slender rostrum (Figure 22h). Dental formula $\frac{2}{3} \frac{1}{1} \frac{2}{2} \frac{3}{3}$.

Figure 26. Wing tip of bent-winged bat.

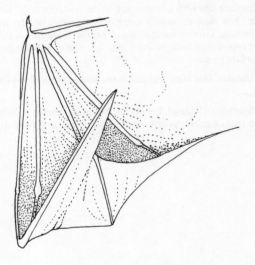

LARGE BENT-WINGED BAT *Miniopterus magnater* Plate 15
(formerly confused with *Miniopterus schreibersii)*

Measurements. FA 47-52, Wt 13-16 (30 specimens). Skull: cbl 15.8-16.8, m-m 7.4-8.0.

Identification. See general description of bent-winged bats (above). Largest of the *Miniopterus,* with an especially wide palate.

Ecology and Habitat. Roosts in caves. Flies above the canopy catching insects — often flies around street lights at 1500 m on G. Kinabalu.

Distribution. Southeast Asia to New Guinea and Australia. **Borneo:** *M. m. macrodens.* Definitely identified only from Sabah, but probably widespread Cave roosts are known from P. Balembangan, Gomantong, Madai and the upper S. Kuamut, and foraging bats have been caught at Poring and Kinabalu.

COMMON BENT-WINGED BAT *Miniopterus schreibersi* Plate 15

Measurements. FA 44-49, Wt 10-12.5 (40 specimens). Skull: cbl 15.1-16, m-m 6.6-7.0.

Identification. See general description of bent-winged bats (above). Forearm length slightly overlaps the range of the Large Bent-winged*M. magnater,* but it is usually shorter, and the body and skull are smaller and narrower.

Ecology and Habitat. Roosts in caves, sometimes mixed with other species of bent-winged bats including *M. magnater* and *M. australis.*

Distribution. Africa and Europe through Asia to Australia. **Borneo:** *M. s. blepotis.* Recorded from Madai and the upper S. Kuamut in Sabah. Specimens from near Kuching in Sarawak were not distinguished from the Large Bent-winged Bat, *M. magnater,* and could represent either species.

SMALL BENT-WINGED BAT *Miniopterus pusillus* Plate 15
(formerly mistaken for a subspecies of *M. australis)*

Measurements. FA 40-43 (7 Thailand specimens). Skull: cbl 12.8-13.3.

Identification. See general description of bent-winged bats (above). Similar to the Lesser Bent-winged Bat, *M. australis,* but with a longer forearm — skull shorter than in *M. a. witkampi.*

Ecology and Habitat. Unknown.

Distribution. Nicobar Is, India, Thailand, Indonesia through New Guinea. **Borneo:** One specimen has been reported from somewhere in Kalimantan.

MEDIUM BENT-WINGED BAT *Miniopterus medius* Plate 15

Measurements. FA 41-42, Wt. 7.3-8.3 (3 specimens). Skull: cbl 13.8-14.5.

Identification. See general description of bent-winged bats (above). Intermediate in size between the Common and Lesser Bent-winged Bats, *M. schreibersi* and *M. australis.* Skull larger than the Small Bent-winged Bat, *M. pusillus.* Fur tends to be more grey-brown and less blackish than the Lesser Bent-winged Bat, *M. australis.*

219

Ecology and Habitat. Roosts in caves, sometimes mixed with the Lesser Bent-winged Bat, *M. australis.*

Distribution. Thailand, Peninsular Malaysia, Java, New Guinea. **Borneo:** *M. m. medius.* Small numbers were caught near Tepadong Caves in Sabah; one specimen was collected in a cave near Kutai in East Kalimantan.

LESSER BENT-WINGED BAT   *Miniopterus australis*   Plate 7

Measurements. FA 35-39, Wt 5-6.5. Skull: cbl 13.5-14.0 *(M. a. witkampi);* cbl 11.8-12.6 *(M. a. paululus).*

Identification. See general description of bent-winged bats (above). Fur usually very dark or black sometimes with large reddish patches. Smallest of the bent-winged bats. *M. a. paululus,* found on P. Balembangan and in the Philippines, has a slightly shorter forearm and much smaller skull. It may prove to represent a separate species.

Ecology and Habitat. Roosts in large colonies in caves, often mixed with other species of bent-winged bats. Roosts individually, except during the breeding season when females gather their young in very large dense clusters of up to 100,000.

Distribution. Philippines, Indonesia through to New Guinea and Australia. **Borneo:** *M. a. witkampi.* Found in large numbers in most cave systems in Sabah and Sarawak as well as Kutai in East Kalimantan. *M. a. paululus.* Colonies found in small caves on P. Balembangan.

Family MOLOSSIDAE   Free-tailed Bats

Medium small to large bats distinguished by their thick tail which protrudes for well over half its length from the interfemoral membrane (Figure 16b). The muzzle lacks a noseleaf and projects well beyond the lower jaw. Lips often somewhat wrinkled. Ears thick, sometimes joined over the top of the head by a band of skin. Wings long and narrow.

Premaxillary bones of skull well developed and attached to the palate and the maxillaries, forming small foramina.

Genus *Cheiromeles:* large and naked with only scattered hairs on the skin. Ears separate. Skull very robust with a prolonged sagittal crest (Figure 17d). Anterior lower premolar minute. Dental formula $\frac{1}{2}\ \frac{1}{1}\ \frac{2}{2}\ \frac{3}{3}$.

NAKED BAT   *Cheiromeles torquatus*   Plate 8

Measurements. FA 74-83, Wt 150-175 (5 specimens).

Identification. Body almost completely naked except for scattered short hairs and a cluster of long hairs around a scent gland in its neck. Bare skin of body dark grey. In flight can often be recognized by its large size, strong flight and the audible clicking of its echolocation call as it searches for insects. Exposed tail and large separate ears can sometimes be seen as well.

Ecology and Habitat. Roosts in large caves or hollow trees, sometimes associated with Free-Tailed Bats, *Tadarida mops.* Feeds in open areas over streams or clearings or high over the forest canopy.

Distribution. Peninsular Thailand and Malaysia, Philippines, Sumatra, Java and nearby small islands. **Borneo:** *C. t. torquatus.* Recorded from scattered localities in the north and west, including P. Banggi, Sandakan, Tabin and Tenom in Sabah; near Bandar Seri Begawan in Brunei; Niah, the Baram district and the Kuching area in Sarawak.

Genus *Tadarida:* fur thick and short. The **subgenus *Chaerephon*** has an extra small upper premolar which is lacking in the **subgenus *Mops*** (Figure 27). Upper incisors long and well-developed, evenly spaced between the canines. Dental formula $\frac{1}{1}\ \frac{1\cdot2}{2}\ \frac{3}{3}\ \frac{1}{2}$.

FREE-TAILED BAT   *Tadarida (Mops) mops*   Plate 8

Measurements. FA 43-46 (4 Peninsular Malaysian and Bornean specimens). Skull: cbl 19.1-19.4, mt 7.0-7.4, c-c 5.2-5.7.

Identification. Upperparts and underparts uniform dark brown to reddish brown; crown of head nearly naked. Ears large and rounded, joined across the top of the head by a narrow flap of skin. Upper lip heavily wrinkled. Only one upper premolar; posterior molar reduced (Figure 27b). **Similar Species:** the Wrinkle-lipped Bat, *T. plicata,* has shorter fur, paler underparts, and a smaller skull with two upper premolars and a well developed posterior molar (Figure 27a).

Ecology and Habitat. In Peninsular Malaysia roosts in hollows in trees, sometimes in association with the Hairless Bat, *Cheiromeles torquatus.*

Distribution. Peninsular Malaysia, Sumatra. **Borneo:** two specimens were reported from an unspecified location in Sarawak.

Figure 27. Upper toothrow of a. *Tadarida plicata*
  b. *Tadarida mops*

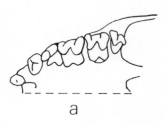
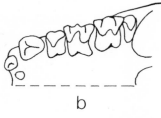

a   b

x 4

WRINKLE-LIPPED BAT   *Tadarida (Chaerephon) plicata*   Plate 8

Measurements. FA 40-43.5, Wt 10.5-18 (20 specimens). Skull: cbl 16.5-17.7, mt 6.5-6.8, c-c 4.4-5.0.

Identification. Upperparts covered in short dark brown fur; underparts paler with grey tips to the fur. Upper lip heavily wrinkled; ears moderate, joined across top of head by narrow flap of skin. Two upper premolars, the anterior quite small; posterior upper molar well developed and about half the area of the second molar (Figure 27a). **Similar Species:** the Free-tailed Bat, *T. mops*, is larger with a slightly longer forearm, darker fur and a massive skull with only one upper premolar and a reduced posterior upper molar (Figure 27b).

Ecology and Habitat. Roosts in caves in large densely packed colonies, sometimes containing hundreds of thousands of individuals. Often fly out before darkness in dense flocks.

Distribution. Sri Lanka, India through southern China, Southeast Asia, Philippines, Sumatra, Java. **Borneo:** *T. p. plicata*. Large cave roosts known from Gomantong and Madai in Sabah; G. Mulu in Sarawak. Also collected near Kuching in Sarawak.

Order PRIMATES
Prosimians, Monkeys and Apes

The primates are represented in Borneo by six families including the Hominidae, the family of Man. All primates have hands and feet which can grasp, digits generally with nails rather than claws, and both eyes on the front of the face. The Lorisidae and Tarsiidae are strictly nocturnal. The monkeys (family Cercopithecidae) and apes (families Hylobatidae and Pongidae) are diurnal and, along with tree squirrels and treeshrews, are the only mammals active in trees during the daytime.

Family LORISIDAE
Lorises

Lorises are small, stockily built primates with a very short tail, and unlike most other members of their order they climb slowly and deliberately, never jumping under normal circumstances. All the digits have nails, with the exception of the second digit of the foot, which has a short claw.

SLOW LORIS
Nycticebus coucang
Plate 19

Measurements. HB 199-275, T 13-25, HF 48-63 (5 specimens). Wt 230-610.

Identification. General coloration varies from pale grey-brown to reddish-brown, with a brown stripe from top of head to middle of back or base of tail. Usually has a dark-coloured ring around each eye. Fur soft and dense. Eyes reflect torchlight clearly at night with a reddish colour.

Ecology and Habitat. Nocturnal and usually arboreal, mostly in small to medium-sized trees. Feeds on small animals, mostly insects, and on pulpy fruits, including cocoa. Occurs in tall and secondary forests, gardens and cocoa plantations. Mainly solitary.

Distribution. North-eastern India, South-east Asia, Sumatra, Java, southern Philippines. **Borneo:** *N. c. borneanus.* Known from many lowland and hill localities throughout the area. Highest record above 1300 m on G. Kinabalu.

Family TARSIIDAE
Tarsiers

Tarsiers are small, long-tailed primates which jump from tree to tree and feed exclusively on small animals. The distribution of the family, which contains only the genus *Tarsius*, is restricted and unusual: in addition to the Western Tarsier, *T. bancanus*, two other species are recognised, one in Sulawesi and offshore islands, the other in Mindanao, Bohol, Leyte and Samar in the southern Philippines.

WESTERN TARSIER
Tarsius bancanus
Plate 19

Measurements. HB 121-154, T 181-224, HF 59-71 (12 specimens). Wt 86-135.

Identification. General coloration varies from pale olive- or reddish-brown to pale or dark grey-brown (possibly varying with age). Fur soft. Tail hairless except at the end. Digits slender with large terminal pads and pointed nails, except for second and third toes on hind feet, which bear a large claw. The eyes, although large, do not reflect torchlight.

Ecology and Habitat. Nocturnal. Active from ground level up to at least 7 m, often leaping betwen vertical supports at lower levels. Diet mainly large insects.

223

Apparently forages for food singly, making high-pitched calls frequently. Found in a variety of tall and secondary forests.

Distribution. Southern Sumatra and nearby islands. **Borneo:** *T. b. borneanus.* Known from many lowland sites in Sabah, Brunei, Sarawak and West Kalimantan, · and above 900 m in the Kelabit uplands in northern Sarawak. Elsewhere, recorded only from Kutai and Peleben in East Kalimantan and Tumbang Maruwe in Central Kalimantan.

Family CERCOPITHECIDAE   Monkeys

Monkeys in Borneo are represented by two distinct groups: the langurs or leaf monkeys and the Proboscis Monkey (subfamily Colobinae) and the macaques (subfamily Cercopithecinae). The colobines are mainly arboreal, have a long tail, lack cheek pouches and have a large, sacculated stomach which permits breakdown of leafy material into digestible substances and helps detoxify poisonous leaves. The macaques are partly terrestrial, with a short or long tail, cheek pouches for temporary storage of food and a simple stomach capable of breaking down only a limited amount of leafy material.

Figure 28. Skull of a Hose's Langur, *Presbytis hosei*.

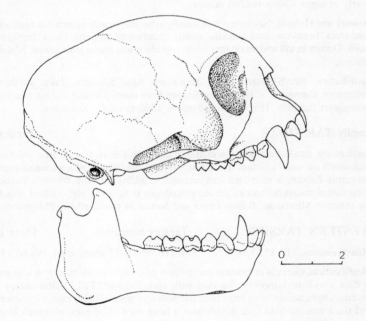

224

BANDED LANGUR   *Presbytis melalophos*   Plate 20
(also called *Presbytis femoralis*)

Measurements. HB 460-593, T 695-765, HF 170-185 (8 specimens).

Identification. Adults black and white, or black, red and white. There is a black band across each cheek, visible in the field under clear conditions. Infants white with black lines down the back and across the shoulders. Adult male loud call: a staccato "ke-ke-ke. .". *P. m. chrysomelas:* black with whitish at base of tail and on inner surfaces of limbs. *P. m. cruciger:* dark red with black markings on the back and limbs; whitish at base of tail and on inner surfaces of limbs. **Similar species:** the Silvered Langur, *P. cristata*, has no white markings, although parts of the body may appear whitish in bright sunlight, the face is entirely blackish or dark grey with no black cheek bands, and infants are orange coloured.

Ecology and Habitat. Diurnal and arboreal. Groups at Samunsam in Sarawak contain 5-6 individuals. Occurs in dipterocarp forests.

Distribution. Peninsular Burma, Thailand and Malaysia; Sumatra and adjacent islands. **Borneo:** Confined to the lowlands and hills of the west coast (Map 3). *P. m. chrysomelas:* recorded between central Sarawak and S. Kapuas in West Kalimantan. *P. m. cruciger:* recorded in central Sarawak as far north as the Baram area. Also *P. m. natunae:* on P. Natuna Besar.

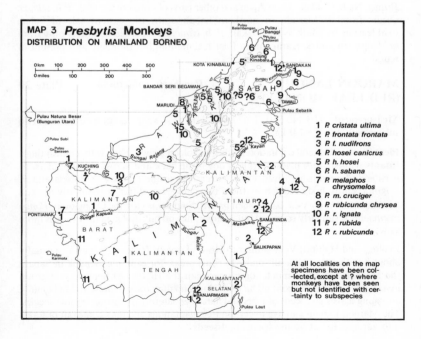

MAP 3 *Presbytis* Monkeys
DISTRIBUTION ON MAINLAND BORNEO

1 *P. cristata ultima*
2 *P. frontata frontata*
3 *P. f. nudifrons*
4 *P. hosei canicrus*
5 *P. h. hosei*
6 *P. h. sabana*
7 *P. melaphos chrysomelos*
8 *P. m. cruciger*
9 *P. rubicunda chrysea*
10 *P. r. ignata*
11 *P. r. rubida*
12 *P. r. rubicunda*

At all localities on the map specimens have been col-lected, except at ? where monkeys have been seen but not identified with cer-tainty to subspecies

HOSE'S LANGUR (GREY LEAF MONKEY) *Presbytis hosei* Plate 20

Measurements. HB 480-557, T 646-840, HF 172-185 (7 Sabah specimens of *P. h. sabana).* Wt 6-7 kg.

Identification. Upperparts grey; underparts white, with blackish hands and feet. Face pinkish with a distinct black band across each cheek. Infants white with black lines down the back and across the shoulders. Groups (probably the adult male) sometimes give a unique gargling call. *P. h. hosei:* adult male with forehead, sides of head and neck white, prominent black crest on top of head; adult female with more black. *P. h. sabana:* both sexes pale grey head and dark grey crest. *P. h. canicrus:* brownish crest and back of neck. **Similar species:** adult Silvered Langurs, *P. cristata,* are entirely grey, infants orange.

Ecology and Habitat. Diurnal. Active throughout the tree canopy, occasionally descending to the ground and visiting natural mineral sources. In Sabah and Brunei, most often encountered in groups of 6-8 individuals (but 12 or more reported from Temburong) containing one adult male and two or more adult females. Diet seeds and leaves. Occurs in tall and, less abundantly, secondary forests. Occasionally enters plantations. Ecologically very similar to the Maroon Langur, *P. rubicunda,* but in some areas (for example, Tabin in Sabah) Hose's Langur is common while the Maroon is rare; in other areas the reverse is true.

Distribution. Confined to Borneo in the lowlands and hill ranges of the north and east (Map 3). *P. h. hosei:* known from western Sabah as far north as G. Kinabalu; Brunei; Niah, G. Dulit, Usun Apau and other parts of northern Sarawak. *P. h. sabana:* occurs from T. Marudu in northern Sabah down the eastern side of Sabah to at least as far south as Kalabakan. *P. h. canicrus:* recorded definitely only from G. Talisayan and S. Karangan in East Kalimantan but probably also present in Kutai.

MAROON LANGUR *Presbytis rubicunda* Plate 20
(RED LEAF MONKEY)

Measurements. HB 440-580, T 673-800, HF 175-185 (5 Sabah specimens of two subspecies). Wt 5.5-7.0 kg.

Identification. General coloration reddish to golden brown. Face with a bluish tinge. Infants whitish with black markings down the back and across the shoulders. *P. r. rubicunda:* reddish with blackish extremities to the limbs. *P. r. rubida* and *P. r. ignita:* entire body reddish — these two subspecies differ only slightly in skull dimensions. *P. r. chrysea:* pale golden brown. **Similar species:** the Orang-utan, *Pongo pygmaeus,* is similarly coloured but is larger, has no tail, and generally moves more slowly.

Ecology and Habitat. Very similar to Hose's Langur, *P. hosei.* Group size usually about 8 with only one adult male. In some areas (for example, Sepilok in Sabah) the Maroon Langur is much commoner than the Hose's. At Sepilok, one group investigated occupied about 60 ha of tall lowland dipterocarp forest and fed mainly on young leaves and seeds of trees and lianas, apparently preferring legume species. The Maroon Langur can live in certain tree plantations and may come out of forest into gardens to eat young leaves and seeds.

Distribution. Confined to P. Karimata and Borneo, where it is the most widespread langur species, apparently occurring throughout most of the lowlands, hills and mountains, including the Kelabit uplands and up to nearly 2000 m on G. Kinabalu (Map 3). There are no records, however, from extreme western Borneo between Kuching and Pontianak, or Central Kalimantan. *P. r. rubicunda:* recorded throughout eastern Borneo and most of Sabah, excluding the range of *P. r. chrysea,* which occurs between S. Kinabatangan and approximately S. Kalabakan. *P. r. rubida* and *P. r. ignita:* recorded in western Borneo (Map 4). *P. r. carimatae:* found only on P. Karimata.

WHITE-FRONTED LANGUR   *Presbytis frontata*   Plate 20

Measurements. HB 470-540, T 630-740, HF 165-180 (3 Sarawak and Kalimantan specimens).

Identification. Mainly grey-brown, with a distinct bare white spot on the forehead. *P. f. frontata:* brownish, with darker arms, legs, top and sides of head and tail; chin and lower cheeks greyish. The white spot on the forehead is roughly triangular in shape. *P. f. nudifrons:* dark greyish, with blackish hands, feet and base of tail; underparts and distal end of tail paler grey-brown; throat white. The white spot on the forehead is rather square and divided by a vertical line of short black hairs.

Ecology and Habitat. Diurnal. Ecology unknown but probably similar to the Maroon and Hose's Langurs, *P. rubicunda* and *P. hosei.* Occurs in tall lowland and hill dipterocarp forests.

Distribution. Restricted to Borneo south of about 3°N and east of S. Barito in Central Kalimantan. *P. f. frontata:* recorded in the east between S. Kayan and Banjermasin in the south. *P. f. nudifrons:* recorded from central Sarawak between the upper S. Rajang and upper Batang Lupar, including Lanjak-Entimau Wildlife Sanctuary.

SILVERED LANGUR   *Presbytis cristata*   Plate 20

Measurements. HB 415-540, 600-760, HF 145-174, Wt 4.0-6.5 kg (4 specimens).

Identification. Entirely dark, metallic grey. Face dark grey or black. Appears totally black under some field conditions. Infants are bright orange. A reddish-coloured form of the adults has been recorded from the mouth of S. Kinabatangan in eastern Sabah, where groups may contain both grey and red forms. **Similar species:** the Banded and Grey Langurs, *P. melalophos* and *P. hosei,* have some white on the body and black bands across the cheeks.

Ecology and Habitat. Diurnal and generally arboreal. Diet includes leaves, shoots and fruits. Average group size at Samunsam in Sarawak about 5 or 6. Occurs in many kinds of coastal, riverine and swamp forests, both tall and secondary. Also reported from inland hill forest in Sarawak, although normally only other langur species occur in non-coastal, non-riverine habitats.

Distribution. Peninsular Burma, Thailand, and Malaysia; Sumatra, Java and adjacent uslands. **Borneo:** *P. c. ultima.* Recorded from coastal areas around most of the island, and also along the banks of rivers far inland. One record at 900 m on G. Dulit in Sarawak.

PROBOSCIS MONKEY   *Nasalis larvatus*   Plate 21

Measurements. (adult males) HB 555-651, T 674-745, HF 210-225, Wt 12-23 kg (4 specimens); (adult females) HB 550-555, T 620-570, HF 190-193 (2 specimens), Wt about 10 kg.

Identification. Upperparts generally dull, pale greyish-yellow to red-brown, darker on the upper back, with a reddish-brown cap on top of the head; underparts paler. Tail and rump whitish, especially in adult males. Adult males have a pale collar around the front and sides of the neck and a much larger nose than females. When sitting in a tree, tail usually hangs vertically downwards. Infants have a dark blue face. Makes a wide range of distinctive noises, including honks, groans, squeals and loud roars. **Similar species:** other monkeys are smaller and have dark tails.

Ecology and Habitat. Diurnal, but most active early morning and late afternoon when leaving or moving to sleeping sites, usually on a river bank. Mostly arboreal, but will swim across rivers or walk across open areas to reach isolated patches of forest. Social structure apparently flexible, with small parties often joining into temporary large groups. Diet includes leaves, fruits and shoots. In eastern Sabah, most often found in mangrove forests, mixed mangrove and nipah and in river edge forests. Seldom encountered in pure stands of nipah, *Casuarina*, coastal heath or swamp forests. In Sarawak and Kalimantan, may be more common in riverine and peat swamp forests. Solitary males occasionally seen in other forest types many kilometres from any mangrove or large river. Function of large nose unknown.

Distribution. Restricted to Borneo and a few inshore islands, notably those at the mouth of S. Brunei and on P. Sebatik off the Sabah/East Kalimantan border. Usually found near large water courses. On the larger rivers of eastern Sabah occurs far upriver (for example, above S. Danum on the upper S. Segama). There are old reports from the upper S. Kapuas in West Kalimantan, at Tumbang Maruwe on S. Barito in Central Kalimantan, and on S. Mahakam and S. Kayan in East Kalimantan. The present situation in interior Kalimantan is uncertain, but the species is present in many coastal parts of West, Central, South and East Kalimantan, notably on the lower S. Barito. The distribution in western Sabah, Brunei and Sarawak is sparse and patchy, probably reflecting both habitat distribution and hunting pressure. In Brunei, locally abundant at the mouth of S. Brunei but there are no records from the mouth of S. Temburong further east.

LONG-TAILED (CRAB-EATING)   *Macaca fascicularis*   Plate 21
MACAQUE

Measurements. HB 400-470, T 500-600 (7 specimens), HF about 140. Wt: Adult males 5-7 kg. Adult females 3-4 kg.

Identification. Grey-brown to reddish-brown, always paler on the underparts. Cheek-whiskers often prominent. Infants blackish. Groups often detected by their calls, the most common being "krra!". Individuals tend to be less noisy than langurs when travelling through the tree canopy, but groups are more noisy. **Similar species:** the Silvered Langur, *Presbytis cristata*, (often in the same habitat) is entirely dark (infants orange) and has a distinct crest of hairs on top of the head; the Pig-tailed Macaque, *M. nemestrina*, has a short tail.

228

Ecology and Habitat. Active periodically from dawn until dusk. Often travels in groups of 20 to 30 or more individuals containing 2 - 4 adult males, 6 - 11 adult females and the remainder immatures. Usually only part of the group can be seen at one time. Males sometimes solitary or in small groups. A group occupies an area of up to several tens of hectares, travelling from 150 - 1500 m daily. Unlike other monkeys, spends a large proportion of the time active in low trees and thick scrub. Common in coastal forests including mangrove and beach, and along rivers. Also around gardens, villages and plantations. Diet mostly ripe fruits and a wide array of animal material including insects, frogs' eggs, crabs and other coastal invertebrates. Sometimes a pest in commercial crops.

Distribution. Peninsular Burma, Thailand, and Malaysia; southern Indochina, Philippines, Sumatra, Java and adjacent islands. **Borneo:** *M. f. fascicularis.* Known throughout the lowlands, especially coastal regions, but up to 1300 m on some mountains.

PIG-TAILED MACAQUE   *Macaca nemestrina*   Plate 21

Measurements. HB 495, T 180, HF 158 (1 adult male). Wt: adult males 7-9 kg, adult females 4-6 kg (Peninsular Malaysian specimens heavier).

Identification. Olive-brown with whitish underparts and dark brown on top of head and neck. Short tail distinctive; other Bornean monkeys have a long tail, while apes have no tail at all. This is the only primate which often descends to the ground to flee from man.

Ecology and Habitat. Diurnal. Group size usually 15-40 monkeys, but solitary males are also encountered. Diet includes fruits and small vertebrate and invertebrate animals. Most often found in hill forests, sometimes entering plantations and gardens in adjacent lowlands where they can cause considerable damage to grain and fruit crops.

Distribution. North-eastern India, southwest China, South-east Asia, Sumatra and adjacent islands. **Borneo:** *M. n. nemestrina.* Known throughout the lowlands and hills up to at least 1300 m.

Family HYLOBATIDAE   Gibbons

Gibbons are slender totally arboreal primates which, like other apes, lack a tail. They can travel very rapidly in the canopy of rain forest, swinging by their long arms.

BORNEAN GIBBON   *Hylobates muelleri*   Plate 22

Measurements. HB 420-470, HF 128-150 (7 specimens). Wt 5.0-6.4 kg.

Identification. Basically grey-brown but with a wide range in coat colour and pattern. No tail. Most often detected by the loud, bubbling call of the adult female, heard during the first hours of daylight and carrying for a distance of over 2 km under suitable conditions. *H. m. funereus:* usually mid grey-brown, with black underparts, and with a blackish "cap" on top of the head; sometimes nearly all black. Hands and feet coloured as the upperparts. *H.m. muelleri:* similarly coloured, but with hands and feet blackish. *H. m. abbotti:* entirely pale greyish. A population of mixed colours occurs in the Lanjak-Entimau Wildlife Sanctuary in southern interior Sarawak. **Similar species:** the Agile Gibbon, *H. agilis,* is very similar in appearance, but occurs only in south-western Borneo and the loud call of the female is different.

Ecology and Habitat. Diurnal and completely arboreal. Unlike monkeys, gibbons usually cease activity about two hours before dusk. Usually found in small groups of one adult male, one adult female and one to three young. Each group defends a territory of 20 - 30 ha. Diet consists of ripe fleshy fruits, young leaves and small insects. Normally found only in tall and selectively logged dipterocarp forests.

Distribution. Confined to Borneo in the lowlands and hills, up to 1500 m on G. Kinabalu. *H. m. funereus:* occurs in the north, south to the Saribas region of Sarawak and the S. Karangan region of East Kalimantan. *H. m. muelleri:* recorded between S. Barito and S. Karangan. *H. m. abbotti:* recorded between the Saribas region and S. Kapuas in West Kalimantan.

AGILE GIBBON   *Hylobates agilis*   (see Plate 22)

Identification. Similar in size and form to the Bornean Gibbon. Upperparts, particularly the lower back, buffy; top of head and underparts, notably the chest, dark brown. Loud call of female a series of high-pitched rising and falling notes. **Similar species:** the Bornean Gibbon, *H. muelleri,* has a different distribution, and the adult female has a "bubbling" loud call.

Ecology and Habitat. Same as the Bornean Gibbon, *H. muelleri*.

Distribution. Northern Peninsular Malaysia, southern Sumatra. **Borneo:** *H. a. albibarbis.* Believed to occur only in the region between S. Kapuas in West Kalimantan and S. Barito in eastern Central Kalimantan. Hybrids with the Bornean Gibbon, *H. muelleri,* have been reported from the upper S. Barito, to the north of Muara Julai.

Family: PONGIDAE   Great Apes

This family includes the Chimpanzees and Gorillas of Africa and the Orang-utan of Borneo and Sumatra, all large, intelligent tail-less primates. The Orang-utan differs from the other apes and monkeys in that adults lead a mostly solitary existence, although the ranges of several individuals may overlap.

ORANG-UTAN   *Pongo pygmaeus*

Plate 22

Measurements. Largest males (above 15 years age) up to 1.4 m tall, with a reach between the outstretched arms up to 2.4 m, and weight 50-100 kg. Adult females much smaller, 35-50 kg. Independent (but immature, 7-10 years age) Orang-utans of both sexes 20-40 kg.

Identification. Coloration generally reddish-brown, varying from orange to dark reddish-brown in old individuals. Calls useful for identification in the field include something like a long belch, made by adult females, and loud roars, made by adult males, both by day and night. Often detected by its nests — a rough array of bent and broken twigs and small branches partially woven together. No other primates make nests, but Sun Bears, *Helarctos malayanus*, make a similar nest, usually lower in trees and less neatly woven; the nest of the Giant Squirrel, *Ratufa affinis*, is more neat and compact when fresh, and made of smaller twigs. Orang-utans can sometimes also be detected by footprints on bare soil or discarded wadges of epiphytic fibres which they sometimes chew. **Similar species:** the Maroon Langur, *Presbytis rubicunda*, is similar in colour, but smaller, has a long tail and is usually in groups; the Proboscis Monkey, *Nasalis larvatus*, is usually paler and has a long pale tail.

Ecology amd Habitat. Diurnal and usually arboreal. Diet mainly fruits with young leaves and insects. Usually solitary, but young remain with mother until 5 or 6 years of age. Found in montane, secondary and swamp forests including nipah, but reaches highest densities (up to 2 individuals per sq. km.) in tall lowland dipterocarp forests — density in hill forest may be only 1 individual per 2 sq. km. Sometimes enters gardens and plantations.

Distribution. Northern Sumatra. **Borneo:** *P. p. pygmaeus.* It seems likely that the Orang-utan was once distributed throughout most of Borneo up to about 1500 m and the present widespread but patchy distribution could be a result of hunting by man coupled with loss of forest habitat. There are at least three substantial regions in Borneo from which there have been no records of Orang-utans in recent historical times: (1) between S. Rajang in Sarawak and S. Padas in south-western Sabah, except for some upland records near the Kalimantan border, (2) the lowlands between S. Barito in south-eastern Borneo and S. Mahakam in East Kalimantan, (3) the Tawau region in Sabah. There are Orang-utan remains at all levels in cave deposits at Niah, however, in the middle of the first of these three regions. These peculiar gaps in distribution may be a result of disease, such as malaria, which in the past appears to have limited the range of human populations in tropical areas. A high altitude record of 2400 m is reported from G. Kinabalu but most records are from below 1000 m.

Order PHOLIDOTA
Family MANIDAE
Pangolin

The Pangolin is unique among Bornean mammals in having scales covering the entire upperparts, a prehensile tail and lacking teeth. The infant travels clinging to the upper side of the base of the mother's tail.

Figure 29. Skull of a Pangolin, *Manis javanica*.

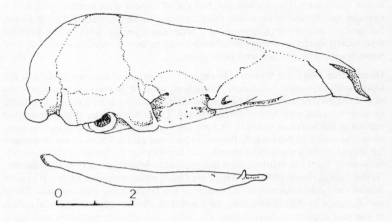

PANGOLIN or SCALY ANTEATER   *Manis javanica*   Plate 19

Measurements. HB 397-645, T 351-565, HF 61-97 (4 specimens). Wt up to 7 kg.

Identification. A distinctive brownish, scaly mammal, with long claws on the forefeet. Head and tail long and tapering, held below level of body while travelling on the ground. Tail wrapped around body when animal is disturbed, to protect the non-scaly underparts.

Ecology and Habitat. Usually nocturnal, sleeping during the daytime in underground burrows. Food consists exclusively of ants and termites taken from nests in trees, on the ground or below ground. The insect nests are opened with the strongly clawed feet and the contents licked up with the long, sticky tongue. Known from tall and secondary forests and from cultivated areas including gardens. Most often seen on roads at night, where it is slow-moving and conspicuous, although the eyes reflect very little torchlight.

Distribution. South-east Asia, Palawan, Sumatra, Java and smaller Indonesian islands. **Borneo:** known from lowlands and hills throughout the island, up to 1700 m on G. Kinabalu.

232

Order RODENTIA   Squirrels, Rats and Porcupines

Rodents can be recognised by their dentition, with large, curved, chiselling incisors
in both the upper and lower jaw, no canines and a wide diastema (= toothless
gap) before the cheek teeth (Figures 30 and 32). Unlike insectivores and treeshrews,
all the Bornean rodents have only four long, clawed digits on each front foot, and
a short thumb with a nail instead of a claw.

Family SCIURIDAE   Squirrels

Subfamily SCIURINAE   Tree squirrels and ground squirrels

Many of the squirrels appear quite similar, but can usually be identified based on
differences in colour patterns if they are seen clearly. Conditions are rarely idéal,
though, and many ground squirrels are glimpsed only briefly in dim light, while
tree squirrels are often obscured by leaves or silhouetted against the sky. Binoculars
are helpful for viewing squirrels, and many species, with the exception of giant
and pygmy squirrels, can be trapped fairly easily in cage traps for closer study.

The Shrew-faced Ground Squirrel, *Rhinosciurus laticaudatus*, could be mistaken
at a distance for a *Tupaia* treeshrew because of its pointed muzzle, but can be
distinguished by its shorter bushy tail.

GIANT SQUIRREL *Ratufa affinis*   Plate 23

Measurements. HB 320-380, T 370-444, HF 67-86 (18 specimens). Wt 875-1500.

Identification. The largest tree squirrel in Borneo. Coloration variable, but upperparts
usually dark in the middle; underparts pale. Four subspecies are recognized, although
there is some colour variation within each form, partly obscuring the differences.
R. a. sandakanensis: upperparts very dark in the midline; underparts very pale,
almost white; sides of body speckled with buff; normally no reddish tinge. *R. a.
baramensis:* upperparts less dark along midline; underparts buff; thighs grizzled.
The whole body with a reddish tinge, especially the sides. Giant Squirrels
intermediate in coloration between these two forms have been collected from the
Kelabit uplands and the Lawas district in northern Sarawak. *R. a. cothurnata:*
resembles *baramensis* but thighs pale, not grizzled. *R. a. ephippium:* resembles
cothurnata but upperparts with a very dark midline. Island forms variable, but
one from P. Laut is entirely pale brown. Three colour forms have been reported
(but not collected) from the upper Temburong region of Brunei: one resembles
baramensis, another is similar but with grey underparts and the third is entirely
pale brown. When moving quickly through the tree canopy, the tail is held out
horizontally but when sitting on a branch it hangs vertically. The loud call is a
short, harsh chatter, often audible for several hundred metres. It also has a distinctive
soft call, a series of "hgip . . .hgip . ." audible from several tens of metres.

Ecology and Habitat. Diurnal, usually emerging from the nest well after dawn
and retiring for the night before dusk. The nest, a neat rather globular array of
twigs, is usually built in the crown of a tall tree. Mostly active in tall trees, descending
to the ground only to cross gaps in the tree canopy. Diet mainly seeds with some
leaves and bark. Occurs in dipterocarp and lower montane forests, also secondary
forests. Rarely enters plantations.

Distribution. Peninsular Burma, Thailand and Malaysia; Sumatra and smaller Indonesian islands. **Borneo:** widespread throughout the lowlands and hills, up to 1500 m on G. Kinabalu. *R. a. sandakanensis.* Recorded throughout Sabah and in the northern part of East Kalimantan. *R. a. baramensis.* Found in Sarawak between the Saribas region and S. Baram — population between S. Baram and the Sabah-Sarawak border probably mixed. In the east, this subspecies occurs approximately between S. Karangan and S. Kayan. *R. a. cothurnata.* Recorded to the south of the Saribas region and S. Karangan, except in the extreme southeast. *R. a. ephippium.* Found between Banjarmasin and T. Pamukan in the southeast. Also found on several offshore islands: P. Banggi *(R. a. banguei),* P. Panebangan *(R. a. griseicollis),* P. Laut *(R. a. vittata),* and P. Sebuku *(R. a. vittatula).*

PREVOST'S SQUIRREL *Callosciurus prevostii*   Plate 24

Measurements. HB 200-267, T 202-273, HF 45-61 (45 specimens of 3 subspecies). Wt 250-500.

Identification. All forms have dark reddish or orange underparts, but coloration varies considerably between and within subspecies. *C. p. pluto, C. p. caedis* and *C. p. rufonigra:* upperparts entirely black, sometimes with a faint white side-stripe. *C. p. atrox:* upperparts grizzled olive-buff; tail black. *C. p. atricapillus:* upperparts grizzled olive-buff; face and rump black; tail usually grizzled black. *C. p. caroli:* upperparts and tail grizzled grey, face and front parts of body usually with a red tinge; has a white side-stripe sometimes with a thin black stripe below it; thighs paler than body. This subspecies is quite variable — individuals from coastal regions are very pale while those further inland are much darker. *C. p. borneoensis* and *C. p. coomansi:* upperparts black with thighs grizzled grey; tail black with heavy white grizzling; white side-stripe distinct, sometimes with a thin black stripe below; shoulder region with a reddish tinge. *C. p. palustris:* like *borneoensis* but with no trace of red on the shoulders. *C. p. sanggaus:* similar to *borneoensis* but shoulder region paler and tail entirely black. *C. p. waringensis:* similar to *sanggaus* but shoulder region only slightly reddish and thighs paler. The subspecies probably overlap in some areas. For example, both *pluto* and *caroli* occur in the Lawas district near the Sabah-Sarawak border, while possible *plutos-atrox* hybrids occur north of S. Kayan in East Kalimantan. **Similar species:** the Kinabalu Squirrel, *C. baluensis,* is the same size and shape, but differs in colour pattern; the Horse-tailed Squirrel, *Sundasciurus hippurus,* is usually found in small trees and has a reddish brown back and greyish head.

Ecology and Habitat. Diurnal, most active in the early morning and late afternoon. Usually arboreal, descending to the ground only to cross gaps in the tree canopy. Diet includes fruits, especially those with a sweet or oily flesh, and insects, notably ants, termites and beetle larvae which are gnawed out of dying wood. Occurs in tall and secondary forests. Enters gardens and plantations from adjacent forest to feed on fruits.

Distribution. Peninsular Thailand and Malaysia, Sumatra, Sulawesi and smaller Indonesian islands. **Borneo:** widespread in the lowlands and hills, but there are no records from South Kalimantan nor from the lowlands of Central Kalimantan between S. Barito and S. Seruyan. Highest altitude records are 1220 m on Usun

234

Apau and somewhat higher on G. Mulu. Prevost's Squirrel is replaced by the Kinabalu Squirrel at high altitudes in the mountains of north-western and central Borneo, but the two species overlap on G. Kinabalu, G.Trus Madi, G. Mulu, G. Dulit, Usun Apau and probably on other mountains. The subspecies are distributed as shown on Map 4: 1. *C. p. pluto*, 2. *C. p. atrox*, 3. *C. p. atricapillus*, 4. *C. p. caroli*, 5. *C. p. borneoensis* and *C. p. coomansi*, 6. *C. p. palustris*, 7. *C. p. sanggaus*, 8. *C. p. waringensis*. Other subspecies occur on some offshore islands including *C. p. caedis* on P. Banggi and P. Balembangan, *C. p. rufonigra* on P. Labuan and *C. p. carimatae* on P. Karimata.

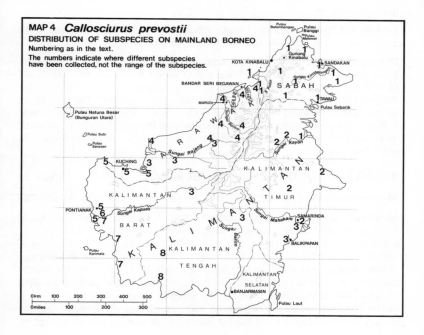

MAP 4 *Callosciurus prevostii*
DISTRIBUTION OF SUBSPECIES ON MAINLAND BORNEO
Numbering as in the text.
The numbers indicate where different subspecies have been collected, not the range of the subspecies.

KINABALU SQUIRREL *Callosciurus baluensis* Plate 24

Measurements. HB 210-255, T 215-260, HF 48-55 (4 specimens).

Identification. Upperparts grey-black with fine buffy-red speckling especially on the face and legs. Short white and black side-stipes. Underparts dark reddish. Some individuals have a dark line along the centre of the belly. *C. b. baramensis* differs from *C. b. baluensis* (illustrated) in having the tail speckled like the body. **Similar species:** Prevost's Squirrel, *C. prevostii*, is usually found at lower altitudes, and differs in coloration: upperparts of *C. p. atrox* and *C. p. atricapillus* are speckled olive buff; upperparts of *C. p. caroli* are speckled grey with no red tinge on the hind quarters.

Ecology and Habitat. Diurnal. Usually arboreal but occasionally descends to the ground. Occurs in montane oak and lower moss forests.

Distribution. Found only in the mountains of northwestern Borneo. *C. b. baluensis.* Known from G. Kinabalu (300-1800 m), the Crocker Range (above 1300 m) and G. Trus Madi (above 1300 m) in Sabah. *C. b. baramensis (including C. b. medialis).* Recorded from Usun Apau (above 1070 m), the upper slopes of G. Dulit, G. Mulu, and G. Murud (1980 m) in Sarawak, and the upper S. Baleh, near the Sarawak-Kalimantan border. Overlaps with the upper range of Prevost's Squirrel, *C. prevostii*, on G. Kinabalu, G. Trus Madi, G. Mulu, G. Dulit, Usun Apau and probably on other mountains.

PLANTAIN SQUIRREL *Callosciurus notatus* Plate 25

Measurements. HB 175-223, T 160-210, HF 42-52 (51 specimens). Wt 150-280.

Identification. Upperparts finely speckled brownish. Side-stripes buff and black. Underparts vary from dark to light, but always reddish or orange, never grey. *C. n. dilutus* is said to have paler underparts than *C. n. dulitensis*, but the range of variation overlaps considerably. *C. n. conipus* differs in having the legs and feet greyish. **Similar species:** the Ear-spot Squirrel, *C. adamsi*, is slightly smaller, usually has a grey tinge on the underparts, and has a pale spot behind each ear — often difficult to see in the field; the Red-bellied Sculptor Squirrel, *Glyphotes simus*, is similar in coloration, but is much smaller and (in the hand) has distinctive incisors (Figure 30c); the Bornean Black-banded Squirrel, *C. orestes*, has greyish underparts.

Ecology and Habitat. Diurnal, most active early morning and late afternoon. Travels and feeds mainly in small trees. Diet includes a wide variety of fruits and insects, mostly ants. The most abundant, and often the only squirrel species in gardens, plantations and secondary forests. Can live and breed entirely in monoculture plantations. Rare, often absent, from tall dipterocarp forests, but usually common in coastal and swamp forests.

Distribution. Peninsular Thailand and Malaysia, Sumatra, Java and most intervening islands. **Borneo:** Widespread in the lowlands and hills. Up to 1600 m on G. Kinabalu. *C. n. dilutus:* recorded from Sabah, the Kelabit uplands and eastern Borneo. *C. n. dulitensis:* recorded from Sarawak and West Kalimantan. *C. n. conipus:* collected only from T. Pamukan and T. Kelumpang on the coast of south-eastern Borneo. The species also occurs on many offshore islands.

236

EAR-SPOT SQUIRREL *Callosciurus adamsi*   Plate 25

Measurements. HB 166-183, T 152-167, HF 36-40 (6 specimens). Wt 115-154.

Identification. Closely resembles the Plantain Squirrel, *C. notatus,* but somewhat smaller and with a distinct pale buffy patch behind each ear. Hairs on the underparts tend to be grey with dull reddish tips, rather than entirely reddish. The ear spots can be seen from a distance with binoculars under clear viewing conditions. **Similar species:** the Red-bellied Sculptor Squirrel, *Glyphotes simus,* is similar in colour, but is smaller and confined to higher altitudes; the Bornean Black-banded Squirrel, *C. orestes,* has grey underparts.

Ecology and Habitat. Diurnal. Active mainly in small trees but, unlike the Plantain Squirrel, *C. notatus,* found mainly in dipterocarp forests.

Distribution. Confined to Borneo. Known from scattered localities throughout Sabah and Sarawak north of the S. Rajang and S. Baleh. Records include Sandakan Bay area, S. Danum, foothills of G. Kinabalu and G. Trus Madi, and near Tenom in Sabah; the Kelabit uplands (up to 900 m), G. Dulit (at 600 m), Niah, upper S. Baram and S. Baleh in Sarawak.

Figure 30. Skulls and incisors of squirrels:
- **a)** *Callosciurus notatus,*
- **b)** *Callosciurus orestes,*
- **c)** *Glyphotes simus.*

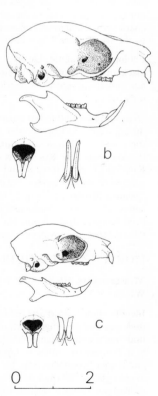

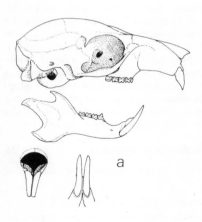

0   2

237

BORNEAN BLACK-BANDED SQUIRREL   Plate 25
Callosciurus orestes

(Formerly called the Black-banded Squirrel, *Callosciurus nigrovittatus*, and the Grey-bellied Sculptor Squirrel, *Glyphotes (Hessonoglyphotes) canalvus*)

Measurements. *C. o. orestes:* HB 132-140, T 128-146, HF 32-35 (4 specimens). *C. o. venetus:* HB 140-170, T 147-170, HF 35-39 (6 specimens). The type and only known specimen of *C. nigrovittatus atristriatus* (a juvenile) may also belong to this species: HB 127, T 145, HF 34.

Identification. Upperparts finely speckled brownish. A pale buffy spot behind each ear. Hairs on the underparts grey, sometimes with a reddish tinge in *C. o. orestes;* dark grey with whitish tips in *C. o. venetus.* Has a black and buffy-white side-stripe. **Similar species:** the Plantain and Ear-spot Squirrels, *C. notatus* and *C. adamsi,* are larger and have reddish underparts; the Red-bellied Sculptor Squirrel, *Glyphotes simus,* is smaller with reddish underparts; other small squirrels lack black and white side stripes. The Black-banded Squirrel, *C. nigrovittatus,* of Peninsular Thailand, Malaysia and Sumatra, is superficially similar, but can be distinguished by its larger size, absence of conspicuous pale ear spots, relatively longer skull and rounded, not angled, outer face to the incisors. The Bornean Black-banded Squirrel has skull characteristics intermediate between *Callosciurus* and *Glyphotes,* but appears closer to the former (see Figure 30).

Ecology and Habitat. Diurnal. Active in small and medium-sized trees. Fruits and black ants were found in the stomachs of two G. Kinabalu specimens. *C. o. orestes* and *venetus* appear to be restricted to lower montane forests and possibly to upper dipterocarp forest.

Distribution. Confined to Borneo. *C. o. orestes.* Known from G. Dulit (above 1000 m) and reported from similar altitudes on Usun Apau, the Kelabit uplands and the upper S. Terusan, all montane localities in northern Sarawak. A record from the lowlands near Kuching is probably in error. *C. o. venetus.* Known from G. Kinabalu (1000-1700 m) and G. Trus Madi (about 1500 m) in Sabah. More specimens are needed to confirm the identity of the squirrel originally named as *"Sciurus atristriatus"* which, unlike other *orestes* squirrels, came from a lowland site on the lower S. Mahakam, East Kalimantan. *"Callosciurus nigrovittatus"* has been reported from Kutai Nature Reserve, about 100 km north-east of the site where *atristriatus* was collected, but the identity has not been confirmed.

HORSE-TAILED SQUIRREL *Sundasciurus hippurus*   Plate 26

Measurements. HB 213-238, T 176-257, HF 52-61 (19 specimens of two subspecies). Wt 260-365.

Identification. Upperparts reddish brown with grey head and shoulders. *S. h. pryeri:* underparts white, tinged with red in some individuals; tail grizzled. *S. h. inquinatus:* underparts dull orange. *S. h. hippurellus* underparts dark reddish; tail entirely dark. *S. h. borneensis* similar to *hippurellus* but heavily grizzled grey on the shoulders and thighs. Specimens from the upper S. Baleh in central Sarawak are intermediate in coloration. Tail thick and bushy, but not very similar to that of a horse. In some individuals it has a reddish tip. The most commonly heard call is "CHEK! ... CHEK! ... chekchekchekchek ...". **Similar Species:** Prevost's Squirrel, *Callosciurus prevostii,* never has a reddish back with a grey head and shoulders.

Ecology and Habitat. Diurnal. Most often seen in small trees but sometimes travels on the ground. Diet includes seeds, fruits and insects. Occurs in tall and secondary forests.

Distribution. Peninsular Thailand and Malaysia, Sumatra. **Borneo:** recorded throughout the lowlands and hills, except South Kalimantan and the eastern parts of Central Kalimantan. Up to 1500 m on G. Dulit. *S. h. pryeri.* Occurs throughout Sabah. *S. h. inquinatus.* Ranges from Lawas in northern Sarawak to S. Sebuku and S. Sembakung in northern East Kalimantan. *S. h. hippurellus.* Found in the coastal areas between S. Kapuas in West Kalimantan and S. Rajang in Sarawak. *S. h. borneensis.* Occurs elsewhere in Kalimantan.

LOW'S SQUIRREL *Sundasciurus lowii*   Plate 26

Measurements. HB 132-157, T 77-106 (about 60-70% of HB), HF 32-37 (21 Sabah specimens). Wt 60-120.

Identification. Upperparts speckled brown; underparts buffy-white, sometimes with a reddish tinge. Pale reddish-buff ring around each eye is rarely clear from a distance. Tail short and bushy. The most commonly heard call consists of a series of bird-like "chik's". **Similar species:** other small squirrels have a significantly longer tail or greyish underparts.

Ecology and Habitat. Diurnal. Most active in the early morning and late afternoon. Diet includes fruits, insects and fungi. Travels and feeds in small standing trees, in fallen trees and on the ground. Occurs in tall and secondary forests.

Distribution. Peninsular Malaysia, Sumatra and smaller Indonesian islands. **Borneo:** *S. l. lowii.* Recorded throughout the lowlands and hills, up to 1400 m in the Kelabit uplands, but usually below 900 m. Also on P. Labuan and P. Banggi.

SLENDER SQUIRREL *Sundasciurus tenuis*   Plate 26

Measurements. 131-155, T 125-132 (85-95% of HB), HF 32-35 (7 specimens).

Identification. Upperparts speckled brownish; hair of underparts normally grey with white or buffy tips, but an immature specimen from Brunei has entirely dull buff underparts. Pale around the eyes and above the facial whiskers. Usually has an indistinct pale spot behind each ear. Tail rather long and slender. **Similar species:** Jentink's Squirrel, *S. jentinki,* has distinct creamy-white markings on the face and ears; Low's Squirrel, *S. lowii,* has a short, bushy tail and whitish (never grey) underparts; the Ear-spot and Bornean Black-banded Squirrels, *Callosciurus adamsi* and *C. orestes,* have black and pale stripes along each side of the body and lack pale markings on the face; the Lesser Treeshrew, *Tupaia minor,* has a more pointed muzzle and relatively longer tail.

Ecology and Habitat. Diurnal. Active mainly in small trees. Diet includes inner bark and insects from tree trunks, and fruits and seeds. Occurs in tall and secondary forests.

Distribution. Peninsular Malaysia, Sumatra and smaller Indonesian islands. **Borneo:** *S. t. parvus.* Occurs throughout the lowlands and hills except most of Sabah, northern East Kalimantan, and the south-east. The most northern records are at

Sipitang on the west coast and at Badang on S. Kayan in East Kalimantan. Recorded at 1650 m on G. Pueh but most records are from lower altitudes. The Slender Squirrel appears to be replaced ecologically by Jentink's Squirrel, *S. jentinki*, in the mountain ranges of northern and central Borneo.

JENTINK'S SQUIRREL *Sundasciurus jentinki*   Plate 27

Measurements. HB 120-144, T 110-133 (96-100% of HB), HF 30-34 (8 Sabah specimens).

Identification. Upperparts rather pale speckled brownish; underparts creamy-white on grey underfur. Tail very thin, appearing banded dark and pale due to reddish, black and white bands on the hairs. Has a distinctive creamy-white "moustache", eye-ring and border to the ears. *S. j. subsignanus* differs from *S. j. jentinki* in having buff rather than white tips on the tail hairs. **Similar species:** the Slender Squirrel, *S. tenuis*, and other small squirrels lack the prominent creamy-white facial and ear markings.

Ecology and Habitat. Diurnal. Active mainly in the crowns of small trees. Often follows mixed species flocks of birds. Confined to montane forests.

Distribution. Confined to Borneo in mountains above 900 m. *S. j. jentinki.* Known from G. Kinabalu (900-3140 m), the Crocker Range and G. Trus Madi in Sabah; the Sabah-Sarawak border hills; G. Mulu, G. Murud, the Kelabit uplands, Usun Apau and G. Dulit in Sarawak. *S. j. subsignanus.* Reported from Long Petak, S. Telen (1170 m) and (probably this subspecies) Badang, S. Kayan in East Kalimantan.

BROOKE'S SQUIRREL *Sundasciurus brookei*   Plate 27

Measurements. HB 140-205, T 108-170 (70-106% of HB), HF 32-38 (13 specimens). Wt 103-128.

Identification. Upperparts speckled brown; underparts grey (hairs grey with whitish tips) with an orange patch between the hind legs. Tail barred. **Similar species:** Jentink's Squirrel, *S. jentinki*, has creamy-white facial and ear markings; the Bornean Mountain Ground Squirrel, *Dremomys everetti*, has a relatively shorter tail without distinct barring; the Slender Squirrel, *S. tenuis*, has buffy-grey underparts. No other small squirrel has a distinct orange patch between the hind legs.

Ecology and Habitat. Diurnal and primarily arboreal. Found in tall forests in hill ranges.

Distribution. Occurs only in Borneo in the northern, central and western mountains. Recorded from G. Kinabalu (600-1070 m), the Crocker Range (above 1200 m), G. Trus Madi (750-900 m) and the upper S. Padas in Sabah; the upper S. Baram, G. Batu Song, Usun Apau, Bt. Kalulung, G. Dulit (600-1500 m) and G. Penrisen (1220 m) in Sarawak; S. Kayan (600 m) in East Kalimantan.

RED-BELLIED SCULPTOR SQUIRREL *Glyphotes simus* Plate 29

Measurements. HB 94-144, T 95-106, HF 27-33 (9 specimens).

Identification. Coloration very similar to the Ear-spot Squirrel, *Callosciurus adamsi*, with finely speckled brownish upperparts; dull orange-buff underparts usually tinged with grey on the belly. Distinctive teeth, especially the lower incisors, which diverge in a shape and are slightly concave on the anterior (outer) surface (Figure 30c). **Similar species:** the Ear-spot Squirrel, *C. adamsi*, is significantly larger; the Bornean Black-banded Squirrel, *C. orestes*, is also larger and has greyish underparts.

Ecology and Habitat. Diurnal. Habits and function of unusually shaped teeth unknown.

Distribution. Known only from Borneo with all records from the mountains in the northwest, including G. Kinabalu, northern Sarawak and the Kelabit uplands, mostly from 1300-1700 m.

THREE-STRIPED GROUND SQUIRREL *Lariscus insignis* Plate 28

Measurements. HB 170-230, T 122-138, HF 33-46 (3 specimens).

Identification. Upperparts brown with three black stripes along the back; underparts white or buff (turning dark yellow in old skins), sometimes with a faint red tinge. **Similar species:** the Four-striped Ground Squirrel, *L. hosei*, has two pairs of black and buff stripes on each side of the back.

Ecology and Habitat. Diurnal and terrestrial. Diet includes fruit and insects. Occurs in tall and secondary forests.

Distribution. Peninsular Malaysia, Sumatra, Java and intervening islands. **Borneo:** *L. i. diversus.* Known from scattered lowland sites in most areas except Sabah and the northern part of East Kalimantan. The highest altitude record is 370 m on G. Sidong in Sarawak.

FOUR-STRIPED GROUND SQUIRREL *Lariscus hosei*   Plate 28

Measurements. HB 172-190,T 110-142, HF 42-46 (4 Sabah specimens). Wt 145-215.

Identification. Upperparts speckled brown with nine prominent stripes along the back: a middle reddish brown stripe and two pairs of black and buff stripes on each side. Underparts orange. The pattern of stripes is diagnostic and usually clear in the field.

Ecology and Habitat. Diurnal and terrestrial. Occurs in tall and secondary forests but with a very patchy distribution.

Distribution. Confined to Borneo. Recorded from a few, scattered lowland and montane sites in Sabah (up to 1530 m on G. Kinabalu) and in the mountains of northern Sarawak, including G. Dulit, Bt. Kalulung, G. Batu Song and the Kelabit uplands.

BORNEAN MOUNTAIN GROUND SQUIRREL   Plate 27
Dremomys everetti

Measurements. HB 160-190, T 92-130 (up to 70% of HB), HF 38-42 (29 specimens). Wt 75-185.

Identification. Upperparts rather dark speckled brown; hairs of underparts grey with buffy-white tips. Tail hairs black with buffy-red bases and tips, but not creating a barred pattern. Muzzle more pointed than other small squirrels except the Shrew-faced Ground Squirrel, *Rhinosciurus laticaudatus*. **Similar species:** other montane squirrels have a longer, less bushy tail with pale and dark bars; the Mountain Treeshrew, *Tupaia montana*, has a more pointed muzzle and longer tail.

Ecology and Habitat. Diurnal. Mainly terrestrial, but sometimes arboreal. Diet includes insects, earthworms and fruits. Found in montane forests.

Distribution. Occurs only in Borneo in the mountains of the northwest above 980 m, including G. Kinabalu (up to 3400 m), G. Trus Madi and the Crocker Range in Sabah; the Sabah-Sarawak border region; G. Mulu, the Kelabit uplands, Usun Apau, G. Dulit, G. Penrisen and G. Pueh in Sarawak.

SHREW-FACED GROUND SQUIRREL   Plate 28
Rhinosciurus laticaudatus

Measurements. HB 195-233, T 131-170 (usually less than 70% of HB), HF 40-46 (3 specimens).

Identification. Upperparts dark brown; underparts white or buff, turning to yellow in old skins. Tail short and bushy, often held upwards with fluffed-out hairs when the squirrel is active. **Similar species:** the Bornean Mountain Ground Squirrel, *Dremomys everetti*, has a shorter muzzle and greyish underparts; *Tupaia* treeshrews have a relatively long tail and darker underparts.

Ecology and Habitat. Diurnal and terrestrial. Diet includes insects taken from fallen trees and branches. Occurs in tall and secondary forests. Rarely seen or trapped.

Distribution. Peninsular Malaysia, Sumatra and adjacent islands. **Borneo:** *R. l. laticaudatus.* Known only from the lowlands and hills in the west, from Pontianak in West Kalimantan northwards; one record from Betotan near Sandakan in eastern Sabah.

BLACK-EARED PIGMY SQUIRREL   Plate 29
Nannosciurus melanotis

Measurements. HB 61-87, T 60-71, HF 19-20 (5 Sarawak specimens).

Identification. Distinguished from other pigmy squirrels by broad buff line across face with black above. *N. m. pallidus* has duller and paler coloration on the head than *N. m. borneanus*. Call is distinctive: an irregular series of loud, high-pitched, piercing "chik"s or "cheep"s, followed by a very high-pitched descending twitter which gradually dies out without a clear ending.

Ecology and Habitat. Diurnal. Active mostly on tree trunks and branches. Several individuals may be heard or seen at one locality. At Samunsam in Sarawak, most often seen in medium to large sized trees. Found only in tall forests.

Distribution. Sumatra, Java and adjacent islands. **Borneo:** Occurs in lowlands and hills up to 1070 m but absent from the north. *N. m. borneanus:* known from Sarawak as far north as G. Dulit; West Kalimantan; the coastal regions of Central Kalimantan; and South Kalimantan. *N. m. pallidus:* known from Buntuk on the upper S. Barito in Central Kalimantan; S. Mahakam, S. Telen and S. Karangan in East Kalimantan.

PLAIN PIGMY SQUIRREL *Exilisciurus exilis*   Plate 29

Measurements. HB 62-82, T 42-62, HF 18-23 (14 specimens). Wt 12-26.

Identification. Upperparts speckled olive-brown; underparts pinkish-buff. Call is a single high-pitched squeak. **Similar Species:** other pigmy squirrels have ear tufts or markings on the head.

Ecology and Habitat. Diurnal. Active mainly in small to medium sized trees, often on tree trunks, but ranges up to the canopy of tall trees. Diet includes various material from the surfaces of trees and lianas such as bark and small insects. Occurs in tall and logged dipterocarp forests.

Distribution. Confined to Borneo. *E. e. exilis:* Known from many localities throughout the lowlands and hills, usually below 750 m but up to 1700 m on G. Pueh in Sarawak. *E. e. retectus:* on P. Banggi.

WHITEHEAD'S PIGMY SQUIRREL   Plate 29
Exilisciurus whiteheadi

Measurements. HB 83-93, T 65-73, HF 17-22 (8 specimens).

Identification. Distinctive ear tufts. Upperparts dark greyish brown with long hair; underparts slightly paler. Call very similar to that of the Plain Pigmy Squirrel, *E. exilis:* a single, shrill squeek, falling slightly in pitch.

Ecology and Habitat. Diurnal. Active mainly in small to medium sized trees, but ranges from tree buttresses up to the canopy of tall trees. Diet includes mosses and lichens. Occurs in hill dipterocarp and lower montane forests.

Distribution. Confined to Borneo. Known only from mountains, including G. Kinabalu (900-3000 m), G. Madalon (above 800 m), the Crocker Range (above 600 m) and G. Trus Madi in Sabah; the Sabah-Sarawak border area; G. Mulu, G. Batu Song, G. Murud, the Kelabit uplands, G. Dulit, Usun Apau, Lanjak-Entimau (possibly as low as 300 m) and G. Pueh in Sarawak; G. Liang Kubung in West Kalimantan.

TUFTED GROUND SQUIRREL *Rheithrosciurus macrotis* Plate 30

Measurements. HB 335-352, T 299-342, HF 81-88 (7 specimens). Wt 1170-1280.

Identification. Upperparts very dark brown, with a blackish and pale stripe on each side of the body; underparts pale grey-buff. Tufts of hair on the tips of the ears. Large, bushy, grizzled tail, held high when the squirrel is active, distinguishes this squirrel from all other Bornean mammals — when glimpsed briefly in the forest, the tail may even give the impression of a larger animal such as a small pig running away.

Ecology and Habitat. Diurnal. Found primarily on the ground or lower tree trunks, but sometimes feeds in tall trees. The few observations available suggest a diet of fruit and seeds. This squirrel is rarely seen and seems to occur in small numbers even under optimum conditions. Most often encountered on steep slopes. Most records are from tall dipterocarp forests, but also recorded in old orchards and recently logged forest.

Distribution. Confirmed to Borneo. Known from many scattered localities throughout the island, except in the south-east to the south of S. Mahakam in East Kalimantan. Most records are from hills, up to 920 m on G. Madalon in Sabah and 1070 m on Usun Apau in Sarawak.

Subfamily PETAURISTINAE   Flying squirrels

Flying squirrels, although unable to truly fly like bats, have membranes between the fore and hind legs which enable them to glide long distances between trees. Unlike the Colugo or Flying Lemur, which also glides, the tail is not enclosed by a membrane.

Flying squirrels are mainly nocturnal, and most active in trees, so they are very difficult to see. The larger flying squirrels are often particularly active just around dusk. If the light is adequate, or if a powerful headlamp or spotlight is available, the four largest species can usually be distinguished, especially with binoculars. However, several of the small to medium-sized flying squirrels are very similar in appearance, especially Vordermann's, the Grey-cheeked and the Red-cheeked, and difficult to identify. In museum specimens, the smaller *Petinomys* can be distinguished from *Hylopetes* by the shape of the skull, notably the auditory bullae viewed from the rear end (Figure 31). Pigmy flying squirrels have a diagnostic white tip to the tail.

Small flying squirrels can occasionally be captured in mist nets at night, but are usually caught only by searching nest holes in tree trunks. A high proportion of flying squirrels caught this way are immature and thus difficult to identify.

Figure 31. Skulls of small flying squirrels — rear view showing bullae:
a) *Hylopetes spadiceus,* b) *Petinomys vordermanni*

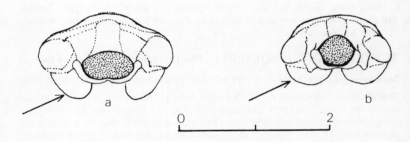

HOSE'S PIGMY FLYING SQUIRREL *Petaurillus hosei* Plate 31

Measurements. HB 80-87, T 80-98, HF 19-20 (4 specimens). Skull: cbl 25.2, mt 4.7-4.8 (2 specimens).

Identification. Upperparts very dark grey with pale buff streaks, especially in the midline; underparts off-white on grey underfur. Tail buffy at base, becoming blacker near the end, with a white tip. Cheeks buffy white with a strong grey tinge beneath the eye. A whitish spot behind each ear. **Similar species:** the Lesser Pigmy Flying Squirrel, *P. emiliae*, is smaller and has totally pale cheeks; immatures of larger flying squirrels do not have a white tail tip.

Ecology and Habitat. Nocturnal. Four individuals were found in a nest hole about 6 m above the ground in a dead tree at the edge of tall dipterocarp forest.
Distribution. Known only from Borneo at a few lowland sites including Sepilok in Sabah; Tasek Merimbun in Brunei; the Baram district and Niah in Sarawak. May be the same species as the Selangor Pigmy Flying Squirrel, *P. kinlochi*, known only from Selangor in Peninsular Malaysia.

LESSER PIGMY FLYING SQUIRREL *Petaurillus emiliae* Plate 31

Measurements. HB 68, 72, T 67, 62, HF 16, 17 (2 specimens — skull measurements not available).

Identification. Very similar to Hose's Pigmy Flying Squirrel, *P. hosei*, but 15% smaller in linear dimensions; cheeks entirely buffy white without grey below the eyes.

Ecology and Habitat. Unknown.

Distribution. Known only from one adult male and one adult female collected in the Baram district, Sarawak, in 1901.

HORSFIELD'S FLYING SQUIRREL *Iomys horsfieldi* Plate 32

Measurements. HB 165-231, T 160-207, HF 33-40 (13 specimens). Wt 135-215.

Identification. Upperparts brown to dark grey, hairs with buff or dull orange tips; underparts orange-buff or whitish, without grey. Gliding membrane fringed with rusty brown. Tail rusty brown. Cheeks buffy or rusty on grey. **Similar species:** Vordermann's Flying Squirrel, *Petinomys vordermanni*, is much smaller and *Hylopetes* flying squirrels have a white margin to the gliding membranes.

Ecology and Habitat. Nocturnal. Occurs in forests, plantations and gardens with tall trees. Although flying squirrels generally sleep in tree holes, one collector reported shooting this species from a leafy nest in the crown of a 6 m tall tree.

Distribution. Peninsular Malaysia, Sumatra and Java. **Borneo:** *I. h. thomsoni.* Known from scattered localities throughout the west, from G. Kinabalu in Sabah south to Batu Jurong in West Kalimantan. Also one record from Sandakan, but none from East, South or Central Kalimantan. Most records from lowlands and hills, but also recorded from the Kelabit uplands in Sarawak and up to 1800 m on G. Kinabalu.

245

BLACK FLYING SQUIRREL *Aeromys tephromelas*   Plate 33

Measurements. HB 355-426, T 410-470, HF 67-78 (6 specimens). Wt about 900.

Identification. Upperparts, tail and cheeks dark grey-brown, almost black, with fine, pale speckling on the back; underparts slightly paler, with sparse, fluffy hair. **Similar species:** the Smoky Flying Squirrel, *Pteromyscus pulverulentus*, is smaller and has creamy underparts.

Ecology and Habitat. Nocturnal. Occurs in tall and secondary forests.

Distribution. Peninsular Malaysia, Sumatra. **Borneo:** *A. t. phaeomelas.* Known from a few scattered localities in the northern part of Borneo, including the foothills of G. Kinabalu, Tenom, and Tawau in Sabah; northern Sarawak and Kuching; near Samarinda in East Kalimantan.

THOMAS'S FLYING SQUIRREL *Aeromys thomasi*   Plate 34

Measurements. HB 350-403, T 340-430, HF 60-70 (3 specimens). Wt 1380-1490.

Identification. Entirely reddish-brown. **Similar species:** the Red Giant Flying Squirrel, *Petaurista petaurista*, has black on the face, tip of the tail and feet.

Ecology and Habitat. Nocturnal. Diet includes fruits. Occurs in tall and secondary forests.

Distribution. Confined to Borneo. Known from the lower slopes of G. Kinabalu (up to 1600 m), Sandakan and Tawau in Sabah; S. Baram in Sarawak; G. Liang Kubung in West Kalimantan; S. Kayan in East Kalimantan.

HAGEN'S FLYING SQUIRREL *Petinomys hageni*   (not illustrated)

(The only known Bornean specimen of this species has been lost and the following description is based on the an old Sumatran skin in the British Museum (Natural History), which is stretched and slightly faded).

Measurements. HB about 280, T about 230, HF about 45.

Identification. Upperparts dull reddish-brown, with buffy tips to hairs; underparts off-white. A broad band of red-brown extends between and around eyes to ears. Long, stiff hairs behind and in front of ears. Tail thickly haired; blackish red above, buffy with blackish-red hair tips below.

Ecology and Habitat. Unknown.

Distribution. Sumatra. **Borneo:** *P. h. ouwensi.* Known from only one specimen collected near Pontianak in West Kalimantan.

WHISKERED FLYING SQUIRREL *Petinomys genibarbis*   Plate 33

Measurements. HB 160-180, T 155-188, HF 31-32 (2 specimens).

Identification. Upperparts reddish-brown with grey underfur, speckled with grey anteriorly, and with reddish posteriorly, giving an unusual pinkish tinge; underparts cream or dull orange-buff. Gliding membrane with a white margin. Tail rusty coloured with darker brown streaking. Whitish hairs at the base of each ear and a distinct tuft of long whiskers on the cheek behind the eye. **Similar species:** no other flying squirrels have a pinkish rump or prominent tuft of whiskers behind the eye.

Ecology and Habitat. Nocturnal. Occurs in tall and secondary forests.

Distribution. Peninsular Malaysia, Sumatra, Java. **Borneo:** *P. g. borneoensis.* Known from Tuaran in Sabah; Tasek Merimbun in Brunei; Baram, Bakong, S. Baleh, G. Penrisen and Lanjak-Entimau in Sarawak; the upper S. Telen in East Kalimantan.

TEMMINCK'S FLYING SQUIRREL *Petinomys setosus*   Plate 31

Measurements. HB 105-127 T 93-115, HF 21-25 (4 Bornean and 9 Peninsular Malaysian specimens). Skull: cbl 27.6-29.6, io 5.0-6.7, mt 5.0-5.2 (5 specimens).

Identification. Upperparts dark grey or black with pale buff tips; underparts white with grey underfur. Fur soft, and silky. Margin of gliding membrane not distinctly pale. Tail dark brownish-grey, with whitish hairs at the base. Cheeks greyish. **Similar species:** other small flying squirrels have at least traces of orange on the upperparts, base of tail or cheeks.

Ecology and Habitat. Nocturnal. One record of a nest hole, 19 mm wide, in a tree trunk at 0.5 m above the ground (Peninsular Malaysia). Occurs in tall and secondary forests.

Distribution. Burma, Peninsular Malaysia, Sumatra. **Borneo:** *P. s. setosus.* Recorded from the foothills of G. Kinabalu, Sandakan Bay and Tawau in Sabah; Tasek Merimbun in Brunei; Baram and near Kuching in Sarawak.

VORDERMANN'S FLYING SQUIRREL   Plate 31
Petinomys vordermanni

Measurements. HB 92-105, T 98-103, HF 21 (2 specimens). HB 93-120, T 89-115, HF 21-23 (16 Peninsular Malaysian specimens). Skull: cbl 28.2- 30.0, io 5.9, mt 5.5-6.2 (2 specimens).

Identification. Hair of upperparts blackish with rusty coloured tips; underparts buffy white. Gliding membrane with a buff (not white) margin. Tail brown with buffy hairs at the base; convex above, about 2 cm wide. Cheeks orange. Black ring around each eye. Tufts of whiskers at the base of each ear. **Similar species:** the *Hylopetes* flying squirrels have white margins on the gliding membranes; Horsfield's Flying Squirrel, *Iomys horsfieldi,* is larger.

Ecology and Habitat. Nocturnal. Nest holes recorded at 0.3-6.0 m above the ground (Peninsular Malaysia). Occurs in tall and secondary forests.

Distribution. Peninsular Malaysia, islands off eastern Sumatra. **Borneo:** *P. v. vordermanni.* Known only from Tasek Merimbun in Brunei and S. Boh off the upper S. Mahakam in East Kalimantan.

GREY-CHEEKED FLYING SQUIRREL *Hylopetes lepidus* Plate 32

Measurements. HB 117-135, T 118-120, HF 29-30 (2 specimens). Skull: cbl 29.8, io 8.0-8.1, mt 7.1-7.2 (2 specimens).

Identification. Upperparts blackish or dark grey-brown with rust-coloured markings, especially in the midline; underparts white or buffy white on grey underfur. Gliding membrane with a thin white margin.Tail somewhat broader at the base than at the tip, dark brownish-grey to black. Cheeks and patch on each side of the base of the tail pale grey, often tinged with yellow but never distinctly orange. **Similar species:** the Red-cheeked Flying Squirrel, *H. spadiceus*, has orange cheeks and base of tail; Vordermann's Flying Squirrel, *Petinomys vordermanni*, has a buff coloured margin to the gliding membrane.

Ecology and Habitat. Nocturnal. Occurs in tall and secondary forests.

Distribution. Burma, Thailand, Peninsular Malaysia, Sumatra, Java. **Borneo:** *H. l. platyurus.* Known only from G. Kinabalu (1370 m) in Sabah; and the Kelabit uplands (900-1070 m) in Sarawak.

RED-CHEEKED FLYING SQUIRREL   Plate 32
Hylopetes spadiceus

Measurements. HB 157-184, T 152-166, HF 29-35 (11 specimens). Wt 80-157. Skull: cbl 31.4-36.4, io 7.8-8.7, mt 6.8-7.6 (5 specimens).

Identification. Upperparts blackish or dark grey-brown, with rust-coloured markings, especially in the midline; underparts white on grey underfur, with a faint orange tinge. Gliding membrane with a thin white margin.Tail dark, slightly orange brown with buffy underfur; distinctly orange at the base. Cheeks orange brown on grey. **Similar species:** the Grey-cheeked Flying Squirrel, *H. lepidus,* is somewhat smaller and has only traces of a yellowish tinge on the cheeks and base of tail; Vordermann's Flying Squirrel, *Petinomys vordermanni,* has a buff margin to the gliding membrane.

Ecology and Habitat. Nocturnal. Nest holes, about 32 mm wide, recorded at 0.3-3.3 m above the ground (Peninsular Malaysia). Occurs in tall and secondary forests.

Distribution. Burma, Thailand, southern Indochina, Peninsular Malaysia, Sumatra, Java. **Borneo:** *H. s. everetti.* Known from the southern slopes of G. Kinabalu in Sabah; Sarawak; S. Kayan in East Kalimantan. Also on P. Natuna Besar.

SMOKY FLYING SQUIRREL *Pteromyscus pulverulentus*   Plate 33

Measurements. HB 221-290, T 215-235, HF 41-44 (9 specimens). Wt 232-305.

Identification. Upperparts very dark grey-brown with fine pale greyish speckling; underparts creamy with some grey. Tail as upperparts but grey-buff at the base. Cheeks greyish. **Similar species:** the Black Flying Squirrel, *Aeromys tephromelas*, is larger and has greyish, fluffly hair on the underparts.

Ecology and Habitat. Nocturnal. Seven nest holes recorded at Poring were all 3-4 m above the ground in trees. Occurs in tall forests.

Distribution. Peninsular Thailand and Malaysia, Sumatra. **Borneo:** *P. p. borneanus.* Known from Poring (about 550 m) in the eastern foothills of G. Kinabalu in Sabah; Marudi, G. Dulit and west of Batang Lupar in Sarawak.

RED GIANT FLYING SQUIRREL *Petaurista petaurista*   Plate 34

Measurements. HB 370-430,T 365-470, HF 69-78 (6 specimens, 2 subspecies). Wt 1070-2900.

Identification. Entire body dark reddish except for black on the nose, chin, eye-ring, behind the ears, feet and tail tip. *P. p. lumholtzi* is distinguished from *P. p. rajah* by less conspicuous black hairs behind the ears and by restricted black on the limbs. *P. p. nigrescens* has darker, duller overall coloration. **Similar species:** other large reddish flying squirrels lack a black tip to the tail.

Ecology and Habitat. Mostly nocturnal, becoming active shortly before dusk, but occasionally active during the day or seen resting on exposed parts of tall trees until mid-morning. Can make continuous glides of about 100 m. Nest holes usually at least 10 m above the ground. Found alone or in small groups. Diet includes leaves and seeds. Occurs in forests, open areas with only a few tall trees, gardens and plantations.

Distribution. Sri Lanka, India, southern China, South-east Asia, Sumatra, Java. **Borneo:** *P. p. rajah.* Recorded from many localities throughout Sabah and Sarawak, up to 900 m on G. Kinabalu, excluding the range of *P. p. nigrescens*, which is known only from the forests around Sandakan Bay north of S. Kinabatangan. *P. p. lumholtzi.* Recorded from Purukcahu, upper S. Barito in Central Kalimantan and from G. Talisayan in East Kalimantan, but probably widespread throughout the Kalimantan provinces.

SPOTTED GIANT FLYING SQUIRREL   Plate 34
Petaurista elegans

Measurements. HB 338-365, T 340-365, HF 60-66 (6 specimens). Wt 840-1240.

Identification. Upperparts black in the middle with many white specks; reddish laterally and on the gliding membrane; underparts reddish. Tail black. An immature specimen from G. Kinabalu (HB 240, T 303, HF 59) has a mix of black, brown and reddish on the upperparts, with only a few, faint white specks. **Similar Species:** the Red Giant Flying Squirrel, *P. petaurista*, has a red back with no white and a red tail with a black tip.

Ecology and Habitat. Nocturnal. Occurs in hill dipterocarp and lower montane forests.

Distribution. Highland areas in Nepal, north-eastern India through South-east Asia, Sumatra, Java. **Borneo:** *P. e. banksi.* Known only from G. Kinabalu (1070-1680 m) and the Crocker Range (1140 m) in Sabah; G. Dulit in Sarawak.

Rats and mice can be found nearly everywhere. The distinction between rats and mice is not clearly defined zoologically. In general, the former are larger and the latter smaller, but the smallest rat is only slightly larger than the largest mouse.

Some rats and mice are confined to human settlements or to vegetation that has been disturbed or modified by man. Others are strictly forest-dwellers either terrestrial or partially or mainly arboreal. All Bornean rats and mice are mainly active at night. Only 3 are confined to mountains, although others can occur at high altitudes.

It is normally necessary to catch rats and mice for positive identification. In some dubious cases it may be necessary to prepare the animal as a museum specimen and measure the skull in order to confirm the identity.

Immature rats are frequently caught and can be difficult to identify as they often differ in appearance from the adults. Not only are the measurements smaller, but the colour and texture of the fur is different — usually fluffier and darker. Any rat or mouse which differs from all of the illustrated species, and is distinctly smaller than the most similar species described, is probably immature. Immatures can often be recognized by their unworn teeth which are not fully erupted from the gums. In addition, their skull bones are not solidly fused, and tend to fall apart if the animal is prepared as a museum specimen.

A rat or mouse which does not seem to fit any description and yet appears to be mature could be an undescribed species. If possible the animal should be collected and either prepared as a skin and skull or preserved in formalin or alcohol. The colours should be described as accurately as possible, as they tend to change with time — red sometimes fades, and the fur can turn yellowish, especially in alcohol or formalin. The specimen should be labelled with date, location and habitat of capture, then sent to a reputable museum for identification.

Although rats become easier to identify with experience, many of the closely-related species are very similar and can be difficult to identify even for experts. The House, Malaysian Field and Ricefield Rats *Rattus rattus, R. tiomanicus,* and *R. argentiventer,* appear very similar, and the differences between them are often apparent only when all 3 are available for comparison. Differences in their habitat preferences sometimes provide the best clue to their identity, although there is some overlap. The Red and Brown Spiny Rats, *Maxomy rajah* and *M. surifer,* can also be difficult to distinguish, particularly immatures. The group comprising the Mountain Spiny Rat, Chestnut-bellied Spiny Rat, Small Spiny Rat and Whitehead's Rat, *Maxomys alticola, M. ochraceiventer, M. baeodon,* and *M. whiteheadi,* can usually be distinguished readily, but the underparts may turn yellow if preserved with formalin.

The presence and relative density of spines in the fur is important for identifying many rats. The spines are often hard to see, but are easily detected by feel — they are stiff, but not sharp, and can be found by running a finger back to front along the fur.

Formerly, all of the rats were thought to belong to the same genus, *Rattus*, as superficially they are very similar. Recent research has shown that actually there are several distinct groups. The Bornean species fall into six genera, which can be distinguished as follows:

Rattus — tail entirely dark (except in some Norway Rats); spines numerous on upperparts, scarce on underparts, but generally soft, like stiff hairs.

Sundamys — tail entirely dark, usually 110-120% of head and body length; prominent long black guard hairs on upperparts.

Niviventer: — tail at least 125% of head and body length, and slightly tufted with hairs at the tip; spines rather stiff.

Maxomys: — tail bicoloured; spines on the upperparts (in some cases also on the underparts) very stiff and prominent.

Leopoldamys: — large, with a very long tail; spines numerous but soft and hair-like.

Lenothrix — dense, woolly hair without spines; tail entirely white at the end distal from the body.

Figure 32. Skull of a Malaysian Field Rat, *Rattus tiomanicus*.

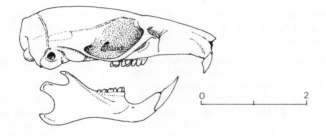

HOUSE RAT *Rattus rattus*   Plate 35

Measurements. HB 122-219, T 121-220 (95-120% of HB; usually just over 100%), HF 32-39 (30 Sabah specimens). Wt about 100-200. Skull: cbl 33.8-42.9, io 5.8-7.4, mt 6.2-7.0 (5 specimens).

Identification. Upperparts finely grizzled olive-brown; underparts usually slightly paler, buffy-brown with grey bases, but may be very pale brown to dull grey-brown. Tail entirely brownish. Some individuals are oddly-coloured: one specimen from G. Kinabalu had a grey "collar" and greyish underparts with a dull reddish stripe in the middle. **Similar species:** the Malaysian Field Rat, *R. tiomanicus,* and Ricefield Rat, *R. argentiventer,* differ in coloration of the underparts, usually lack long, black guard hairs on the rump, have somewhat softer fur and are usually in different habitats.

Ecology and Habitat. Nocturnal and sometimes diurnal. Diet includes a wide range of plant and animal matter. Strictly confined to human settlements, plantations and gardens near settlements.

Distribution. World wide. **Borneo:** *R. r. diardii.* Known to occur in most areas of human activity including towns, villages, houses (up to 1700 m on G. Kinabalu), rice fields (at 1280 m on G. Kinabalu) and oil-palm plantations near Tawau in Sabah.

MALAYSIAN FIELD RAT *Rattus tiomanicus*   Plate 36

Measurements. HB 140-188, T 120-181 (75-120% of HB), HF 28-35 (27 Sabah and Sarawak specimens). Wt 78-125. Skull: cbl 34.3-36.9, io 5.9-6.5, mt 6.0-6.8 (8 specimens).

Identification. Upperparts finely grizzled olive-brown; underparts variable, but hairs usually either pale grey with buffy-white tips *(R. t. sabae)* or white *(R. t. jalorensis).* Intermediate coloration has been recorded. Fur soft and close, with black guard hairs of moderate length distributed evenly through the pelage. Tail entirely dark brownish. Feet relatively broad with a distinct pattern of fine ridges on the pads of the underside. *R. t. banguei* and *R. t. mara* are darker, duller and slightly larger than other races. **Similar species:** the House Rat, *R. rattus,* and Ricefield Rat, *R. argentiventer,* differ in habitat and coloration of underparts; the Ricefield Rat has a slightly longer maxillary toothrow and lacks ridges on the underside of the feet.

Ecology and Habitat. Usually nocturnal and mostly terrestrial although often seen in low bushes. Diet includes a wide range of plant and animal matter. Occurs in secondary and coastal forests, plantations, gardens, scrub and grassland, but rarely in houses or tall dipterocarp forests.

Distribution. Peninsular Malaysia, Sumatra, Java and many adjacent islands. **Borneo:** Widespread through the lowlands and hills, up to 1700 m on G. Kinabalu. *R. t. sabae.* Recorded from Sabah, northern Sarawak and G. Talisayan in East Kalimantan. *R. t. jalorensis.* Recorded from Sarawak as far north as the Baram region; West Kalimantan and S. Telen in East Kalimantan. Specimens with intermediate coloration have been collected at Niah and in the Kelabit uplands in Sarawak. *R. t. banguei.* Recorded from P. Banggi and P. Malawali. *R. t. mara.* Recorded from the Maratua archipelago off eastern Borneo. The species also occurs on many other offshore islands.

RICEFIELD RAT *Rattus argentiventer*   Plate 36

Measurements. HB 140-210, T 130-192 (80-125% of HB, usually just under 100%), HF 32-36 (1 Sabah and 47 Peninsular Malaysian specimens). Wt 85-180. Skull: cbl 35.1-39.7, io 5.6-6.6, mt 7.0-7.1 (4 Bornean specimens).

Identification. Upperparts pale brown with fine black speckling; underparts wholly silvery-grey, often with a dark streak along the middle. Tail entirely dark brownish. Feet rather slender and smooth on the underside. Mature females have 12 mammae. Young individuals have an orange-coloured tuft in front of each ear. **Similar species:** the House Rat and Malaysian Field Rat, *R. rattus* and *R. tiomanicus*, differ in habitat and coloration of underparts. Females of both have only 10 mammae and the latter has ridges on the pads of the feet.

Ecology and Habitat. Active mostly on the ground; burrows extensively — nests in holes in the ground. Diet includes rice plants, grain, oil-palm fruit and flowers, and insects. Occurs in ricefields, grassland and plantations.

Distribution. Indochina, Thailand, Peninsular Malaysia, Sumatra, Java, Sulawesi, Philippines, New Guinea and intervening islands. **Borneo:** recorded from scattered localities throughout the island, including G. Kinabalu and Tenom in Sabah; Balingian, Saribas and Kuching in Sarawak; Pontianak in West Kalimantan; Hantakan in South Kalimantan; and S. Telen in East Kalimantan.

SUMMIT RAT *Rattus baluensis*   Plate 37

Measurements. HB 150-188, T 145-205, HF 21-34 (25 specimens). Wt 80-135. Skull: cbl 38.2-40.5, io 6.0-6.6, mt 6.5-7.0 (5 specimens).

Identification. Upperparts dark greyish brown with pale reddish brown speckling. Hair soft, 30-35 mm long. Underparts grey-buff. Tail entirely dark brownish. **Similar species:** all similar rats occur at lower altitudes and have shorter, coarser hair.

Ecology and Habitat. Mainly terrestrial. Occurs in montane forests.

Distribution. Sumatra. **Borneo:** *R. b. baluensis*. Known only from the upper slopes of G. Kinabalu from 2100 m to at least 3360 m.

POLYNESIAN RAT *Rattus exulans*   Plate 35

Measurements. HB 101-138, T 118-159 (about 110% of HB), HF 22-28 (15 specimens). Wt 45-65. Skull: cbl 26.8-29.2, io 4.6-4.9, mt 4.7-5.6 (5 specimens).

Identification. Upperparts greyish to reddish brown with coarse, spiny fur; underparts greyish-white. Spines white with dark brown tips. Tail entirely brown. Females with only 8 mammae. **Similar species:** the House Rat, *R. rattus,* and House Mouse, *Mus musculus,* are larger and smaller respectively, have darker underparts and, along with the Malaysian Field Rat, *R. tiomanicus,* and Ricefield Rat, *R. argentiventer,* have soft, hair-like spines.

Ecology and Habitat. Diet includes plant and animal material. Associated with man, in houses, gardens, plantations, rice fields and secondary growth.

Distribution. South-east Asia, Sumatra, Java, Sulawesi, southern Philippines to New Guinea, Pacific Islands. **Borneo:** *R. e. ephippium.* Known from throughout the area, up to 1650 m on G. Kinabalu. Recorded from P. Labuan.

NORWAY RAT *Rattus norvegicus*   Plate 35

Measurements. HB 163-265, T 170-230 (79-97% of HB), HF 37-45 (7 Peninsular Malaysian specimens). Wt 150-400. Skull: cbl 41.4-50.9, io 6.3-7.4, mt 7.0-7.4 (4 Peninsular Malaysian specimens).

Identification. Upperparts brown; underparts grey-brown. Tail either entirely dark or dark above and slightly paler below. Females have 12 mammae. All-white forms (albinos) have been reported from western Sabah. **Similar species:** the House Rat, *R. rattus*, is smaller and has finely-grizzled upperparts, with only 10 mammae in females.

Ecology and Habitat. Mostly nocturnal. Diet includes plant and animal material. Usually in coastal towns but also reported from ricefields.

Distribution. World wide. **Borneo:** Recorded from towns and ricefields on the western coast of Sabah; coastal towns in Sarawak; Pontianak and Banjermasin in Kalimantan.

MULLER'S RAT *Sundamys muelleri*   Plate 36

Measurements. HB 179-244, T 191-277 (usually 110-120% of HB), HF 37-49 (59 specimens). Wt 160-305. Skull: gl 44.1-54.2, io 6.0-8.0, mt 8.2-10.0 (62 specimens).

Identification. Upperparts grizzled brown with coarse fur and prominent long black guard hairs; underparts distinctly paler, usually dull buffy-white, but may be whitish or pale greyish. Tail entirely dark brown. **Similar species:** all similar rats have shorter, sleeker fur, with short guard hairs.

Ecology and Habitat. Mostly nocturnal and terrestrial. Often found near streams. Feeds on plant and animal matter. Occurs in forests, forest edge and lightly wooded areas.

Distribution. Peninsular Burma, Thailand and Malaysia, Sumatra and adjacent islands, and Palawan. **Borneo:** *S. m. borneanus.* Known from lowlands and hills throughout the area, up to 1130 m in the Kelabit uplands and 1650 m on G. Kinabalu. Also reported from P. Labuan. Other subspecies have been recorded from offshore islands, including *S. m. otiosus* from P. Banggi and P. Balembangan and *S. m. sebucus* from P. Sebuku off South Kalimantan.

MOUNTAIN GIANT RAT *Sundamys infraluteus*   Plate 37

Measurements. HB 226-295, T 260-343 (about 120% of HB), HF 52-61 (17 specimens). Wt 237-600. Skull: gl 55.9-63.3, io 7.8-9.1, mt 10.6-11.6 (13 specimens).

Identification. Upperparts dark brown with buffy speckling with long hair and longer black guard hairs; underparts grey with a strong orange tinge. Tail entirely dark brown. **Similar species:** the Summit Rat, *Rattus baluensis,* is much smaller.

Ecology and Habitat. Predominantly terrestrial. Diet includes plant and animal matter. Occurs in montane forests.

Distribution. Sumatra. **Borneo:** *S. i. infraluteus.* So far known only from G. Kinabalu (920-2930 m) and G. Trus Madi in Sabah; and G. Mulu (at 1680 m) in Sarawak.

DARK-TAILED TREE RAT *Niviventer cremoriventer* Plate 38

Measurements. HB 106-160, T 143-219 (at least 125% of HB), HF 23-28 (49 specimens). Wt 53-100. Skull: gl 31.5-35.4, io 5.3-6.1, mt 5.6-6.6 (17 specimens).

Identification. Upperparts pale brown, usually with a yellowish tinge but often fading to grey-brown in museum specimens, sometimes with patches of white hairs; underparts whitish, usually with a yellow or buff tinge, especially on the chest. Distinct long, black guard hairs and numerous rather stiff spines on both upper and underparts. Tail entirely dark brown, or dark above and pale below; tip sometimes entirely pale. Tail covered in short hairs with longer, more prominent hairs on the terminal 2 cm. Long facial whiskers. *N. c. malawali* is said to be duller in coloration than *N. c. kina*. **Similar species:** all similar rats except the Long-tailed Mountain Rat, *Niviventer rapit*, have a relatively shorter tail without a tuft of hairs at the end. *N. rapit* is more distinctly red-brown above and white below, and is somewhat larger.

Ecology and Habitat. Nocturnal. Active in small trees to at least 5 m above the ground, in thickets of climbers and on the ground. Occurs in tall and secondary forests, forest edge and lightly wooded areas.

Distribution. Peninsular Burma, Thailand and Malaysia; Sumatra, Java and adjacent islands. **Borneo:** *N. c. kina.* Recorded in lowlands and hills throughout the area, up to 1130 m in the Kelabit uplands and 1530 m on G. Kinabalu. *N. c. malawali.* Recorded from P. Banggi, P. Balembangan and P. Malawali.

LONG-TAILED MOUNTAIN RAT *Niviventer rapit* Plate 39

Measurements. HB 122-163, T 183-211 (usually about 140% of HB), HF 27-34 (5 specimens). Skull: cbl 30.9-36.9, io 5.7-6.5, mt 5.8-6.1 (5 specimens).

Identification. Upperparts reddish-brown, darker and duller along the midline, with inconspicuous grey underfur and numerous rather stiff spines; underparts white or creamy-white. Tail hairy, especially at tip; usually darker above, paler below, but may be entirely dark. **Similar species:** the Long-tailed Giant Rat, *Leopoldamys sabanus*, is larger, lacks any trace of a tuft at the end of the tail and has soft spines; the Dark-tailed Tree Rat, *Niviventer cremoriventer*, is somewhat smaller and has more prominent black guard hairs; other rats have shorter tails.

Ecology and Habitat. Believed to be largely nocturnal and active in small trees. Reported carrying young in danger from a snake, during daylight hours in a bamboo thicket at Poring. Also reported from ricefields in the Kelabit uplands.

Distribution. Peninsular Malaysia, Sumatra. **Borneo:** *N. r. rapit.* Known from only a few scattered localities in the north, including Poring (550 m) and G. Kinabalu (940-3360 m) in Sabah; G. Api near G. Mulu (1200 m), the Kelabit uplands, Lawas and Niah (both lowland sites), G. Dulit and G. Penrisen in Sarawak; S. Kayan in East Kalimantan.

BROWN SPINY RAT *Maxomys rajah* Plate 38

Measurements. HB 139-218, T 162-210 (usually slightly longer than HB), HF 35-43 (21 specimens). Wt 95-218. Skull: gl 40.9-48.6, iob 6.6-7.4, mt 6.9-8.1 (13 specimens).

Identification. Upperparts brown, sometimes tinged reddish or orange; darker in the midline and with numerous stiff grey-brown spines; underparts white, with many short, soft, white spines, usually with a dark brown streak along the middle in adults. White on inner side of thigh normally extends unbroken to the feet. Tail brown above, pale below, thinly haired. **Similar species:** the Red Spiny Rat, *Maxomys surifer,* is brighter reddish, lacks a dark streak on the underparts, and usually has an orange collar under the neck and an orange band around the leg. Immature Brown and Red Spiny Rats are very difficult to distinguish.

Ecology and Habitat. Nocturnal and predominantly terrestrial. Occurs in tall and secondary forests. Records suggest that this species may be more associated with sandy, lowland sites than the Red Spiny Rat, *R. surifer.*

Distribution. Peninsular Thailand and Malaysia, Sumatra and adjacent islands. **Borneo:** *M. r. rajah.* Recorded from many localities in the coastal regions of eastern and western Sabah, Brunei, Sarawak, Kutai in East Kalimantan and Riam in Central Kalimantan. *M. r. hidongis.* Recorded from P. Natuna.

RED SPINY RAT *Maxomys surifer* Plate 38

Measurements. HB 160-202, T 187-215 (usually slightly longer than HB), HF 38-43 (30 specimens). Skull: gl 39.4-46.1, io 5.6-6.9, mt 5.8-6.8 (29 specimens).

Identification. Upperparts distinctly orange- or reddish-brown, slightly darker along the midline, with numerous short, stiff, dark spines; underparts white with soft, white spines. Coloration of upperparts usually extends around part or all of the neck, forming a "collar", and around the inner side of the leg above the ankle. **Similar species:** the Brown Spiny Rat, *Maxomys rajah,* is less brightly coloured, usually has a dark brown streak in the middle of the underparts and lacks the orange-brown "collar" and band around the leg. Immature Red Spiny Rats are very similar to Brown Spiny Rats but slightly more brightly coloured.

Ecology and Habitat. Nocturnal and predominantly terrestrial. Occurs in forests and, in the Kelabit uplands, in grassland and ricefields.

Distribution. South-east Asia, Sumatra, Java and adjacent islands. **Borneo:** *R. s. bandahara.* Recorded from localities in lowlands and hills throughout the area, up to 1220 m in the Kelabit uplands and 1680 m on G. Kinabalu. The species also occurs on many offshore islands, including: *M. s. panglima* on P. Banggi, P. Balembangan and P. Malawali; *M. s. perflavus* on P. Laut; *M. s. ubecus* on P. Sebuku; and *M. s. carimatae* on P. Karimata Besar.

MOUNTAIN SPINY RAT *Maxomys alticola* Plate 37

Measurements. HB 139-176, T 128-180, HF 32-37 (30 specimens). Skull: gl 37.0-41.7, io 7.0-8.1, mt 5.4-6.1 (23 specimens).

Identification. Upperparts dark grey-brown along the midline, paler along the sides of the body; underparts whitish to creamy-buff, or grey in young rats. Entire upper- and underparts covered with numerous stiff spines giving a flecked appearance below. Tail dark above, pale below. **Similar species:** the Chestnut-bellied Spiny Rat, *Maxomys ochraceiventer,* has grey and yellowish on the underparts; the Small Spiny Rat, *Maxomys baeodon,* is significantly smaller.

Ecology and Habitat. Diet includes ants and other insects. Occurs in montane forests.

Distribution. Known only from G. Kinabalu (1070-3360 m) and G. Trus Madi in Sabah. Overlaps with the Chestnut-bellied Spiny Rat, *Maxomys ochraceiventer.*

CHESTNUT-BELLIED SPINY RAT   Plate 40
Maxomys ochraceiventer

Measurements. HB 140-171, T 128-175, HF 29-35 (32 specimens). Skull: gl 35.3-39.6, io 6.2-7.4, mt 5.4-6.0 (13 specimens).

Identification. Upperparts generally reddish-brown; underparts greyish with a strong yellow or buffy-red tinge; often turn bright yellow in old skins. Extent of grey at bases of hairs variable — underparts sometimes appear entirely yellowish. Numerous stiff spines on entire body. Tail dark above, pale below. **Similar species:** the adult Mountain Spiny Rat, *Maxomys alticola,* has whitish underparts without any grey or strong yellow tinge. Whitehead's Rat, *Maxomys whiteheadi,* is smaller and much less spiny on the underparts.

Ecology and Habitat. Occurs in dipterocarp and lower montane forests.

Distribution. Known only from northern Borneo, mainly in the hills. *M. o. ochraceiventer.* Recorded from G. Kinabalu below 1700 m and near the lower S. Padas in Sabah; the Kelabit uplands, upper S. Tinjar, G. Dulit and G. Sidong in Sarawak. *M. o. perasper.* Recorded from Labuhan Kelambu and the upper S. Belayan in East Kalimantan.

SMALL SPINY RAT *Maxomys baeodon*   Plate 39

Measurements. HB 126-140, T 119-133, HF 25-28 (6 specimens). Skull: gl 33.2-35.2, io 6.7-6.9, mt 4.1-5.0 (5 specimens).

Identification. Upperparts brown, dark along the midline; progressively paler towards the underparts, which are pale buff coloured. Whole body covered in soft fur intermixed with numerous stiff spines. Tail dark above, pale below. **Similar species:** the Mountain Spiny Rat, *Maxomys alticola,* is larger and found only in montane forest; Whitehead's Rat, *M. whiteheadi,* is less spiny and is grey and yellowish or pinkish on the underparts.

Ecology and Habitat. Unknown.

Distribution. Known only from a few scattered localities in northern Borneo, including the Tenom area, G. Kinabalu (900-1400 m) and Sandakan Bay in Sabah; the Kelabit uplands (above 1200 m) in Sarawak.

WHITEHEAD'S RAT *Maxomys whiteheadi*   Plate 39

Measurements. HB 103-150, T 87-125 (always shorter than HB), HF 23-30 (35 specimens). Wt 30-83. Skull: gl 29.2-33.7, io 5.2-5.8, mt 5.1-6.2 (21 specimens).

Identification. *M. w. whiteheadi:* upperparts reddish-brown with grey underfur and numerous stiff pale grey spines with black tips; underparts orange-buff with grey underfur and numerous soft, pale spines; tail dark above, pale below. *M. w. piratae:*

larger than *whiteheadi,* with a dark grey tinge on the entire body and somewhat orange underparts; tail entirely dark. **Similar species:** the Polynesian Rat, *Rattus exulans,* has an entirely dark tail significantly longer than the body.

Ecology and Habitat. Nocturnal. Diet includes ants and other insects. Occurs in tall and secondary forests, usually on the ground. Also reported from rice fields.

Distribution. Peninsular Thailand and Malaysia, Sumatra and adjacent islands. **Borneo:** *M. w. whiteheadi.* Recorded from localities throughout the area including lowlands, hills and mountains. Up to 2100 m on G. Kinabalu and above 1000 m in the Kelabit uplands in Sarawak and the upper S. Telen in East Kalimantan. *M. w. piratae.* Occurs on P. Banggi, P. Malawali and P. Balembangan.

LONG-TAILED GIANT RAT *Leopoldamys sabanus*   Plate 40

Measurements. HB 215-273, T 327-402 (at least 135% of HB; shorter tails may have been broken), HF 40-52 (26 specimens). Wt 250-532. Skull: cbl 46.0-52.3, io 8.0-8.5, mt 9.1-10.0 (5 specimens).

Identification. Upperparts generally reddish-brown with grey underfur and numerous soft hair-like spines; underparts creamy-white. Tail dark, sometimes with pale, irregular blotches. Specimens from above 1700 m on G. Kinabalu are larger than lowland specimens and duller with a blackish midline and top of head — their taxonomic status is unclear. **Similar species:** the Long-tailed Mountain Rat, *Niviventer rapit,* has a smaller hindfoot, stiffer spines and a somewhat tufted tail tip.

Ecology and Habitat. Nocturnal. Lives in the trees up to at least 3 m but often active on the ground. Occurs in tall and secondary forests.

Distribution. South-east Asia, Sumatra, Java and adjacent islands. **Borneo:** *L. s. sabanus.* Recorded throughout the lowlands and hills, up to 3100 m on G. Kinabalu.

GREY TREE RAT *Lenothrix canus*   Plate 39

Measurements. HB 165-220, T 200-265, HF 30-37 (3 Bornean and 48 Peninsular Malaysian specimens). Wt 80-220. Skull: cbl 42.0-44.5, io 6.1-6.6, mt 8.2-8.6 (5 Peninsular Malaysian specimens).

Identification. Upperparts grey; underparts white. Fur thick and soft. Tail dark near the body, white near the tip — a feature unique among Bornean rats.

Ecology and Habitat. Nocturnal. Active mainly in small trees and on fallen trees and branches. Occurs in tall and secondary forests.

Distribution. Peninsular Malaysia, Banyak Islands. **Borneo:** *L. c. malaisia.* Recorded only from Sepilok and Poring (550 m) in Sabah; near Kuching in Sarawak.

258

ASIAN HOUSE MOUSE *Mus castaneus*   Plate 35
(formerly confused with *Mus musculus*)

Measurements. HB 67-79, T 80-84 (over 100% of HB), HF 16 (2 specimens). Skull: cbl 18.5, io 4.1, mt 3.2 (1 specimen).

Identification. Upperparts brown with grey underfur; underparts slightly paler. Fur soft. Tail entirely dark brownish. Runs very fast. Rarely enters cage traps. **Similar species:** the Polynesian Rat, *Rattus exulans*, is larger and spiny; the Ricefield Mouse, *M. caroli*, has whitish underparts and a pale undertail.

Ecology and Habitat. Nocturnal. Diet includes a wide range of plant and animal material. Restricted to buildings in towns.

Distribution. Asia. **Borneo:** Occurs around Kota Kinabalu and Sandakan in Sabah; Kuching in Sarawak.

RICEFIELD MOUSE *Mus caroli*   Plate 35
(unconfirmed in Borneo)

Measurements. HB 76, T 78, HF 18 (average of 15 Thai specimens).

Identification. Upperparts brownish-grey; underparts whitish. Tail dark above, pale below. **Similar species:** the House Mouse, *M. castaneus*, has grey-brown underparts and an entirely dark tail.

Ecology and Habitat. Diet includes plant and animal material. Occurs in ricefields and grassland.

Distribution. Mainland South-east and East Asia, Taiwan, Ryuku Islands, Sumatra and Java. **Borneo:** one specimen fitting the description of this species was caught at Kampung Kaingaran, 700 m, in the western foothills of G. Trus Madi in Sabah (illustrated). Unfortunately, the specimen was lost, so the identity cannot be confirmed.

COMMON PENCIL-TAILED TREE-MOUSE   Plate 41
Chiropodomys gliroides

Measurements. HB 65-85, T 81-96, HF 16-18 (3 specimens). Wt 14-22. Skull: gsl 19.7, 22.3, io 4.4, 4.4, mt 3.3, 3.3 (2 specimens).

Identification. Upperparts pale grey with a yellow tinge, fading to reddish-grey in old skins; underparts white. Fur short and soft. Tail brown, hairy and with a brush of hairs at the tip. The hallux (big toe) of the hind foot is semi-opposable, with a nail. **Similar species:** the Large Pencil-tailed Tree-mouse, *C. major*, is significantly larger.

Ecology and Habitat. Nocturnal. Active mostly in trees or bamboo clumps. Nests in tree holes, in the internodes of bamboo and similar places. Occurs in tall and secondary forests.

Distribution. North-eastern India through South-east Asia, Sumatra, Java, Bali. **Borneo:** *C. g. pusillus*. Recorded from G. Kinabalu (up to 1220 m) in Sabah; G. Mulu, G. Dulit and the Kelabit uplands in Sarawak; Riam in the Kotawaringin district in Central Kalimantan.

LARGE PENCIL-TAILED TREE-MOUSE Plate 41
Chiropodomys major

Measurements. HB 94-114, T 109-144, HF 21-28 (17 specimens). Skull: gsl 27.5-30.2, io 4.9-5.4, mt 4.2-5.1 (17 specimens).

Identification. Upperparts pale grey with a yellow tinge, fading to reddish-grey in old skins; underparts white. Fur short and soft. Tail brown, sometimes with whitish patches on the underside; hairy and with a brush of hairs at the tip. The hallux (big toe) of the hind foot is semi-opposable, with a nail. **Similar species:** the Common Pencil-tailed Tree-mouse, *C. gliroides*, is smaller.

Ecology and Habitat. Nocturnal. Active mostly in small trees. Occurs in tall and probably in secondary forests.

Distribution. Confined to Borneo. Recorded from G. Kinabalu (up to 1500 m) and Sepilok in Sabah; Balingian and the Kuching region in Sarawak.

GREY-BELLIED PENCIL-TAILED TREE-MOUSE Plate 41
Chiropodomys muroides

Measurements. HB 66-80, T 85-91, HF 15-17 (3 specimens). Skull: cbl 18.0-19.9, io 4.6-4.9, mt 3.0-3.1 (3 specimens).

Identification. Upperparts reddish-brown, base of hairs grey; underparts grey with a buff tinge. Tail brown, hairy and with a brush of hairs at the tip. The hallux (big toe) of the hind foot is semi-opposable, with a nail. **Similar species:** the Common and Large Pencil-tailed Tree-mice, *C. gliroides* and *C. muroides*, have white underparts.

Ecology and Habitat. Unknown.

Distribution. Confined to Borneo. Known only from G. Kinabalu (1100 m) in Sabah; and Long Petak on the upper S. Telen in East Kalimantan.

RANEE MOUSE *Haeromys margarettae* Plate 41

(Note: Medway (1977) recognised two species of Ranee Mice from Borneo, giving the name Lesser Ranee Mouse, *Haeromys pusillus*, to smaller forms. Body and skull measurements (below) suggest that there may be only one species, with specimens from the Sandakan area and G. Penrisen being slightly larger than those from interior localities. Superficially, all Ranee Mice look identical. Further specimens are required to resolve the issue.)

Measurements. The type specimen of *H. margarettae* from G. Penrisen: HB 76, T 144, HF 20. Skull: cbl 23.9, io 4.3, mt 3.7.Two specimens from the Sandakan area: HB -, 77, T 123, 136, HF 17, 18. Skull: cbl -, 20.7, io 4.5, 4.0, mt 3.3, 3.5. Specimens previously recorded as *pusillus:* HB 54-76, T 97-123, HF 15-17 (4 specimens). Skull: cbl 19.6-21.1, io 3.5-4.1, mt 3.3-3.5 (5 specimens).

Identification. Upperparts reddish-brown with grey underfur; underparts white. Tail very long, dark brown, with tiny stiff hairs. The hallux (big toe) of the hind foot is semi-opposable with a tiny claw.

260

Ecology and Habitat. Unknown. A specimen was caught at Sepilok in a pitfall trap in the ground near the edge of tall dipterocarp forest. A closely-related species from Sulawesi is said to build a nest in tree holes.

Distribution. Recorded only from Borneo. *H. margarettae* first collected from G. Penrisen in Sarawak. *"H. pusillus"* recorded from G. Kinabalu (up to 900 m) in Sabah; the Kelabit uplands in Sarawak; and Peleben and Badang on S. Kayan in east Kalimantan. Individuals intermediate in size recorded from Sepilok and the west side of Sandakan Bay.

Family HYSTRICIDAE   Porcupines

Porcupines are larger and more heavily built than squirrels or rats, with characteristic hard spines or quills over most of the upperparts. The incisors and molars are large and powerful. All three species found in Borneo are normally terrestrial and usually nocturnal, sleeping during the daytime in underground holes or burrows.

LONG-TAILED PORCUPINE *Trichys fasciculata*   Plate 42
(formerly called *Trichys lipura)*

Measurements. HB 375-437, T 152-240, HF 61-67 (4 specimens). Wt 1.5-2 kg.

Identification. Upperparts brown; underparts whitish. Spines short and flattened, dark brown towards the end, whitish towards the base. Tail brown and scaly, with a brush of hollow bristles at the end. Gives the overall impression of a large rat. Part or all of tail sometimes missing.

Ecology and Habitat. In Sabah, observed feeding on seeds of the belian or ironwood tree , *Eusideroxylon zwageri,* at Sepilok, and on bamboo shoots on steep terrain in the Crocker Range. Occurs in forests and cultivated areas.

Distribution. Peninsular Malaysia, Sumatra. **Borneo:** *T. f. lipura.* Known from many localities throughout the lowlands and hills, up to 900 m on G. Kinabalu.

COMMON PORCUPINE *Hystrix brachyura*   Plate 42

Measurements. HB 590-630, T 95-130, HF 80-95 (4 Sumatran specimens).

Identification. Generally black; long spines or quills white with a black band towards the tip; short spines on front parts of body mostly blackish, some with a paler base and tip. Both males and females have hollow quills on the tail, which are shaken to make a noise. **Similar species:** the Thick-spined Porcupine, *Thecurus crassispinis,* appears generally dark brown from a distance with the white quill tips not prominent.

Ecology and Habitat. Feeds on fallen fruits including oil palm, roots and stems. Occurs in forests and cultivated areas.

Distribution. Peninsular Thailand and Malaysia, Sumatra. **Borneo:** *H. b. longicauda.* Known from many localities throughout the lowlands and hills. Up to 900 m on G. Kinabalu.

THICK-SPINED PORCUPINE *Thecurus crassispinis*   Plate 42

Measurements. HB 550-665, T 90-135, HF 80-90 (4 specimens).

Identification. Generally dark brown; long spines or quills dark brown with white tip and base; short spines on front part of body grey-brown with a pale tip and base. Both males and females have hollow quills on the tail, which are shaken to make a noise. **Similar species:** the Common Porcupine, *Hystrix brachyura*, appears blackish with the white parts of the quills prominent from a distance.

Ecology and Habitat. Feeds on fallen fruits and other vegetable material. Occurs in forests and cultivated areas.

Distribution. Confined to Borneo. Recorded from many localities in the lowlands and hills to the north of S. Rajang on the west coast and Samarinda in the east. Up to 1200 m in the Kelabit uplands.

Order: CETACEA   Whales, dolphins and porpoises

Although the cetaceans include the largest animals in the world, there are many small forms as well. Because they live completely in the water they are often thought to be fish, but they are true warm blooded mammals which have lost their legs and most of their hair, and acquired fins and other modifications for living in the sea. They still breathe air, give birth to live young, and feed them on milk.

If not seen well, some whales could be mistaken for sharks, as the dorsal fin sometimes appears similar. However, amongst other differences, whales have a blowhole on top of the head, visible when the animal breathes, and horizontal tail flukes instead of a vertical tail.

Whales and dolphins are often difficult to identify as they are usually hard to see well in the water. Even experienced observers familiar with the behaviour of the animals cannot identify every cetacean seen, and it can be especially difficult for a beginner. However, some species are quite tame, allowing good views, while others show themselves several times, eventually allowing enough to be seen for identification.

Very few people have studied whales around Borneo, and the few confirmed records available are mostly stranded specimens. However, there appear to be many small porpoises and dolphins in the offshore waters, and several species of large whales are likely to pass through Bornean waters at least occasionally. Because of this, all of the species known to occur in the tropical Pacific or Indian Ocean are included here, even if they have not definitely been recorded from Bornean waters.

Family: BALAENOPTERIDAE   Rorquals or Baleen Whales

The rorquals include some of the largest whales and can be recognized by their huge size and small dorsal fins near the back of the body. They feed by filtering food and water through huge baleen plates in their mouths. They can often be distinguished from the Sperm Whale at a long distance by the shape of the spout when they breathe — tall and conical or low and bushy as opposed to the Sperm Whale's spout which is angled forwards and to the left. This, however, is less conspicuous in warm tropical air.

The various rorquals can only be separated when they are seen well. Key features include size, the shape and position of the dorsal fin, the shape of the head and the coloration. The size and colour of the baleen can be helpful for distinguishing dead whales found stranded on beaches.

BLUE WHALE *Balaenoptera musculus*   Plate 55

Measurements. TL 22-24 m, formerly up to 30.5 m, but excessive hunting has led to the extermination of most of the larger, older individuals. Females slightly larger than males.

Identification. Largest of the whales. General colour light bluish-grey mottled with greyish-white; belly sometimes yellowish. Head flat from the side, broad and U-shaped from above. Dorsal fin tiny, in last quarter of back — rarely visible until whale dives. Flukes lifted only slightly out of the water or not at all when diving.

Baleen relatively short, stiff and all black. **Similar Species:** the Fin and Sei Whales, *B. physalus* and *B. borealis*, are smaller; the Fin has a plain grey back and asymmetrical white on the underparts, a more V-shaped head and larger dorsal fin; the Sei has a taller, more conspicuous dorsal fin.

Ecology and Habitat. Feeds mainly on krill (small crustaceans) within 100 m of the surface. Migrates long distances between tropical seas and cold waters.

Distribution. Worldwide, but most common in temperate to cold waters. **Borneo:** no definite records, but unconfirmed sightings just north of Sabah.

FIN WHALE *Balaenoptera physalus* Plate 55

Measurements. TL 18-20 m, maximum 24-27 m. Females slightly larger than males.

Identification. Dark grey to brownish black above with little or no mottling; whitish below. Asymmetrical head colour — right lower lip and palate white, left dark. Right front baleen white, remainder striped dark grey and whitish; up to 72 cm long and 30 cm wide. Dorsal fin somewhat variable in shape, shallowly angled; usually conspicuous shortly after blow. Head broadly V-shaped from above, with a central ridge. Tail flukes rarely raised before diving. Tall cone-shaped blow. **Similar Species:** the Blue Whale, *B. musculus*, is mottled blue-grey with a U-shaped head and tiny dorsal fin; Bryde's Whale, *B. edeni*, has 3 ridges on the rostrum; the Sei Whale, *B. borealis*, can be difficult to distinguish, but the lower lips and baleen are all grey, the dorsal fin is steeper (over 40°), and usually visible at the same time as the blow.

Ecology and Habitat. Eats a wide variety of food including crustaceans, squid and small fish. Can dive up to 200 m, but feeds near the surface as well. Winters in tropical areas and migrates to colder richer feeding areas in summer.

Distribution. Worldwide. **Borneo:** Several unconfirmed strandings on the Sarawak coast may have been this species.

SEI WHALE *Balaenoptera borealis* Plate 55

Measurements. TL 12-14 m, maximum 17-21 m. Females larger than males.

Identification. Body uniform dark-grey with ovoid white scars; belly whitish. Conspicuous dorsal fin about one third of way forward from tail; angle of front of fin usually more than 40°. Single prominent ridge from blowholes to front of rostrum; tip of snout slightly down-turned in profile. Fin usually visible at same time as blow. Baleen uniform grey-black with white fringes; sometimes a few half-white plates near front of mouth. **Similar Species:** Fin Whales, *B. physalus*, have a more shallow dorsal fin visible just after the blow, and asymmetric white lower lips; Bryde's Whale, *B. edeni*, has a slightly smaller more pointed fin and 3 ridges on top of head.

Ecology and Habitat. Rarely dives very deeply, often feeding near the surface. Eats krill, squid, and small fish. Often in small groups. Migrates annually from high-latitude feeding grounds to low-latitude wintering grounds.

Distribution. Worldwide. **Borneo:** One specimen stranded at Pusa, S. Saribas in Sarawak.

BRYDE'S (TROPICAL) WHALE *Balaenoptera edeni*   Plate 55

Measurements. TL 12-14 m, females slightly larger than males.

Identification. Dark grey above; whitish below. 3 prominent ridges on top of head. Baleen slate-grey, up to 42 cm long by 24 cm wide. Rolls sharply to expose fin and base of tail before diving. **Similar Species:** other large whales have only one ridge on the head; the Fin Whale, *B. physalus*, is larger and has a white right lower lip; the Sei Whale, *B. borealis*, often feeds closer to the surface, breathing smoothly at regular intervals, while Bryde's usually dives deeply and breathes irregularly.

Ecology and Habitat. Primarily feeds on schooling fish, often diving deeply.

Distribution. Throughout tropical and subtropical seas. **Borneo:** Two strandings reported on the Sarawak coast in 1956 and 1957.

MINKE (PIKED) WHALE *Balaenoptera acutorostrata*   Plate 55

Measurements. TL 7—8 m, up to 9.8 m (males) and 10.7 m (females).

Identification. Smallest of the rorquals with narrow pointed V-shaped rostrum and a single head ridge. Black to dark grey above, white below, usually with pale grey areas on the sides or back; white bands on flippers (sometimes lacking). Baleen about 20 cm long, by 12 cm wide — usually whitish in northern populations, dark grey in the south. **Similar Species:** the Fin, Sei and Bryde's Whales, *B. physalus*, *B. borealis* and *B. edeni*, are much larger with more rounded heads, but could be confused at a distance; beaked whales have similar dorsal fins, but distinctive head shapes.

Ecology and Habitat. Feeds mainly on krill in the south, but also on small shoaling fish in the north. Populations in colder seas migrate seasonally to warmer waters.

Distribution. Worldwide. **Borneo:** not yet recorded.

HUMPBACK WHALE *Megaptera novaeangliae*   Plate 55

Measurements. TL 11.4-12.4 m, maximum 16 m (females); 11-12 m, maximum 15 m (males).

Identification. Generally black or dark-grey, with varying amount of white on belly. Dorsal fin variable, sometimes similar to Blue or Fin Whales, *Balaenoptera musculus* or *B. physalus*, but often stepped. Very long flippers, white below and usually partially white above. Tail raised high out of the water on deep dives — distinctive deep notches in middle and white markings. Baleen generally all black, 70 cm x 30 cm. Tall bushy blow. **Similar Species:** other rorquals have ridges instead of knobs on the head, smaller flippers and do not raise their tail very high or at all before diving; the Sperm Whale, *Physeter macrocephalus*, can also appear "hump-backed" when diving, but its tail is all dark and even along the edge and the head shape is quite different when seen well.

Ecology and Habitat. Feeds on krill and schooling fish. Migratory.

Distribution. Worldwide. **Borneo:** One sight record off Sarawak.

Family: PHYSETERIDAE   Sperm Whales

This family includes one of the largest whales as well as some of the smallest, but they appear to be related. They all have a huge bulbous forehead containing a "spermacetti" organ, full of oil highly valued by whalers. The lower jaw is relatively small and underslung, with a row of well developed teeth which fit into sockets in the upper jaw.

(GREAT) SPERM WHALE *Physeter macrocephalus*   Plate 55

Measurements. TL: 10-12 m, maximum 18 m (males); 8-9 m, maximum 12 m (females).

Identification. Head huge, with a large square forehead. Overall colour dark brownish-grey to brown; "wrinkled" skin. Distinct dorsal hump with a series of low bumps leading to the tail — clearly visible when tail is thrown high before a deep dive. Tail flukes square, all dark below. Teeth on lower jaw only. Distinctive blow, angled forwards and to the left. **Similar Species:** the Humpback Whale, *Megaptera novaeangliae*, could appear similar when diving at a distance but tail flukes differ in shape and colour; beaked whales, *Mesoplodon* spp., have a high forehead, but with a long beak and prominent dorsal fin; blowhole well back on head.

Ecology and Habitat. Feeds primarily on large squid. Usually in deep water— sometimes dives to over 1000 m.

Distribution. Worldwide. **Borneo:** Not yet recorded.

PIGMY SPERM WHALE *Kogia breviceps*   Plate 57

Measurements. TL 2.7-3.4 m (males and females similar).

Identification. Head appears sharklike with underslung lower jaw. General colour dark bluish-grey fading to whitish on belly, with a gill-shaped light and dark mark at the side of the head. Dorsal fin low, behind the centre of the back. Teeth thin, curved inwards and sharp; twelve to sixteen pairs in lower jaw, none in upper; up to 30 mm long, 4.5 mm in diameter. Usually swims slowly and sluggishly on the surface. **Similar Species:** the Dwarf Sperm Whale, *K. simus,* is smaller, has a taller dolphin-like fin and fewer, smaller teeth; some beaked whales, *Mesoplodon* spp. might appear similar at a distance, but have a quite different head shape.

Ecology and Habitat. Feeds mainly on squid and octopus, but also some fish and crabs. Usually alone or in small groups. Often in shallow water — frequently stranded.

Distribution. Most parts of the world in temperate to tropical waters. **Borneo:** one specimen was stranded at Buntal in Sarawak.

DWARF SPERM WHALE *Kogia simus*   Plate 57

Measurements. TL 2.1-2.7 m.

Identification. Coloration and shape very similar to Pigmy Sperm Whale, *K. breviceps* — dark grey above, whitish below — but slightly smaller, dorsal fin larger

266

and further forward (as in Bottlenose Dolphin, *Tursiops truncatus)*, sometimes a few creases or grooves on throat, and teeth smaller. **Similar Species:** dolphins with similar fins have beaked heads; the Pigmy Killer Whale, *Feresa attenuata*, and Melon-headed Whale, *Peponocephala electra*, have different-shaped heads, but could appear similar at a distance — both are much more active and usually in groups.

Ecology and Habitat. Feeds mainly on squid, but also fish and crustaceans. Can dive up to 300 m, but often in inshore waters.

Distribution. Throughout the world in tropical to temperate seas, but until recently confused with the Pigmy Sperm Whale and many records have not been separated. **Borneo:** Not yet recorded.

Family ZIPHIIDAE   Beaked Whales

A poorly known group of medium to small whales, with an indistinct beak. The lower jaw has a few large teeth in males, only vestigial teeth in females. Bodies often covered with long pale scars.

CUVIER'S BEAKED (GOOSEBEAK) WHALE
Ziphius cavirostris   Plate 56

Measurements. TL 5.5-7.5 m.

Identification. Sloping forehead; poorly defined beak — lower jaw longer than upper. Colour extremely variable from dark rust brown to slate grey or fawn; belly usually paler; head sometimes whitish in older adults; back and sides usually covered with linear scars. Males have two conical teeth at front of jaw. **Similar Species:** Blainville's Beaked Whale, *Mesoplodon densirostris*, has a longer beak, teeth at side of jaw; the Southern Bottlenose Whale, *Hyperoodon planifrons*, of a similar size although not known to occur in the tropics, has a large bulbous forehead and long beak like a dolphin.

Ecology and Habitat. Feeds mainly on squid and deepwater fish. Can probably dive very deeply — submerges for up to 30 minutes. Often raises flukes before diving. Apparently wary of boats and hard to observe.

Distribution. Worldwide except in Arctic waters, though less common in the tropics. **Borneo:** Not yet recorded.

BEAKED WHALES *Mesoplodon* spp.   Plate 56

Measurements. TL up to about 5 m.

Identification. The various species of *Mesoplodon* are very poorly known, and can rarely be identified at sea. Blainville's (Dense) Beaked Whale, *M. densirostris*, and the Ginkgo-toothed Beaked Whale, *M. ginkgodens* are the two species most likely to occur in Bornean waters. They are generally black or dark grey, paler below, often with extensive pale blotches and white scars (presumably from fighting). Forehead low with a distinct beak; lower jaw highly arched, especially in males which have a large tooth in the middle of the arch. Blainville's has a single massive tooth, while the Gingko-toothed has a bilobed tooth. **Similar Species:** Cuvier's Beaked Whale, *Ziphius cavirostris*, has a less prominent beak, more sloped forehead in profile and an unarched jaw.

267

Ecology and Habitat. Almost unknown.

Distribution. *M. densirostris* has been reported from tropical and temperate seas in most parts of the world. *M. ginkgodens* is known from a few specimens from the Indian Ocean around to Japan. Further research may reveal other species in the tropics. **Borneo:** Not yet recorded.

Family DELPHINIDAE   Oceanic Dolphins

This family includes all of the well-known dolphins as well as the large Killer Whale. They have rows of peg-like teeth in both jaws, well developed dorsal fins and often a distinct beak.

IRRAWADDY (SNUBFIN) DOLPHIN *Orcaella brevirostris*Plate 58

Measurements. TL 2-2.5 m.

Identification. Overall grey to dark slate-blue, paler underneath — no distinctive pattern. Dorsal fin small and rounded behind middle of back. Forehead high and rounded; beak lacking. Broad rounded flippers. **Similar Species:** the Finless Porpoise, *Neophocaena phocaenoides*, is smaller and has no back fin; the Hump-backed Dolphin, *Sousa chinensis*, is larger, has a longer beak and larger dorsal fin.

Ecology and Habitat. Prefers inshore waters and estuaries, including very muddy and murky waters. Quiet and inconspicuous, rarely leaping or jumping.

Distribution. India through Indonesia to Australia. **Borneo:** Often seen in estuaries and bays, with sightings from Sandakan in Sabah; most parts of Brunei and Sarawak; a specimen was collected at S. Mahakam in East Kalimantan.

MELON-HEADED WHALE *Peponocephala electra*   Plate 57

Measurements. TL 2.2-2.7 m.

Identification. No prominent beak; forehead smoothly curved downward in profile; head triangular from above. Dorsal fin tall and curved. Flippers long, slim and pointed. Colour generally black, sometimes paler on the belly. 20-25 teeth in each row. **Similar Species:** the False Killer Whale, *Pseudorca crassidens*, is much larger, has a slightly more rounded profile, and bent flippers; the Pigmy Killer Whale, *Feresa attenuata*, has rounded flippers and a grey-brown cape contrasting with paler sides — a pattern rarely present in the Melon-headed Whale.

Ecology and Habitat. Often found in large herds of up to several hundred animals which can travel very quickly. Feeds on squid and small fish.

Distribution. Throughout the tropics and subtropics — common in some areas of the Philippines. **Borneo:** Not yet recorded.

PIGMY KILLER WHALE *Feresa attenuata*   Plate 57

Measurements. TL 2.2-2.7 m.

Identification. General colour dark grey-brown to black with paler sides giving an indistinct caped appearance; irregular patches of white on the belly, chin and lips.

Head rounded with no beak. Dorsal fin tall and curved back in centre of back; flippers rounded at tips. Upper jaw has 8-11 teeth on each side, lower jaw has 11-13. **Similar Species:** the Melon-headed Whale, *Peponocephala electra*, can be hard to separate but the head shape is slightly different and the flippers are more pointed; the False Killer Whale, *Pseudorca crassidens*, is much larger and more uniformly dark.

Ecology and Habitat. Often forms large groups; very active, but wary of boats. May sometimes attack other cetaceans.

Distribution. Throughout the world in tropical and subtropical seas. **Borneo:** Not yet recorded.

FALSE KILLER WHALE *Pseudorca crassidens*   Plate 56

Measurements. TL 3.2-4 m; females up to 4.9 m, males up to 6.1 m.

Identification. Mainly black, sometimes slightly paler around the head and on the chest. Long slender body with relatively small, rounded head. Conspicuous dorsal fin, curved backwards; flippers with hump on leading edge, unlike other black whales. 8-11 large conspicuous teeth in each row. **Similar Species:** the Killer Whale, *Orcinus orca*, is larger with a tall triangular fin, broad rounded head and large white patches; the pilot whales, *Globicephala* spp. have a more rounded, bulbous head, broader lower dorsal fin and long pointed flippers; the Pigmy Killer and Melon-headed Whales, *Feresa attenuata* and *Peponocephala electra*, are smaller and have paler markings, often white on the lips.

Ecology and Habitat. Gregarious, often forming large herds; very active, frequently playing near boats. Eats mainly squid and larger fish.

Distribution. Throughout the tropical seas, into the warmer temperate areas. **Borneo:** Not yet recorded.

(GREAT) KILLER WHALE *Orcinus orca*   Plate 56

Measurements. TL adult males up to 9.5 m, females up to 7 m, but usually smaller.

Identification. Tall triangular dorsal fin, lower and more curved in females. General colour black with large well-marked white areas on the underparts, behind the eye and behind the dorsal fin — pattern varies with each individual. Eye patch often visible when swimming. Flippers broad and rounded. Adult males easily recognized, but females are smaller with a more dolphin-like fin. **Similar Species:** the False Killer Whale, *Pseudorca crassidens*, is more slender with no white markings and a more rounded head; Risso's Dolphin, *Grampus griseus*, is much smaller, usually paler and greyer in adults with a rounded beakless head; Pilot Whales, *Globicephala* spp., have a bulbous forehead and low broad-based dorsal fin.

Ecology and Habitat. Eats most marine animals including fish, penguins, seals and other cetaceans. Very social, usually in groups of a few up to 30 or more. In seas from the tropics to polar ice regions.

Distribution. Worldwide. **Borneo:** One specimen stranded at Miri in Sarawak.

SHORT-FINNED PILOT WHALE
Globicephala macrorhynchus **Plate 56**

Measurements. TL 4.2-5.4 m (males), 3-4 m (females).

Identification. Generally black with greyish-white marks under the throat and often pale marks behind the eye and behind the dorsal fin. Dorsal fin long and low. Thick, bulbous forehead with small beak. Flippers sickle-shaped. Teeth 7 to 9 in each row. **Similar Species:** the False Killer Whale, *Pseudorca crassidens*, has a more tapered head and a more slender, erect dorsal fin; the Long-finned Pilot Whale, *Globicephala melaena*, is extremely similar, but not known to occur in the tropics: it is slightly larger, has 8-12 teeth in each row and longer flippers, but can rarely be distinguished at sea.

Ecology and Habitat. Found in small groups, often in the company of dolphins. Feeds mainly in deep waters, but often comes close to shore.

Distribution. Worldwide in tropical and warm-temperate waters. **Borneo:** a few were stranded near Kota Kinabalu in Sabah; several sight records off the Sarawak coast.

ROUGH-TOOTHED DOLPHIN *Steno bredanensis* **Plate 58**

Measurements. TL 1.8-2.8 m.

Identification. Forehead and sides of head slope evenly into long, slender beak. Generally dark grey to blackish, with white lips and underparts and variable pale blotches on the sides. Often has pale streaks along the sides forming an indistinct narrow saddle. **Similar Species:** Other dolphins have a distinct crease between the bulbous forehead and the beak; the Bottlenose Dolphin, *Tursiops truncatus*, has a shorter beak and more uniform grey coloration; the Spotted Dolphin, *Stenella attenuata*, generally has more spots on the body and a more complex colour pattern; the Spinner Dolphin, *Stenella longirostra*, has a taller dorsal fin; the Hump-backed Dolphin, *Sousa chinensis*, which sometimes lacks the hump, has a different-shaped head.

Ecology and Habitat. Eats octopus, squid and fish. Usually prefers deeper offshore water.

Distribution. Widely distributed in tropical and warm-temperate seas. **Borneo:** not yet recorded.

INDO-PACIFIC HUMP-BACKED DOLPHIN *Sousa chinensis* **Plate 58**
(includes *S. plumbea*, *S. lentiginosa*, and *S. borneensis*)

Measurements. TL up to 2.8 m.

Identification. Adults usually have a long low hump on the back with a small triangular fin on top, but some forms lack the hump and have a larger fin. Quite variable in coloration, from uniform dull grey to pure white, with some speckled individuals. The colour variation is partly related to age, but the taxonomy is not well understood and several species may be involved. **Similar Species:** the Bottle-nosed Dolphin, *Tursips truncatus*, can be very similar to forms without a hump, but is always dark grey — humpless dolphins appear to be most frequently of the white form; the Finless Porpoise, *Neophocaena phocaenoides*, which is also very pale, lacks a dorsal fin and has no beak.

Ecology and Habitat. Eats mainly fish. Usually in inshore waters.

Distribution. Throughout the Indian and western Pacific Oceans, in warm temparate to tropical waters (a closely related species occurs in the eastern Atlantic). **Borneo:** Both the grey and white forms have been reported off the Sarawak coast; one old specimen was reported as *S. lentiginosa* (the speckled form), but the colour may not have been accurately recorded.

FRASER'S (SHORTSNOUT) DOLPHIN *Lagenodelphis hosei*Plate 59

Measurements. TL 2.3-2.7 m.

Identification. Short beak; relatively small flippers and pointed dorsal fin. Generally dark blue-grey above, white below with broad striping on the sides; long dark stripe through eye to anus. Fin, flippers and flukes dark. **Similar Species:** the Spinner Dolphin, *Stenella longirostra*, has a narrower dark side stripe and a forward pointing dark mark below the fin, longer beak and larger fin; the Common Dolphin, *Delphinus delphis*, has a larger fin and a distinctive pale pattern on the side.

Ecology and Habitat. Eats squid, crustaceans and fish, often feeding at night. Usually in large herds, often mixed with other species. Prefers deep water.

Distribution. Tropical seas in most parts of the world. **Borneo:** the type specimen was found stranded in Sarawak. Sight records of Hector's Dolphin, *Cephalorhynchus hectori*, have been reported from Sarawak, but this seems rather unlikely, as the species is otherwise restricted only to New Zealand — these sightings could well have been Fraser's Dolphin.

COMMON DOLPHIN *Delphinus delphis*   Plate 59

Measurements. TL up to 2.5 m, but usually less than 2.3 m.

Identification. Back brownish-black to black, belly white; sides with broad criss-crossing stripes of buff or grey and white; dark V-shaped saddle below dorsal fin distinguishes from all other dolphins if seen clearly. Dorsal fin tall and triangular, all black to white with a black border. Beak long and narrow, usually black but sometimes with a white tip. **Similar Species:** the Striped Dolphin, *Stenella coeruleoalba*, has thin dark stripes from the eye to the anus and the eye to the flippers.

Ecology and Habitat. Feeds mostly at night on deep-sea fish and squid. Very active during the day, often jumping and playing in the water.

Distribution. Throughout the tropical and sub-tropical seas. **Borneo:** sight records off Sabah (in the east and north) and Sarawak.

BOTTLENOSE DOLPHIN *Tursiops truncatus*   Plate 57

Measurements. TL up to 3.9 m, but usually smaller; males slightly larger than females.

271

Identification. Fairly uniform dark brown to grey colour, darkest on the back, forming an indistinct cape; paler on the sides; whitish on the belly. Beak moderately short and thick; dorsal fin tall and curved. **Similar Species:** the Hump-backed Dolphin, *Sousa chinensis*, if it lacks the hump, is usually whiter and has a more triangular dorsal fin; the Rough-toothed Dolphin, *Steno bredanensis*, has a more conical head with no crease separating the beak, and a very narrow cape; Risso's Dolphin, *Grampus griseus*, has no beak or distinct cape — adults are much paler, usually white around the head; the Spotted Dolphin, *Stenella attenuata*, has a more complex pattern, usually with spots, and a longer slimmer beak.

Ecology and Habitat. Eats a wide variety of food, including fish and invertebrates. Found in shallow to oceanic waters, usually in small groups. Often quite tame, approaching ships or swimmers.

Distribution. Worldwide except in very cold waters. **Borneo:** sight records off Sarawak.

RISSO'S (GREY) DOLPHIN *Grampus griseus*   Plate 57

Measurements. TL 3.6-4 m.

Identification. High, domed forehead bisected in the middle by a deep crease; no conspicuous beak. Body generally dark grey when young, turning pale grey to whitish with age, especially around the head. Dorsal fin and flippers dark; extensively covered with long scars. No upper teeth and usually fewer than seven pairs of peg-like lower teeth. **Similar Species:** the Bottlenose and Humpback Dolphins, *Tursiops truncatus* and *Sousa chinensis*, have a long beak; the False Killer Whale, *Pseudorca crassidens*, is darker and generally unscarred, forehead not grooved; beaked whales, *Mesoplodon* spp., have a smaller dorsal fin, tapered head and grow to be much larger.

Ecology and Habitat. Feeds mainly on squid, but also some fish; usually in groups, but sometimes in singles or pairs. Prefers deep water.

Distribution. Throughout the world in tropical to sub-tropical seas. **Borneo:** Many sight records off the Sarawak coast; one skull in the Sarawak museum.

SPOTTED (BRIDLED) DOLPHIN *Stenella attenuata*   Plate 59

Measurements. TL male up to 2.5 m, female up to 2.3 m.

Identification. Dark grey to brownish grey cape, narrow on the forehead, broader below the dorsal fin; underside whitish except dark flippers and a thin stripe from the beak to the flippers. Amount of spotting varies with age and geographical location; generally light to moderate in the western Pacific and Indian Ocean. Beak long and narrow, often with white tip and lips. **Similar Species:** the Bottlenose Dolphin, *Tursiops truncatus*, can be similar to unspotted individuals, but is more robust with a thicker beak and plainer coloration; the spotted form of the Hump-backed Dolphin, *Sousa chinensis*, often has a thickened base to the dorsal fin, and a more uniform mantle pattern.

Ecology and Habitat. Feeds on fish and squid; often congregates in large herds sometimes mixed with other species; both coastal and offshore waters. Very active, often leaping high or "playing" in the water.

Distribution. Throughout tropical waters and sometimes into warm temperate seas, though some Atlantic forms are probably a different species. **Borneo:** not yet recorded.

STRIPED DOLPHIN *Stenella coeruleoalba*   Plate 59

Measurements. TL 1.8-2.7 m.

Identification. Long, narrow black stripes from eye to flipper and eye to anus; broad pale grey streak above eye to below dorsal fin. Back dark grey to bluish grey; sides light grey; belly white. Fin moderate and slightly curved; beak long and distinct. **Similar Species:** the Common Dolphin, *Delphinus delphis*, has a different pattern of stripes; the Bottlenose and Spotted Dolphins, *Tursiops truncatus* and *Stenella attenuata*, sometimes have an indistinct pale blaze on the shoulder, but lack the black stripes on the sides; Fraser's Dolphin, *Lagenodelphis hosei*, has broader black side stripes, a shorter snout and a small dorsal fin.

Ecology and Habitat. Eats many small fish, shrimp and squid. Usually in large groups well off-shore, but sometimes comes near shore. Very active, often jumping clear of the water.

Distribution. Worldwide in tropical to temperate seas. **Borneo:** not yet recorded.

LONG-SNOUTED SPINNER DOLPHIN *Stenella longirostris* Plate 59

Measurements. TL up to 2.2 m but smaller in some areas.

Identification. Dorsal fin generally triangular and not curved, especially in adult males; tail base often strongly keeled; beak long and narrow, with dark lips and tip. Upperparts dark grey, underparts white, sides pale — pattern varies geographically, and some forms are all grey in the eastern Pacific. **Similar Species:** the Bottlenose Dolphin, *Tursiops truncatus*, is larger, has a more curved fin, and a shorter beak with a pale tip and lips; the Common Dolphin, *Delphinus delphis*, has a distinct V-shaped saddle on the side.

Ecology and Habitat. Forms very large, active groups, often jumping and twisting, sometimes mixed with other species. Usually in deep, offshore waters. Feeds mainly on fish and squid.

Distribution. Tropical and subtropical regions of the world's oceans. **Borneo:** not yet recorded.

Family PHOCOENIDAE   Porpoises

Similar to dolphins, but with no beak. The only species found in Bornean waters has no dorsal fin.

FINLESS PORPOISE *Neophocaena phocaenoides*   Plate 58

Measurements. TL 1.6-1.9 m.

273

Identification. Uniform slate grey, sometimes very pale — never black except after death. Rounded head; no dorsal fin. **Similar Species:** all other potentially similar species such as the Irrawaddy Dolphin, *Orcaella brevirostris*, and the Hump-backed Dolphin, *Sousa chinensis*, have a distinct dorsal fin and are usually larger.

Ecology and Habitat. Eats small squid, prawns, and small fish. Found in shallow coastal waters and river estuaries in small groups or singles.

Distribution. Coastal Asian waters from India through to Japan. **Borneo:** reportedly common in estuaries of northern Sarawak, formerly also in southern Sarawak.

274

Order CARNIVORA
Dogs, Bears, Mustelids, Civets, Mongooses and Cats

The carnivores are represented by a diverse array of animals which can be distinguished from other mammals by their large sharp teeth. All Bornean species have three incisors on each side of both the upper and lower jaws. The canines are long, pointed and relatively large. There is always a small gap (diastema) between the row of incisors and the canine in the upper jaw, and in some species a similar gap in the lower jaw. Excluding the Domestic Dog, four families of carnivores occur in Borneo (five if mongooses are placed in their own family separate from civets).

All Bornean carnivores eat at least some animal matter, but some eat a large proportion of fruits.

Family CANIDAE   Dogs

There is no evidence that any truly wild dogs occur in Borneo, although the Domestic Dog, *Canis familiaris*, has been present for a very long time. The Asian Wild Dog, *Cuon alpinus*, which is found on mainland Asia, Sumatra and Java, is absent. The Domestic Dog has a total of 42 teeth, more than any other Bornean carnivore.

DOMESTIC DOG *Canis familiaris*   not illustrated

Measurements. HB about 800-1000, T about 300-350.

Identification. Coloration variable, most commonly dull orange-brown, sometimes black or pied. The footprints can be distinguished by size and the presence of claw marks.

Ecology and Habitat. Always associated with Man, even when feral. Dogs reared for hunting wild mammals normally find their way back to their owner. Untrained dogs which have been abandoned in disused logging camps are sometimes encountered far from human settlements, usually in poor condition.

Distribution. World wide. **Borneo:** Occurs in most areas where there are human settlements.

Family URSIDAE   Bears

Bears are large, powerfully built, omnivorous mammals with a short tail and good sense of smell, but poor sight and hearing. The one species found in Borneo is the smallest in the world and the Bornean subspecies is smaller than that on mainland Asia. Nevertheless, it is one of the few native mammals (as are elephants) potentially dangerous to man, owing to the unpredictability of its behaviour.

SUN BEAR *Helarctos malayanus*   Plate 43

Measurements. HB 1125-1260, T 30-90, Wt 48-63kg (3 specimens).

Identification. Body entirely black, except for grey muzzle and a white or yellowish 'V' or 'C' shaped mark on the upper chest. Chest mark normally prominent but occasionally very faint. A reddish-coloured specimen lacking the chest mark has been found in south-eastern Sabah. Signs more often seen than Bear itself: prominent claw marks gouged into a tree trunk where it has climbed the tree, or the remains of bee or termite nests ripped open in standing or fallen trees. Claw marks much more conspicuous than the faint marks of other carnivores or monitor lizards. Occasionally, utters hoarse grunts or loud roars, which may be confused with those of the adult male Orangutan; rarely short barks like that of a muntjac, *Muntiacus* spp., or Rhinoceros, *Dicerorhinus sumatrensis*. **Similar species:** the Binturong, *Arctictis binturong*, has a prominent long, bushy tail and is much smaller.

Ecology and Habitat. Active periodically during day and night time, on the ground and in tall trees. Builds nests of small branches in tall trees for sleeping, similar to those of the Orang-utan, but usually nearer the trunk and less well woven. Diet includes entire bees' nests, termites, small animals, fruits and the "heart" of coconut palms. Occurs in extensive areas of forests and occasionally enters gardens in remote areas.

Distribution. Burma, Thailand, Peninsular Malaysia, Sumatra. **Borneo:** *H. m. euryspilus*. Recorded at low densities from many localities in the lowlands and hills. Reported up to 1500 m in the Sabah-Sarawak border region and 2300 m on G. Kinabalu.

Family MUSTELIDAE   Martens, Weasels, Badgers and Otters

The mustelids are a rather diverse group and the seven Bornean species are divided into four subfamilies. The subfamily Mustelinae includes the Yellow-throated Marten, *Martes flavigula*, and Malay Weasel, *Mustela nudipes*, both slender, agile mammals adapted to hunting small vertebrate animals, as well as invertebrates. The subfamily Melinae is represented by the Ferret-badger, *Melogale personata*, stockily built, with a short tail and long muzzle. The Teledu, *Mydaus javanensis*, is believed to be closely allied to the skunk subfamily, Mephitinae, of North America. The otters, subfamily Lutrinae, are easily distinguished by their semi-aquatic existence, webbed or partially webbed feet and broad muzzle. The presence of otters may be detected by piles of faeces, known as spraints, consisting of the hard parts of crustaceans, molluscs or fish, deposited on open places near to water courses. All large otters found in Borneo are usually allocated to the genus *Lutra*, although the Smooth Otter, *L. perspicillata*, is sometimes placed in the genus *Lutrogale*. Mustelids appear to be closely related to the Viverridae. They can usually be distinguished by having 34 to 38 teeth, whereas all viverrids (except the Banded Linsang, *Prionodon linsang*) have a total of 40 teeth. Mustelids also tend to have stockier limbs and broader feet, and are generally more strictly carnivorous.

YELLOW-THROATED MARTEN *Martes flavigula*   Plate 44

Measurements. HB 403-463, T 310-375 (about 75% of HB), HF 81-91 (7 specimens; males slightly larger than females). Wt 1000-1370.

Identification. Upperparts brown or pale brown in the front, dark brown at the rear; chin, throat and chest yellowish, whitish or buff, bordered by a dark stripe behind the ear. Tail dark brown, sometimes with a pale tip. In the field, the long, slender body, long tail and lithe, bounding motion are distinctive. Tail may be held

276

down, up with the tip drooping or almost horizontal (if moving quickly). **Similar species:** mongooses rarely climb trees, have a more pointed muzzle, tend to hold the head and tail down while walking, and walk quickly but rarely bound; civets are normally active only at night and have different colour patterns; otters have small rounded ears, tapering tail, webbed feet.

Ecology and Habitat. Active mainly during the day, but sometimes at night. Agile, moving fairly quickly on the ground or in the tree canopy. Diet includes a wide range of small vertebrates and invertebrates, bees's nests and nectar. Rests in tree holes and on large branches. Usually alone or in pairs, but sometimes in family groups. Call a series of soft, rapid 'chuk's. Occurs in tall and secondary forests; often enters plantations and gardens in search of food.

Distribution. Mainland Asia from eastern Siberia south to Peninsular Malaysia, Sumatra, Java. **Borneo:** *M. f. saba.* Recorded from many localities throughout the lowlands and hills including G. Kinabalu (up to 1700 m), the Crocker Range, Sepilok and the Tawau area in Sabah; Brunei; the Kelabit uplands (up to 1500 m), Samunsam and many other sites in Sarawak; G. Palung in West Kalimantan; Kotawaringan in Central Kalimantan; Teluk Pamukan in South Kalimantan; Peleben in East Kalimantan.

MALAY WEASEL   *Mustela nudipes*   Plate 44

Measurements. HB 310,320, T 215,220, HF 49,54 (2 specimens).

Identification. Entire body orange to golden brown, except tail, which is paler near the tip, and head which is whitish. Tail bushy.

Ecology and Habitat. Terrestrial. Apparently active both during the day and at night. Sleeps in holes in the ground. Diet includes small animals. Occurs in forests. Sometimes seen crossing roads.

Distribution. Peninsular Thailand and Malaysia; Sumatra, Java. **Borneo.** Recorded from many scattered localities throughout the lowlands and hills, including G. Kinabalu (up to 1700 m), the Sandakan region and Tabin in Sabah; the Kelabit uplands, G. Kalulung and the Kuching region in Sarawak; Pontianak in West Kalimantan; Riam in Central Kalimantan; Banjarmasin and the upper S. Mahakam in East Kalimantan.

FERRET-BADGER   *Melogale personata*   Plate 44
(formerly called *Melogale orientalis*)

Measurements. HB 300-328, T 125-150, HF 53-55 (3 specimens).

Identification. Body entirely brownish, except the head which has a distinct pattern of blackish brown and whitish.

Ecology and Habitat. Mostly nocturnal and terrestrial. Diet includes earthworms, lizards, birds and rats.Occurs in montane forests.

Distribution. Nepal, Assam, Burma, Thailand, Indochina, Java. **Borneo:** *M. p. everetti.* Known only from G. Kinabalu between 1070 and 3000 m. Probably also occurs on G. Tambayukon, to the north of G. Kinabalu.

277

TELEDU or MALAY BADGER *Mydaus javanensis*   Plate 44

Measurements. HB 370-520, T 34-38, HF 64-70 (4 specimens).

Identification. Black, with a white dorsal stripe. Extent of stripe variable but usually extends from top of head to tail. Muzzle long. Often detected by its strong, pervading odour which is secreted by an anal gland and can be squirted up to a couple of metres.

Ecology and Habitat. Nocturnal and terrestrial. Sleeps in underground burrows. Food obtained mainly by digging with the muzzle and long claws into soft soil. Diet includes earthworms and cicada larvae. Occurs in tall forests, but more often in secondary forest and open ground such as gardens adjacent to forest.

Distribution. Sumatra, Java, P. Natuna. **Borneo:** *M. j. lucifer.* Known from scattered localities in the lowlands and low hills of Sabah, Brunei, Sarawak, West Kalimantan and South Kalimantan. Also recorded from a few higher localities including G. Murud and the Kelabit uplands (1100 m) in Sarawak. Distribution appears to be patchy and is probably related to food supply.

HAIRY-NOSED OTTER *Lutra sumatrana*   Plate 45

Measurements. HB 575, 615, T 375, 385, HF 103, 107 (2 specimens). Skull: cbl 91-101, io 14.4-14.8, mt 31.5-31.6 (3 specimens).

Identification. Entirely brown, except lips, chin and upper throat which are whitish. Fur rather rough but short. Rhinarium (moist part of nose) covered in hair. Tail flattened oval in cross section. Feet fully webbed between the digits. Claws prominent. Penis of adult male not visible externally. Contact call between otters a single syllabic chirp. Adult females call to cubs with a staccato chatter. **Similar species:** the large otters are very similar and can be positively distinguished only by close inspection of the nose and fur, or the skull. In this species, the skull is flatter than that of the Smooth Otter, *L. perspicillata* (Figure 33).

Ecology and Habitat. Occurs in coastal areas and larger inland river systems, including associated lakes and streams. Diet includes fish. May be seen solitary or in groups of up to at least six. Pairing of male and female may be limited to the breeding period.

Distribution. Southern Indochina and Thailand, Peninsular Malaysia, Sumatra, Java. **Borneo:** Recorded from scattered localities in most areas except the south and east, including S. Kinabatangan, S. Segama, Sandakan, Kota Kinabalu and south-western Sabah; S. Tutong in Brunei; the Tg. Sirik and Kuching areas in Sarawak; S. Kapuas and Pontianak in West Kalimantan; and the upper S. Barito in Central Kalimantan.

Figure 33. Skulls of Otters:
  a) *Aonyx cinerea,*
  b) *Lutra perspicillata,*
  c) *Lutra sumatrana*

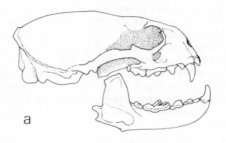

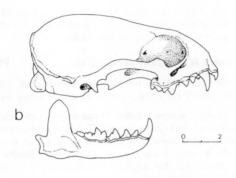

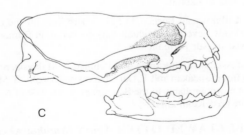

EURASIAN OTTER *Lutra lutra*   not illustrated
(unconfirmed in Borneo)

Measurements. HB 673, T 417, HF 128 (1 specimen from P. Langkawi, off Peninsular Malaysia). Skull: cbl about 97-106 (mainland Asia).

Identification. Upperparts rather dark brown, with paler chin and upper throat. Fur dense, consisting of short hairs and longer guard hairs producing a somewhat grizzled appearance. Rhinarium hairless. Two skins of an otter which may be this species from the Kelabit uplands in Sarawak are darker than Eurasian Otters from elsewhere in Asia. Skulls of both specimens missing, but those of mainland specimens appear intermediate between those of the Smooth and Oriental Small-clawed Otters, *L. perspicillata* and *Aonyx cinerea* (Figure 33a,b), unlike the long flattened skull of the Hairy-nosed Otter, *L. sumatrana*. **Similar species:** the Hairy-nosed and Smooth Otters appear to live primarily in coastal and flatland habitats, and may have a paler, sleeker coat.

Ecology and Habitat. On mainland Asia, diet includes fish, other small vertebrates and crustaceans. Most Asian records, as well as the two Sarawak specimens, are from mountainous areas.

Distribution. Europe, North Africa, mainland Asia, Sri Lanka, Taiwan, Japan, Sumatra, Java. **Borneo:** No definite records, but two skins (without skulls) from the Kelabit uplands in Sarawak may belong to this species.

SMOOTH OTTER *Lutra (Lutrogale) perspicillata*   Plate 45

Measurements. HB 522-750, T 355-450, HF 100-140 (1 immature Sabah and several mature Thailand specimens). Skull: cbl 120.8, io 18.5, mt 40.6 (1 Sabah specimen).

Identification. Upperparts brown; underparts buffy. Throat and sides of neck creamy coloured. Fur short, smooth and sleek. Nose hairless. Tail flattened on underside. Feet large (Figure 42) and webbed up to last joint on digits. Claws prominent. Penis of adult male protrudes beyond body wall. Contact call "wiuk". **Similar species:** the Hairy-nosed Otter, *L. sumatrana*, has smaller footprints (Figure 42), flattened skull (Figure 33c) and greater contrast between the dark upperparts and whitish throat. The Eurasian Otter, *L. lutra*, has a coarser, two-layered coat of fur and, if present, probably differs in habitat.

Ecology and Habitat. Unknown in Borneo, but elsewhere lives on the coast or inland in extensive flatlands. Several individuals may cooperate in fishing. Males and females are believed to pair permanently.

Distribution. Mainland Asia, including India and Peninsular Malaysia, Sumatra. **Borneo:** Recorded only from Sandakan and T. Darvel in eastern Sabah; "S. Mugang" in Sarawak (locality unknown; probably in the Bau region, south-west of Kuching); Badang on S. Bahau in East Kalimantan.

ORIENTAL SMALL-CLAWED OTTER *Aonyx (Amblonyx) cinerea*
Plate 45

Measurements. HB 360-460, T 225-310, HF 85-95 (7 specimens). Skull: cbl 80.5-84.6, mt 24.2-26.0 (6 specimens).

Identification. Upperparts dark brown or greyish-brown; underparts slightly paler. Chin, throat, cheeks and sides of neck buffy. Digits only partially webbed. Claws short, not extending beyond the end of the digits. Contact call is 'wiuk'; various other calls are also made. **Similar species:** the other Bornean otters are larger and have prominent claws.

Ecology and Habitat. Diurnal. Diet includes crabs, other crustaceans and molluscs. Occurs in many habitats where there is permanent water and some tree cover, including the coast, large rivers, small streams in the hills, ponds and lakes. Solitary individuals sometimes encountered, but often in groups. Males and females appear to pair permanently.

Distribution. India to S. China, South-east Asia, Sumatra, Java, Palawan. **Borneo:** *A. c. cinerea.* Known from all regions of Sabah and Sarawak; Brunei; Sampit in Central Kalimantan; Pleihari in South Kalimantan; the upper S. Mahakam in East Kalimantan. Also on P. Laut off South Kalimtanan. Probably occurs in all other parts of Borneo. Up to 1300 m on Usun Apau.

Family VIVERRIDAE   Civets and Mongooses

The twelve viverrids in Borneo from a diverse group without a common diagnostic feature overall. However, some features are common to most species: (1) muzzle rather pointed and tail long relative to body (the Otter Civet, *Cynogale bennettii*, has a broad muzzle and short tail); (2) total of 40 teeth (the Banded Linsang, *Prionodon linsang*, has 38); (3) perineal scent glands (absent in the Banded Linsang, *P. linsang*, male Small-toothed Palm Civet, *Arctogalidia trivirgata*, and mongooses, *Herpestes* spp., although mongooses have small anal glands).

Mongooses can be distinguished in the field from civets by their sharply pointed muzzle, tapering tail with hair longer near the base than at the tip, rather slender legs with long claws, diurnal activity, and posture while walking with hindquarters arched above the level of the forequarters and tail. Some zoologists place the mongooses in their own family, Herpestidae.

The viverrids share many features with the mustelids, but the latter have fewer teeth and lack perineal scent glands.

Figure 34. Skull of an Otter-civet, *Cynogale bennettii*.

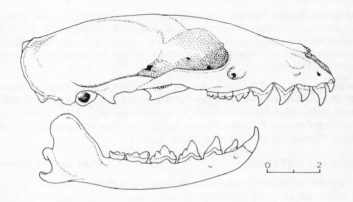

MALAY CIVET or TANGALUNG *Vierra tangalunga*   Plate 46

Measurements. HB 615-665, T 285-355, HF 94-105 (6 specimens).

Identification. Upperparts greyish with numerous black spots; a black stripe along the midline extends to tip of tail; underparts white with bold black markings on the throat. Legs blackish. Tail with about 15 black bands. The throat markings are diagnostic and usually the most prominent feature from a distance in the field at night, when the spots on the body may not be discernible.

Ecology and Habitat. Nocturnal and usually terrestrial, but occasionally climbs into trees. Diet includes a very wide variety of invertebrates and small vertebrates taken mainly from the forest floor. Often visits forest camps at night to feed on food scraps. Occurs in forests and cultivated land adjacent to forest.

Distribution. Peninsular Malaysia, Palawan, Sumatra and adjacent islands, Sulawesi. **Borneo:** *V. t. tangalunga*. Recorded from many localities in the lowlands and hills, up to 900 m on G. Madalon in Sabah and 1100 m on Usun Apau and the Kelabit uplands in Sarawak. Also on P. Karimata and P. Laut.

BANDED LINSANG *Prionodon lisang*   Plate 48

Measurements. HB 350-411, T 295-362, HF 54-66 (3 specimens).

Identification. Whitish to golden or buff, with a pattern of bold dark brown spots and bars on the upperparts and a distinctive barred tail. Small, slender and cat-like. Claws retractile, like a cat's and unlike those of other viverrids. **Similar species:** other Bornean civets and wild cats are larger; the Malay Civet, *Viverra tangalunga*, has prominent black and white throat markings; but no spots, and a mainly black tail; the Leopard Cat, *Felis bengalensis*, and the Marbled Cat. *F. marmorata*, have a blunter muzzle and lack the regular, broad barring along the entire length of the tail.

Ecology and Habitat. Nocturnal. Arboreal and terrestrial. Sleeps during the day in a nest made in a hole either in the ground or in a tree. Diet includes small mammals birds, reptiles and arthropods. Occurs in tail and secondary forests, plantations and gardens.

Distribution. Peninsular Burma, Thailand and Malaysia, Sumatra and adjacent islands, Java. **Borneo:** *P. l. gracilis.* Recorded from G. Kinabalu (up to 1800 m), the Sandakan area and the upper S. Segama in Sabah; Muara in Brunei; Usun Apau and G. Dulit in Sarawak; G. Kenepai in West Kalimantan; South Kalimantan. Rarely seen but probably widespread.

COMMON PALM CIVET *Paradoxurus hermaphroditus* Plate 47

Measurements. HB 420-500, T 330-420 (usually 70-90% of HB), HF 70-76 (10 specimens). Skull: cbl 92.4-99.6, mt 32.4-36.8 (9 specimens).

Identification. Upperparts vary from olive-brown or occasionally reddish-brown to dark grey-brown; underparts paler. Specimens from eastern Sabah tend to be darker than those from western Borneo. Face, limbs and tail dark brownish or black. Usually three indistinct, broken dark stripes along the midline. Adult females with three pairs of mammae. **Similar species:** the Small-toothed Palm Civet, *Arctogalidia trivirgata*, usually has the tail longer than the head and body, a larger skull with relatively smaller and widely-spaced teeth (Figure 35) and two pairs of mammae in females; the Masked Palm Civet, *Paguma larvata*, is larger and has a "mask" on the face.

Ecology and Habitat. Nocturnal. Sleeps during the day in trees or in buildings. Arboreal and terrestrial, but more often active on the ground than the Small-toothed Palm Civet. Diet includes fruits, leaves, arthropods, worms and molluscs. Occurs in secondary forests, plantations and gardens, rarely in tall forests. Often seen near human settlements.

Distribution. Sri Lanka, India, South-east Asia, Philippines, Sumatra, Java, Sulawesi and smaller Indonesian islands. **Borneo:** *P. h. sabanus.* Recorded from many localities in the lowlands but not known from hill ranges or mountains.

Figure 35. Upper toothrows of palm civets:

a) *Paradoxums hermaphroditus,*
b) *Arctogalidia trivirgata.*

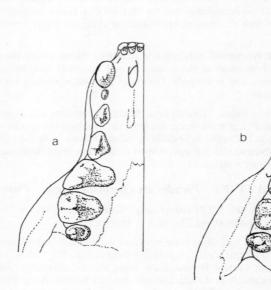

MASKED PALM CIVET   *Paguma larvata*   Plate 47

Measurements. HB 580, 605, T 565, 599, HF 95, 101 (2 specimens).

Identification. Pale to dark reddish-brown with yellow-grey underfur. Neck, ears, limbs and terminal half of tail dark brown. Face yellowish-white with a dark "mask" extending from behind the eyes to the tip of the muzzle. Some individuals have a white or yellow tail tip. **Similar species:** the Common Palm Civet, *Paradoxurus hermaphroditus,* and the Small-toothed Palm Civet, *Arctogalidia trivirgata,* are smaller, lack of distinct face "mask" and rarely have a red tinge; the latter has a relatively longer tail.

Ecology and Habitat. Nocturnal, but occasionally active during the day. Arboreal and terrestrial. Sleeps in tree holes or forks in large trees. Diet includes fruits and small animals. Occurs in tall and secondary forests; enters plantations and gardens to feed.

284

Distribution. Himalayas, southern China, Taiwan, South-east Asia, Sumatra. **Borneo:** *P. l. ogilbyi.* Known from scattered localities in lowlands and hills throughout the north, including G. Kinabalu (up to 2100 m), the upper S. Segama and Tawau region in Sabah; upper Temburong in Brunei; Kuching and northern Sarawak. Southernmost records are from G. Liang Kubung in West Kalimantan and the upper S. Mahakam in East Kalimantan.

BINTURONG or BEARCAT   *Arctictis binturong*   Plate 46

Measurements. HB 610-965, T 500-840, HF 118-180 (4 specimens). Wt 6-7.5 kg (2 specimens).

Identification. Entirely black with a variable amount of whitish or reddish grizzling. Hair coarse and long. Ears with long tufts of hair. Tail long, thickly haired especially near base, and prehensile (able to grasp branches). **Similar species:** the Sun Bear, *Helarctos malayanus*, is larger, has a short tail and no ear tufts; melanistic (dark) forms of cats have shorter hair, a slender, non-prehensile tail and no ear tufts.

Ecology and Habitat. Arboreal and terrestrial. Mainly active at night but sometimes during the day as well. Moves slowly in trees, using the tail for balance and to cling to branches while feeding. Diet includes ripe fruits, especially figs, and small animals. Occurs in tall and secondary forests; sometimes enters cultivated areas near to forest.

Distribution. South-east Asia, Palawan, Sumatra, Java. **Borneo:** *A. b. penicillata.* Known from scattered localities in lowlands and hills throughout the north including S. Kinabalu (up to 1500 m), Sandakan region, Tabin and Kalabakan in Sabah; various lowland sites, the Kelabit uplands and G. Penrisen in Sarawak; the upper S. Kapuas in West Kalimantan; and records south of S. Kapuas or S. Mahakam.

SMALL-TOOTHED PALM CIVET *Arctogalidia trivirgata* Plate 47

Measurements. HB 440-520, T 480-630 (about 110-120% of HB), HF 78-91 (5 specimens). Skull: cbl 100.0-108.7, mt 38.0-41.0 (5 specimens).

Identification. Coloration varies from olive-brown to greyish, rarely reddish-brown. Underfur reddish-brown. Face, ears, feet and much of tail blackish. There are usually but not always three fine dark stripes or series of close, dark spots extending along the midline from the neck to the base of the tail. Unlike Small-toothed Palm Civets elsewhere, Bornean individuals normally do not have a pale stripe down the nose. Females have two pairs of mammae. **Similar species:** the Common Palm Civet has a shorter tail, is stockier and less agile, has a smaller skull but relatively larger teeth (Figure 35), and females have three pairs of mammae.

Ecology and Habitat. Usually nocturnal and arboreal, rarely descending to the ground. Very agile. Diet includes fruits and small animals. Occurs in tall and secondary forests.

Distribution. Northest India, South-east Asia through southern China, Sumatra, Java. **Borneo:** *A. t. stigmatica.* Recorded from many localities in the lowlands and hills, but apparently less common than the Common Palm Civet. Up to 1500 m on G. Kinabalu.

BANDED PALM CIVET   *Hemigalus derbyanus*   Plate 48

Measurements. HB 500-565, T 300-365, HF 72-88 (13 specimens).

Identification. Buffy grey to reddish brown, with distinct dark brown or black bars across the back and stripes on the face. Tail mostly dark brown, banded only at the base. **Similar species:** the Banded Linsang, *Prionodon linsang*, is smaller, with an entirely banded tail and spots on the body in addition to barring.

Ecology and Habitat. Nocturnal. Travels and feeds mainly on the ground but sleeps in holes either in the ground or in trees. Diet includes earthworms, insects and other small animals, both invertebrate and vertebrate. Occurs in tall and secondary forests.

Distribution. Peninsular Burma, Thailand and Malaysia; Sumatra. **Borneo:** *H. d. boiei.* Recorded in many localities in the lowlands and hills. Together with the Malay Civet, the most commonly encountered viverrid in the forests of Sabah. Up to 1200 m on G. Dulit.

HOSE'S CIVET   *Hemigalus hosei*   Plate 48

Measurements. HB 472-540, T 298-335, HF 74-78 (3 specimens).

Identification. Upperparts dark brown; underparts white. Feet partly webbed with patches of hair between the footpads. **Similar species:** the Otter-civet, *Cynogale bennettii,*has dark underparts and a short tail; the Yellow-throated Marten, *Martes flavigula,*lacks white markings on the nose and has a yellow or buff tinge on the throat.

Ecology and Habitat. Unknown. Probably nocturnal and mainly terrestrial. The long facial whiskers and hairs between the footpads suggest it may specialise in foraging for small animals in mossy boulders and streams. One stomach examined contained various small insects. Occurs in lower montane forests.

Distribution. Recorded only from Borneo in the mountains of the north-west, including G. Kinabalu and the Crocker Range above 1200 m in Sabah; the Kelabit uplands (above 1100 m), G. Dulit, G. Kalulung and G. Batu Song (at 600 m) in Sarawak.

OTTER-CIVET   *Cynogale bennettii*   Plate 46

Measurements. HB 575-680, T 120-205, HF 102-110 (Peninsular Malaysian and Thai specimens).

Identification. Entirely dark brown, with faint grey grizzling and pale underfur; lips prominent, broad and white, with very long whiskers; a faint pale spot above each eye. Ears small. Feet with partial webbing between the digits. **Similar species:** Hose's Civet, *Hemigalus hosei*, has a long tail, larger ears and white underparts; otters have longer, tapering tails, a pale chin and throat, no white on the muzzle or above the eyes; the Flat-headed Cat, *Felis planiceps*, is paler with white on the chin and chest, and a short, slender muzzle.

Ecology and Habitat. Little known. Terrestrial and aquatic. Diet includes aquatic animals. Occurs in tall and secondary forests.

Distribution. North Vietnam, Peninsular Thailand and Malaysia, Sumatra, **Borneo:** *C. b.bennettii.* Recorded from scattered localities throughout most of the area including Sepilok, the middle S. Kinabatangan, Tabin, Kalabakan and Sapulut in Sabah; Tasik Merimbun in Brunei; the Kelabit uplands, S. Baram, upper S. Rajang and Mukah in Sarawak; upper S. Kapuas, Simpang and S. Kendawangan in West Kalimantan; Peleben and near Sangkulirang in East Kalimantan.

SHORT-TAILED MONGOOSE *Herpestes brachyurus* Plate 49

Measurements: HB 380-445, T 205-250 (less than 55% of HB), HF 75-86 (8 specimens).

Identification. Entirely blackish-brown with orange speckling, except chin and throat which are pale brown. Head and tail somewhat paler than body. Orange speckling clear at close range but indiscernible from a distance. **Similar species:** Hose's Mongoose, *H. hosei,* is very similar, but possibly smaller and more reddish-distinguished with certainty only by the shape of the coronoid process of the jaw bone (Figure 36); the Collared Mongoose, *H. semitorquatus,* has a longer tail and clear area of yellowish on the underside of the head and neck.

Ecology and Habitat. Mainly diurnal and terrestrial. Diet includes arthropods and small vertebrate animals. Occurs in tall and secondary forests. Sometimes enters plantations and gardens.

Distribution. Peninsular Malaysia, Palawan, Sumatra. **Borneo:** *H. b. rajah.* Recorded in lowlands and hills throughout the area and up to 1500 m in the upper S. Padas in Sabah.

Figure 36. Lower mandible of mongooses, showing coronoid process:
    a) *Herpestes hosei,*
    b) *H. brachyurus*

 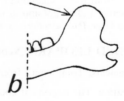

HOSE'S MONGOOSE   *Herpestes hosei*   Plate 49

Measurements. Skull: gl 83, width 46.

Identification. Known from only one (adult female) specimen. Similar to the Short-tailed Mongoose, *H. brachyurus*, but hair shorter and more reddish-brown; claws straighter and more slender; skull smaller with a less rounded coronoid process on the lower jaw (Figure 36).

Ecology and Habitat. Unknown.

Distribution. Only known specimen collected in the Baram district, Sarawak, in 1893.

COLLARED MONGOOSE   *Herpestes semitorquatus*   Plate 49

Measurements. HB 400-455, T 258-303 (over 60% of HB), HF 82-93 (4 specimens).

Identification. Reddish-brown, with fine yellow markings on the back. Lower parts of legs blackish-brown. Underside of head and neck distinctly yellowish. **Similar species:** the Short-tailed Mongoose, *H. brachyurus*, has a shorter tail, is darker coloured and lacks the yellowish neck coloration.

Ecology and Habitat. Mainly terrestrial. Diurnal and probably also nocturnal. Diet includes small animals. Occurs in tall and secondary forests, mixed tree plantations and partially cultivated areas.

Distribution. Sumatra. **Borneo:** *H. s. semitorquatus*. Recorded from scattered localities in the lowlands and hills, including the Sandakan region, Kalabakan and south-western Sabah; most parts of Sarawak (up to 1200 m on G. Dulit); Sukadana in West Kalimantan; Kumai in Central Kalimantan; Badang in East Kalimantan

Family FELIDAE   Cats

All the Bornean wild cat species are basically similar to the domestic cat in body form and have 28-30 teeth. They are distinguished mainly by size, tail length and coloration. All cats have four toes on the hind feet and five on the front feet, but the inner front toe is small and leaves no impression on the ground. The claws are retractile, and do not appear in footprints. There is no definite evidence that either the Tiger, *Panthera tigris*, or the Leopard, *Panthera pardus*, occur in Borneo.

CLOUDED LEOPARD *Neofelis nebulosa*   Plate 50

Measurements. Total length from nose to tip of tail 1.5 m or more.

Identification. The largest cat known to occur in Borneo. Varies from very pale sandy brown to very dark. Almost always has a pattern of cloud-like markings on the sides of the body — totally black specimens have been reported but not confirmed. The upper canines are very large relative to the skull with a clear gap between them and the cheek teeth. **Similar species:** the Marbled Cat, *Felis marmorata*, and other cats are smaller; the Binturong, *Arctictis binturong*, is sometimes mistaken for a black Clouded Leopard, but has long shaggy hair, ear tufts, no coat pattern and a prehensile tail.

288

Ecology and Habitat. Mainly nocturnal and arboreal, but sometimes active during the day. In logged forest, often travels on the ground. Diet includes pigs, deer, monkeys, Orang-utans and smaller mammals. Occurs in tall and secondary forests, sometimes in mangrove; rarely enters plantations.

Distribution. From the Himalayas, southern China and Taiwan south to Peninsular Malaysia, Sumatra. **Borneo:** *N. n. diardi.* Recorded from many scattered localities including the Crocker Range, G. Madalon, Sugut, Sepilok, Tabin, upper S. Segama and Kalabakan in Sabah; many parts of Sarawak; S. Kendawangan in West Kalimantan; upper S. Kahayan in Central Kalimantan; the Kutai region in East Kalimantan. Up to 1500 m on G. Dulit.

MARBLED CAT *Felis marmorata*   Plate 50

Measurements HB 465-490, T 480-495, HF 118-122, Wt 2425-2492 (2 specimens).

Identification. Brownish with black markings, similar in pattern to the Clouded Leopard, *Neofelis nebulosa*, but black-edged blotches on sides of body less distinct and black spots on legs more numerous. Fur soft and thick. **Similar species:** the Clouded Leopard, *Neofelis nebulosa*, is much larger.

Ecology and Habitat. Nocturnal. Arboreal and terrestrial. Diet includes rats. Occurs in tall and secondary forests.

Distribution. Mainland Asia from the Himalayas south to Peninsular Malaysia and Sumatra. **Borneo:** *F. m. marmorata*. Recorded from the Sandakan Bay area, the upper S. Kinabatangan, Kretam and Danum Valley in Sabah; Kuching and Miri in Sarawak; Purukcahu in Central Kalimantan.

BAY CAT *Felis badia*   Plate 50

Measurements. (prepared skins) HB 630-690, T 370-430 (about 60% of HB), HF 120-140 (2 specimens).

Identification. Entire body reddish or dark grey. Few specimens are recorded and it is unclear whether the colour phases are distinct, or represent extremes in a broad range of colour variation. A grey specimen in the British Museum has blackish hair with pale tips on the upperparts merging to reddish and buff on the underparts. Usually has three dark stripes on top of head in both colour forms. **Similar species:** the Flat-headed Cat, *F. planiceps*, has a short tail and white on the chin and chest.

Ecology and Habitat. Unknown.

Distribution. Restricted to Borneo and recorded only from S. Baram, "Entoyat" (probably Long Tuyut on S. Tinjar) and Kuching in Sarawak; upper S. Mahakam in East Kalimantan. One unconfirmed sight record from G. Kinabalu at 1800 m.

FLAT-HEADED CAT *Felis planiceps*   Plate 50

Measurements. HB 446-505, T 130-170 (27-34% of HB), HF 95-107 (6 specimens).

Identification. Appears brownish at a distance, but hair of upperparts brown with fine grey and pale buff speckling. Chin and chest white. Ears small; top of head long and flattened. **Similar species:** the Bay Cat, *F. badia*, has a relatively long tail and lacks white on the chin and chest; the Otter-Civet, *Cynogale bennettii*, is darker and has a very broad muzzle.

Ecology and Habitat. Nocturnal and terrestrial. Probably feeds mainly on fish. Occurs in tall and secondary forests.

Distribution. Peninsular-Thailand and Malaysia, Sumatra. **Borneo:** Recorded from the Sandakan area in Sabah; Tasek Merimbun in Brunei; many parts of Sarawak; several areas in West Kalimantan; South Kalimantan.

LEOPARD CAT *Felis bengalensis*   Plate 50

Measurements. HB 400-435, T. 175-220, HF 100-115 (2 specimens).

Identification. Reddish- or yellowish-buff, with black spots over entire upperparts including tail. **Similar species:** the Marbled Cat, *F. marmorata,* has a different pattern of markings, not just spots; the Banded Linsang, *Prionodon linsang,* is smaller with a different shape, and has a relatively thick tail with bands, not spots, along the entire length.

Ecology and Habitat. Usually nocturnal and terrestrial, but sometimes active in small trees. Diet includes small mammals and large insects. Occurs in forests, plantations and gardens.

Distribution. Northern India to eastern Asia and Siberia, Taiwan, southeast Asia, Sumatra, Java, Bali, Palawan. **Borneo:** *F. b. borneoensis.* Recorded from most areas including some towns.

DOMESTIC CAT *Felis catus*   not illustrated

Measurements. HB about 400-500, T variable, often short and bent.

Identification. Coloration variable, often white with irregular orange patches. Unlike wild cats, feral Domestic Cats rarely flee from people and are often seen during the day. **Similar species:** wild cats have a regular symmetrical coat pattern and are usually very shy of people.

Ecology and Habitat. Always associated with Man. Domestic Cats abandoned in disused temporary settlements fare much better than Domestic Dogs in the same situation and tend to stay near the old buildings, feeding on a variety of small animals.

Distribution. World wide. **Borneo:** found near most human settlements.

Order SIRENIA
Family DUGONGIDAE

Sea Cows
Dugongs

The order Sirenia contains two families: the Trichechidae, found in the Americas, and the Dugongidae in Africa, Asia and Australasia. Like the Cetaceans, they are adapted to a life completely in the water, but they appear to be have evolved separately. Sirenians live in shallow coastal seas, feeding only on plant material. The fore-limbs are flippers and there is a tail flipper or fluke, but no dorsal fin. In adult Dugongs there is only one pair of tusk-like incisors in the upper jaw and none in the lower jaw. There are no canines or premolars, but a total of 10 to 12 molars, only some of which are visible at one time; the deeper ones replace the top ones as they wear out.

DUGONG   *Dugong dugon*   **Plate 43**

Measurements. TL 2.5-3.0 m. Wt 150-250 kg.

Identification. Coloration usually dull brownish-grey. Has a few sparsely scattered hairs on body and stiff bristles on upper lip. Head broad and rounded, with the mouth on the underside. Unlike most cetaceans of similar size, the Dugong has two nostrils and no dorsal fin. Less active than most small cetaceans.

Ecology and Habitat. Usually rests during the day in deep water and feeds on sea grasses and other vegetation in shallow waters at night. Usually found in small groups, which are believed to travel long distances between feeding areas.

Distribution. Seas off East Africa through India, Sri Lanka, South-east Asia, Indonesia, Philippines, New Guinea and northern Australia. **Borneo:** Recorded off Kudat and the north-east coast, in Sandakan Bay, Semporna and near Kota Kinabalu in Sabah; near Lawas in Sarawak (though not recently); Kotawaringin in Central Kalimantan; Samarinda in East Kalimantan. Very few recent records, and possibly approaching extinction in Borneo.

Order PROBOSCIDEA
Family ELEPHANTIDAE

Elephants

There are two living species of elephants: the larger one in Africa, the smaller one now restricted to scattered parts of Asia. The Asian Elephant is the largest land mammal in Borneo, although adults appear to be slightly smaller than those in mainland Asia. There are two sorts of teeth: the tusks and the cheek teeth. The Asian Elephant posesses six sets of four cheek teeth during its lifetime, but only one set at a time, each set being shed when it is no longer functional. The last set emerges at an age of about forty years. Even within its restricted distribution in Sabah, the population is concentrated in flat, fertile areas and comes into conflict with Man by feeding on agricultural crops, particularly palms.

ASIAN ELEPHANT   *Elephas maximus*   **Plate 51**

Measurements. Height: 1.7-2.6 m (12 adult males), 1.5-2.2 m (5 adult females). Most adult males have tusks 0.5-1.7 m long weighing 1.5-15.0 kg each (12 specimens). Most adult females lack tusks or have very short tusks which do not protrude beyond the lips. There are no recorded weights for Bornean Elephants, but adults are unlikely to exceed 3000 kg.

Identification. Distinctive shape with long trunk. Generally grey-brown, but paler when dry and blackish when wet. Infants are covered in black bristly hair.

Ecology and Habitat. Mostly active from about two hours before dusk until two hours after dawn. Diet consists mainly of tender parts of monocotyledonous plants, including soft grasses, the growing parts of palms and banana stems. Fruits and the bark of latex-producing trees are also eaten but only in relatively small quantities. Water and minerals are important to Elephants, and this species' distribution in Sabah is closely correlated with permanent supplies of both resources. Groups usually contain between three and forty individuals, although larger groups up to one hundred are sometimes reported. Groups split and merge, but normally contain one or more adult females with young of both sexes and various ages. Adult males occur loosely attached to herds or as solitary individuals or in groups of two or three. Elephants occur in dipterocarp forests, and sometimes enter swamp forests and nipah to feed. They travel through and feed in gardens and plantations mainly at night or during rainy weather. They can swim across rivers.

Distribution. Once widespread but now restricted to parts of India, Sri Lanka, Burma, Thailand, Indochina, Peninsular Malaysia, Sumatra. **Borneo:** *E. m. sumatrensis:* Occurs only between S. Sugut in north-eastern Sabah and S. Sembakung in northern East Kalimantan. Exterminated from the Tawau-Semporna area and the Sandakan peninsula during the past two decades. Most of the population occurs between S. Labuk and north of a line between the upper S. Kuamut and T. Darvel. Prior to 1983, small groups of Elephants only rarely crossed the S. Labuk, but larger numbers now appear to be moving northwards as a result of rapid forest clearance for agriculture south of the river. The population in Sabah is estimated at 500-2000, but is decreasing rapidly with loss of habitat. The Elephant may have been introduced to Borneo, possibly several hundred years ago by the Sultan of Sulu. The peculiarly restricted distribution, lack of fossil remains and lack of indigenous names for the Elephant elsewhere in Borneo lend support to this theory. However, they are restricted to the region with the most fertile soils and abundant natural mineral sources and the lowest population of indigenous hunting peoples. As there are authentic reports of people in the past killing elephants only with spears both on the upper S. Kinabatangan and near Semporna, it is conceivable that Elephants are native but restricted in range by availability of minerals and prolonged hunting pressure.

Order PERISSODACTYLA   Odd-toed Ungulates

Members of this order are large herbivorous mammals with one or three toes on each foot, each with a hard hoof (except tapirs which have four toes on the front foot). The stomach is rather small and simple, while the caecum (large intestine) is large.

Domesticated horses (family Equidae), with one large hoofed toe, were present on the north-west coast of Sabah before the first recorded European contact with this area, but none have gone wild.

The Malay Tapir, *Tapirus indicus* (family Tapiridae), was present in Borneo up to at least 8000 years ago, as shown by fossils from Niah Caves in Sarawak. However, there are no authenticated records of this species in recent historical times, despite some unconfirmed reports. The reason for its apparent extinction in Borneo is unknown. The Malay Tapir is about 1 m tall at the shoulder, with an elongated, flexible nose. The head, legs and foreparts of the body are black in the adult while the remainder of the body is white. If the species does still exist, it is most likely to be detected by the footprints, which closely resemble those of the Asian Two-horned Rhinoceros, *Dicerorhinus sumatrensis*, but have somewhat more pointed toes and do not exceed about 17 cm in total width. The fourth toe on the front foot often does not show up in the footprint. The ecology and habitat of the Malay Tapir are very similar to that of the Asian Two-horned Rhinoceros; however, although the Malay Tapir often walks and bathes in streams, it does not wallow in mud pools.

Family RHINOCEROTIDAE   Rhinoceros

Rhinoceroses are characterised by a large, stocky body; short, stout legs with three toes on each foot; and either one or two horns made of compacted hairs on top of the muzzle. The rhinoceros family has a long fossil history and of the five living species (two in Africa and three in Asia), the species found in Borneo most closely resembles the primitive forms found in Europe about 30 million years ago. There appears to have been a relatively recent decrease in body size of Bornean rhinos. Bones from Niah caves in Sarawak, which are less than 30,000 years old, are significantly larger than those of living rhinos. All rhinos have been persecuted for their horns and other parts of the body which are falsely believed to have medicinal properties.

Only one species of rhinoceros now occurs in Borneo, but fossil remains of the Lesser One-horned (Javan) Rhinoceros, *Rhinoceros sondaicus*, have been found in Madai cave in south-eastern Sabah, dating from about 10,000 years ago.

ASIAN TWO-HORNED (SUMATRAN) RHINOCEROS
Dicerorhinus sumatrensis   Plate 51

Measurements. Height at shoulder about 1.2-1.3 m. HB about 2.5 m.

Identification. General coloration usually dark brown, but appearance may vary after bathing in water or mud. Hairy, especially when young, but hairs often not apparent in the field. Front horn rarely exceeds 30 cm in length, smaller in females than·in males. Rear horn normally very short, sometimes hardly projecting above the level of the skin; often not visible in the field. Presence usually detected by tracks: footprints of adults on firm soil 18.5-23.5 cm across at widest point, showing 3 clear toe marks. Mud wallows can be distinguished from those of Bearded Pigs, *Sus barbatus*, by the clear, deep horn marks in the sides of the wallow. Dung consists of balls of coarsely chopped woody material about 9 cm in diameter, usually found in small piles, sometimes in mounds frequently used over long periods. When disturbed unexpectedly, this Rhinoceros usually flees rapidly, sometimes giving a series of short, hoarse barks. **Similar species:** Bearded Pigs, *Sus barbatus,* have slender legs, a large head relative to the body and two-hoofed footprints; adult

Malay Tapir, *Tapirus indicus*, and Lesser One-horned Rhinoceros, *Rhinoceros sondaicus* (not presently known to occur in Borneo) have footprints which are respectively smaller and larger.

Ecology and Habitat. Mainly active from late afternoon to mid morning. Usually rests during the hot hours of the day in a mud wallow, shaded spot or ridge top. Feeds on mature leaves and twigs from a wide range of woody plants including saplings, lianas and small trees, which may be pushed over to obtain the leaves. Occasionally eats fallen fruits. Natural mineral sources are visited and all accurate records of rhinos in Sabah are within 14 km of a mineral source. Occurs in tall and secondary forests, including very steep areas. Rarely comes out into open areas.

Distribution. Once widespread through mainland South-east Asia. Now known definitely only from Peninsular Malaysia and Sumatra. **Borneo:** *D. s. harrissoni.* Recorded in recent years only from the eastern half of Sabah, with a small breeding population surviving in Tabin Wildlife Reserve. There may still be scattered individuals in the remote interior of other parts of Borneo. Old records cover all parts of Sabah; scattered parts of Sarawak; G. Liang Kubung and southern parts of West Kalimantan; upper S. Kahayan in Central Kalimantan; and the S. Telen region in East Kalimatan. Rhinoceroses appear to have disappeared from most parts of Borneo as a result of hunting over thousands of years and particularly over the past one hundred years.

Order ARTIODACTYLA   Even-toed Ungulates

The even-toed ungulates are terrestrial mammals with two functional hoofed toes and two small dew toes on each foot. The dew toes are situated well above the main toes and, except in pigs, appear in foot prints only in soft soil or mud. Most species feed only on plant material. The stomach is rather large and complex, with 2 or 3 chambers in pigs, 3 in mouse-deer and 4 in other species. The caecum is small. All Bornean artiodactyls (except pigs) are classed as ruminants — food is partially digested in the stomach and then brought back up into the mouth for further chewing one or more times. This permits the maximum amount of nutrition to be extracted from vegetation containing a large proportion of indigestible material. It also permits ruminants to ingest large amounts of food quickly and move to sheltered places, better protected against predators, for processing.

In comparison to many other regions of the world, both tropical and temperate, Borneo has rather few species of artiodactyls; and even among the species that do occur, population densities are low. Bornean forests, despite their dense and diverse vegetation cover, may not produce very much plant material suitable for ruminants. To support large populations of artiodactyls, plants must not only have a high productivity (that is, a fast growth rate) but also be fairly free of digestion-inhibiting substances such as fibre and tannins, and be available to animals no more than one or two metres above the ground. In Bornean forests, most plants are high in fibre and tannins, and most leafy material is situated well above the ground. Grasses, herbs and shrubs edible to ruminants are very scarce inside forests and occur abundantly only on river banks and cultivated land. Another factor possibly contributing to the rarity in Borneo of all large terrestrial mammals is the scarcity of minerals. Soils in many regions of Borneo are very poor in minerals, and supplementary sources such as salt water springs and mud volcanoes are patchy in distribution.

Unlike other artiodactyls, pigs have incisors in the upper jaw and an omnivorous diet, including animal material. Only the Bearded Pig, *Sus barbatus,* occurs wild in Borneo. The Domestic Pig is believed to have been bred from the Common Wild Pig, *Sus scrofa,* of mainland Asia.

Figure 37. Skull of a Bearded Pig. *Sus barbatus.*

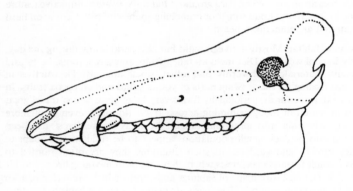

BEARDED PIG   *Sus barbatus*   Plate 51

Measurements. (adult males) HB 1365-1520, T 225-260, HF 277-320 (9 specimens); (adult females) HB 1220-1475, T 170-250, HF 265-290 (11 specimens). Wt in both sexes usually 57-83 kg, up to 120 kg or more when fat. Height at shoulder about 90 cm in both sexes.

Identification. Coloration variable: young pigs blackish; adults paler, from reddish brown or yellow-grey to almost buffy white. Colour of mud wallow also affects apparent colour of pigs.Head long with a "beard" of bristles along the lower jaw and a fleshy protuberance above each side of the mouth with upward-pointing bristles. Body size varies greatly with food supply. Females with five pairs of mammae. Foot prints more rounded and symmetric than those of deer, with imprints of the dew toes apparent even on hard ground. Mud wallows are a distinctive feature of Bearded Pig activity. Loud snorts or crunching sounds (of pigs feeding on hard plant material) are sometimes heard.

Ecology and Habitat. Mostly active at night but also periodically during the day, especially in cool weather. Diet includes fallen fruits and seeds, roots, herbs and other plant material, earthworms and other small animals. Destructive in plantations, feeding on the growing parts of young palms and on cocoa fruits. In regions of extensive forest, periodically forms very large herds which travel great distances in search of food, swimming acrosss rivers (formerly even to offshore islands) and climbing into mountain ranges. In areas where forest has been fragmented into patches, small populations appear to be resident and adapt to secondary growth and gardens. In such situations they are often hunted to extinction. Adult females make nests where they give birth to young (from 3 to 11) at one time). The nests are made of saplings and shrubs which are bitten or torn off and piled up on the ground. These nests are made on sites not liable to flooding, usually on broad ridge-tops but also on raised patches of ground in swamp forests. Males and immatures may sometimes make nests, but no other Bornean animal makes a similar nest.

Distribution. Peninsular Malaysia, Sumatra, larger adjacent islands and the Philippines. **Borneo:** *S. b. barbatus.* Recorded throughout the area including many offshore islands.

DOMESTIC PIG *Sus scrofa*   Plate 60

Measurements. Height up to about 60 cm.

Identification. Fat, with short legs. General coloration grey-black, often with whitish legs and top of muzzle. **Similar species:** the Bearded Pig, *Sus barbatus* is larger with longer legs and a more massive bristly muzzle.

Ecology and Habitat. Feeds on roots, including grass roots and other vegetable and animal matter. Associated with settlements; no truly feral Domestic Pigs have been reported.

Distribution. Worldwide, at least in the domestic state. **Borneo.** Occurs in many coastal and inland settlements.

Family TRAGULIDAE   Mouse-deer

Mouse-deer are small, forest-dwelling deer with slender legs and without antlers. The back is strongly arched. Individuals are sometimes reported with "horns", but these are probably the long canines which protrude out of the mouth from the upper jaw of males.

LESSER MOUSE-DEER   *Tragulus javanicus*   Plate 52

Measurements. HB 425-485, T 60-93, HF 125-148 (including hoof; 22 specimens). Wt 2.0-2.5 kg.

Identification. Overall appearance of upperparts plain reddish brown. Centre of nape usually darker than rest of body. Underparts white with a pale brownish tinge in the middle and distinctive dark brown markings on the throat and upper chest; in profile, white appears as a single line from chin to chest. *T. j. klossi* is said to have slightly duller coloration than *T. j. hosei*, without a bright reddish tinge, but the difference is not well marked. **Similar species:** the Greater Mouse-deer, *T. napu*, is larger, with flecked coloration on the upperparts and different throat markings.

Ecology and Habitat. Active periodically both during the night and day. Diet includes fallen fruits, leaf shoots and fungi. Usually solitary. Both adults and young rest in any sheltered spot under forest cover. Occurs in tall and secondary forests, sometimes entering gardens and mixed scrub.

Distribution. Southwest China, Indochina, Thailand, Peninsular Malaysia, Sumatra, Java and many adjacent islands. **Borneo:** Known mainly from lowland sites, usually below 100 m, with no records above 600 m. *T. j. klossi.* Occurs in Sabah and northern East Kalimantan. *T. j. hosei.* Occurs elsewhere on mainland Borneo and also P. Laut. *T. j. carimatae.* Found on P. Karimata and P. Panebangan.

GREATER MOUSE-DEER *Tragulus napu*   Plate 52

Measurements. HB 520-572,T 60-100, HF 140-157 (including hoof; 22 specimens). Wt 3.5-4.5 kg.

Identification. Hairs on upperparts grey-buff to orange-buff with blackish tips, giving a coarsely flecked overall appearance. Darker in midline and paler on sides of body, but without a distinct darkening on the nape. Intensity of coloration varies between individuals. Underparts white with a pale brownish tinge in the middle and distinctive dark brown markings on the chest; in profile, white on neck usually appears as two more-or-less separate bars. **Similar species:** the Lesser Mouse-deer, *T. javanicus*, is smaller, with relatively plain reddish-brown coloration and different throat markings.

Ecology and Habitat. Very similar to the Lesser Mouse-deer but appears to be more common in upland forest and rarer in flatlands. Occurs in tall and secondary forests, sometimes entering gardens.

Distribution. Indochina, Thailand, Peninsular Malaysia, Sumatra and many adjacent islands; southern Philippines. **Borneo:** *T. n. borneanus.* Occurs in all parts of Sabah, up to at least 1000 m in the upper S. Padas; Sarawak, including the Kelabit uplands; and many parts of Kalimantan. Also on P. Laut and P. Sebatik (at the Sabah-East Kalimantan border). *T. n. banguei.* P. Banggi. *T. n. sebucus.* P. Sebuku.

Family CERVIDAE   Deer

Males have distinctive antlers which are usually shed and regrown at regular intervals (probably annually). They are a form of bone and grow from permanent projections, pedicels, on the skull. In the Bornean Yellow Muntjac, *Muntiacus atherodes*, there is no obvious dividing point or burr between the pedicel and the antler, so it is possible that it never sheds its antlers. Muntjac, *Muntiacus* spp. walk with the head carried low, the back slightly arched and the hindquarters high, lifting the feet high off the ground at every step. Rusa, *Cervus* spp., walk with the head held high and the back fairly straight. Adult males of both species of muntjac have long upper canines which protrude beyond the lip and are loose in their sockets. A rattling noise, probably produced by these loose teeth, is sometimes heard from muntjac observed at close range.

Only two species of large deer (rusa) are known to have occurred in Borneo, but there are no recent records of one, the Javan Rusa, *Cervus timorensis*. Many hunters in Sabah and Sarawak believe there are two or even three species of large deer in northern Borneo. However, all Bornean antlers seen by us belong to Sambar Deer *Cervus unicolor*, and without firm evidence to the contrary, it seems likely that the different forms of deer reported by hunters represent not different species, but a range of variation within one species. Body size, coat colour and antler size can vary with age, diet, condition and time of year.

RED MUNTJAC (COMMON BARKING DEER) *Muntiacus muntjak*
(formerly included Muntiacus atherodes)   Plate 53

Measurements. HB 98-111 cm (4 specimens). Height at shoulder over 50 cm. Antler length 73-130 (24 adult specimens). Pedicel length 69-149 (24 adult specimens).

Identification. Upperparts reddish brown, somewhat darker along the midline; underparts whitish, often with a grey tinge. Tail dark brown above, white below. Males with rough antlers, bearing a small spike near the base and curving sharply near the tip. Pedicel thick and straight, with a burr where the antler joins. Young normally with white spots. Adult males and females give short, loud barking calls, a distinctive sound of forested hill ranges (probably indistinguishable from those of the Bornean Yellow Muntjac, *M. atherodes).* **Similar species:** the Bornean Yellow Muntjac is paler, the males with slender pedicels and tiny smooth antlers; female rusa, *Cervus* spp., are larger, duller coloured and walk with a different posture; mousedeer, *Tragulus* spp., have no antlers and are much smaller.

Ecology and Habitat. Probably similar to the Bornean Yellow Muntjac. Available data suggests that the Red Muntjac predominates in extensive hill and mountain ranges.

Distribution. Sri Lanka, India through southern China, Taiwan, South-east Asia, Sumatra, Java and some adjacent islands. **Borneo:** *M. m. pleiharicus.* Recorded from most parts of Borneo, including the Crocker Range, Poring and upper S. Segama in Sabah. Recorded at over 1000 m at Usun Apau in Sarawak.

BORNEAN YELLOW MUNTJAC *Muntiacus atherodes*
(formerly confused with *Muntiacus muntjac)* **Plate 53**

Measurements. HB 86-92 cm, T 14-20 cm, HF 26-29 cm (6 specimens). Height at shoulder up to 50 cm. Wt 13.5-17.7 kg (5 specimens). Antler length 16-42 (18 adult specimens). Pedicel length 65-87 (18 adult specimens).

Identification. Upperparts yellowish-red with diffuse brownish along the midline especially on the neck; underparts pale yellowish-orange to whitish. Tail dark brown above, white or buff below. Males with tiny, unbranched antlers on slender, curved pedicels, normally without any burr where the antler and pedicel join. Young have lines of white spots or blotches on the upperparts, a coloration retained until at least half adult size. Adults give short, loud barking calls (probably indistinguishable from calls of the Bornean Red Muntjac, *M. muntjac*). Adult females with young give short, high-pitched mewing calls. **Similar species:** the Bornean Red Muntjac, *M. muntjac,* is darker coloured, and males have larger antlers and pedicels; female rusa, *Cervus* spp. are larger, darker or duller coloured and walk with a different posture; mousedeer, *Tragulus* spp. have no antlers and are much smaller.

Ecology and Habitat. Active mainly during the day. Diet includes herbs, young leaves, grasses and fallen fruits and seeds (including those of dipterocarp trees). Often encountered as an adult male/female pair, sometimes alone. Available data suggests that this species predominates over the Red Muntjac in low hill ranges and coastal regions.

Distribution. Occurs only in Borneo, in all regions.

SAMBAR DEER (RUSA or PAYAU) *Cervus unicolor* **Plate 54**

Measurements. HB 154-204 cm, T 21-27 cm (6 specimens; mature males larger than females). Height at shoulder over 100 cm. Length of antlers along greatest curve 29-56 cm (22 specimens).

Identification. Upperparts generally grey-brown, with a variable degree of reddish coloration, usually darker along the midline; underparts pale brown to creamy-white. Tail bushy and entirely blackish. Adult males with long, coarse hair on the neck. Young sometimes with faint pale spots. One to two year old males have antlers with one point; three year old males have antlers with two points; older males have antlers with three or occasionally four, points. Inner branch of terminal fork of antler normally somewhat smaller than the outer, which appears to be a continuation of the main beam of the antler. Call is a distinctive yelp or shrill bark. **Similar species:** the Javan Rusa, *C. timorensis,* is very similar but has more white on the underparts, a thinner tail with a tuft of hair at the tip; unspotted young and different antler shape: the outer branch of the terminal fork is normally much smaller than the inner, which is clearly a continuation of the main beam of the antler.

Ecology and Habitat. Active mainly at night, also early morning and late afternoon. Diet includes grasses, herbs, shrubs, young leaves of woody plants and fallen fruits. Often visits natural mineral sources. Usually solitary, but groups of two or more are sometimes seen, consisting of adult male and female, female and young, or adult females. Nocturnal activity and solitary nature possibly a consequence of

299

heavy hunting pressure. Most common in secondary forests on gently sloping terrain, but also in tall dipterocarp forests on steep terrain and in swamp forests. Enters gardens and plantations to feed.

Distribution. Sri Lanka, India, southern China, South-east Asia, Philippines, Sumatra and many larger adjacent islands. **Borneo:** *C. u. brookei.* Recorded throughout the area including P. Banggi, P. Balembangan and P. Laut. Up to 1200 m in the upper S. Padas and 3000 m on G. Kinabalu in Sabah.

JAVAN RUSA   *Cervus timorensis*   Plate 54

Identification. Very similar to the Sambar Deer, *C. unicolor,* and positively distinguished only by the form of the antlers in the mature male (see above).

Ecology and Habitat. More adapted to open grassland than the Sambar Deer.

Distribution. Java, Sulawesi, Timor, New Guinea and many other islands in the central and eastern part of Indonesia. **Borneo:** *C. t. russa.* Recorded from South Kalimantan during the 19th century. Probably introduced from Java in the 17th century. Present occurrence unknown.

Family BOVIDAE   Cattle, Buffalo and Goats

This family contains cattle, buffalo, antelope, goats and sheep. All are characterised by horns which are never shed and which continue to grow as the animal gets older. Both males and females have horns in all of the species occuring in Borneo.

The Tembadau, *Bos Javanicus,* is the only species known to occur naturally in the wild in Borneo. Water Buffalo, *Bubalus bubalis,* and Cattle, *Bos indicus,* are probably all descended from domestic animals introduced to Borneo. A large goat-like animal with unbranched straight horns has been reported by road-builders in hills about 100 km north of Samarinda in East Kalimantan. If authentic, the report suggests the presence of the Serow, *Capricornis sumatraensis,* previously known only from mainland South-east Asia and Sumatra. This species is not to be confused with the Domestic Goat, *Capra aegagrus,* which is widespread wherever there are people.

TEMBADAU (BANTENG)   *Bos javanicus*   Plate 54

Measurements. Height at shoulder 120-170 cm, adult females smaller than adult males, more slender and with smaller horns.

Identification. Adult males black or blackish; adult females and young males reddish-brown. Both sexes with distinctive white buttocks and "stockings" on the lower part of the legs. **Similar species:** Water Buffalo, *Bubalus bubalis,* and Domestic Cattle, *Bos indicus,* lack white on the buttocks, although the domesticated form of the Tembadau, known as Bali Cattle, and some cross-breeds between Bali and other Domestic Cattle appear almost identical to wild Tembadau.

Ecology and Habitat. Mainly nocturnal, probably partly a result of hunting pressure. Diet mainly grasses, with some herbaceous and low woody vegetation. Visits natural mineral sources, including the sea. In eastern Sabah, most often encountered in groups of about 8-10 individuals, consisting of one mature male with mature females and young; sometimes solitary males, small groups and herds of up to about 40.

Prior to the 1940's, reported as common along the banks of most major rivers in eastern Sabah and in many areas of shifting cultivation in the west and north, even in interior hill ranges. The widespread use of guns led to rapid extermination from most areas. Now, locally common in logged forest on flatland, but again being exterminated as land is cleared for permanent agriculture. Occurs in dipterocarp, swamp and beach forests.

Distribution. Burma, Thailand, Indochina, Java. **Borneo:** *B. j. lowi:* occurs along S. Sugut, S. Kinabatangan, S. Segama, Kretam, Tabin and upper S. Padas in Sabah; Kutai and probably other scattered parts of Kalimantan; extinct in Brunei and no recent reports from Sarawak.

DOMESTIC CATTLE *Bos indicus* Plate 60

Identification. Size similar to Tembadau, *Bos javanicus*, males larger than females; horns generally shorter, thicker and straighter. A hump usually apparent above the shoulders in most Bornean varieties. Coloration variable.

Ecology and Habitat. Associated with many coastal and larger inland settlements. Diet mainly grasses.

Distribution. Throughout much of Asia. Relationship with European and African cattle uncertain.

WATER BUFFALO *Bubalus bubalis* Plate 60

Measurements. Height at shoulder 150-180 cm.

Identification. Entirely greyish, except for a pale shape usually present on the underside of the neck. Horns somewhat triangular in cross section. **Similar Species:** the Tembadau, *Bos javanicus*, has white buttocks and lower parts of the legs.

Ecology and Habitat. Truly wild Water Buffalo on mainland Asia are associated with grassland on alluvial soil; domestic Water Buffalo in Borneo occur in many coastal and larger inland communities.

Distribution. Originates from India and mainland South-east Asia. Now present in many parts of the world. **Borneo:** may be encountered anywhere near human settlement.

DOMESTIC GOAT *Capra aegagrus* Plate 60

Measurements. Height at shoulder up to 50 cm.

entification. Coloration variable, but most often an uneven pattern of brown and white. Horns (if present) curved backwards. **Similar Species:** the Serow, *Capricornis sumatraensis*, which may occur in Borneo, has straight horns and occurs far from human settlements.

Ecology and Habitat. Diet includes a wide range of leafy material. Often seen on roadside verges.

Distribution. Worldwide. **Borneo:** throughout the area wherever there are human settlements.

Appendix 1. Guide to footprints.

Even when mammals are not seen, the presence of some types can be verified by their footprints in soil or sand. In the case of large terrestrial mammals, species can be identified merely by inspection of the footprints. In the case of small mammals, prints can be used generally only as a guide to the family or order to which the mammal belongs. In part, this is because there are so many species with very similar footprints, but mainly because size and form of prints varies with condition of the soil or sand. If footprints are located under ideal conditions, some species may be identified by making plaster of Paris casts and comparing them with the prints of captive mammals or preserved specimens.

Some of the footprints illustrated in the following figures can be used merely as a guide to family or order, while others will be found useful in positive identification of species. Note that in conditions of deep, soft mud, such as river banks, footprints are often prominent and clear, but smaller than those illustrated here because the mud has caved inwards. In shallow mud on a hard substrate, such as on logging roads, however, footprints may be splayed such that they are larger than those illustrated. Prints in sand are likewise splayed, but unclear, so that identification is possible only for a few species of large mammals.

Without considerable study amd experience. probably only the following species can be identified reliably from footprints alone: Sun Bear, (Figure 40), Domestic Dog (Figure 45), Clouded Leopard (Figure 45) and ungulates illustrated in Figure 46. Only rarely are domestic ungulates found in situations where their footprints might be mistaken for those of wild species, but discussion with reliable local residents normally solves uncertain cases. Elephant footprints (not illustrated) are unmistakeable because of their rounded shape, with four nail-prints, and massive size (over 30 cm across in adults).

Note that among the carnivores, cats have four toe prints without any trace of claw marks (Figure 45). The footprints of feral domestic dogs (maximum width more than 40 mm across; Figure 45) and of the Malay Civet or Tangalung, *Viverra tangalunga*, (maximum width less than 35 mm across; not illustrated) have four toes each with a claw mark. The footprints of all other viverrids (Figures 43 and 44), and of all of the mustelids except the Small-clawed Otter (Figures 41 and 42), have five toes, each with a claw mark, always present although sometimes faint. Those of the Oriental Small-clawed Otter, *Aonyx cinerea*, (Figure 42), have five webbed toes without claw marks. Footprints of the Water Monitor Lizard, *Varanus salvator*, (not illustrated), common near water, may be distinguished from those of any similar sized mammal by the presence of five long, thin, clawed toes continuous with and not separated from the underside of the foot.

Among the even-toed ungulates, the dew toes are usually evident only in the footprints of pigs (arrowed in Figure 46), being absent from prints only of very lean pigs travelling on hard soil. In deep, soft mud, the dew toes often appear also in the footprints of mouse-deer, deer and Tembadau, while footprints of running ungulates in hard soil may show only the tips of the hoofs. The Bearded Pig has hoofs which are more rounded than those of the deer, while the hoofs of cervid deer are more pointed and more mobile than those of pigs, the two toes often appearing asymmetrical in deer prints in soft soil.

Figure 38. Footprints of some small mammals.

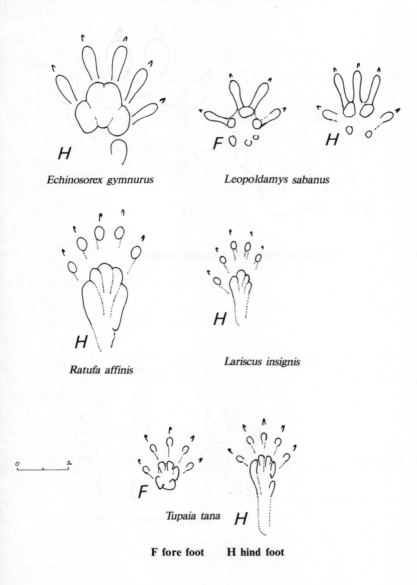

Echinosorex gymnurus

Leopoldamys sabanus

Ratufa affinis

Lariscus insignis

Tupaia tana

F fore foot   H hind foot

Figure 39. Footprints of porcupines.

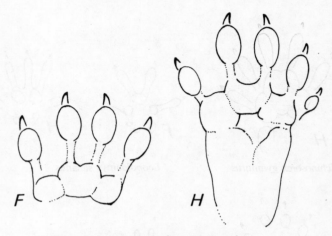

Hystrix brachyura and Thecurus crassipinis

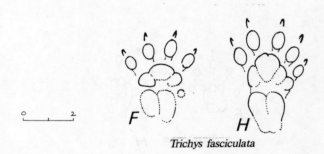

Trichys fasciculata

Figure 40. Hind footprint of a Sun Bear

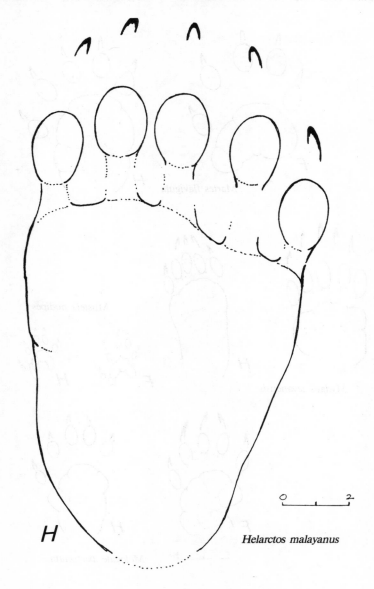

Helarctos malayanus

H

Figure 41. Footprints of mustelids.

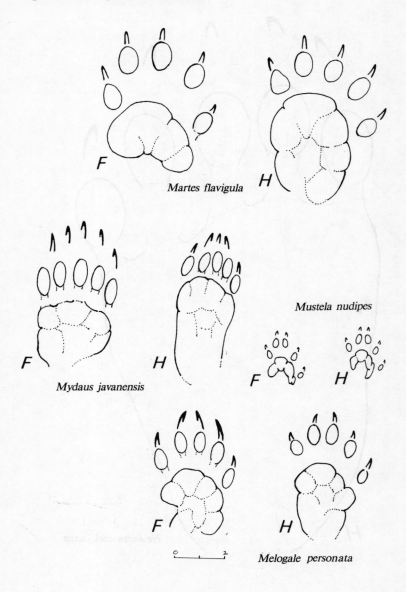

F

Martes flavigula H

Mustela nudipes

F

Mydaus javanensis H

F H

F H

Melogale personata

Figure 42. Footprints of otters.

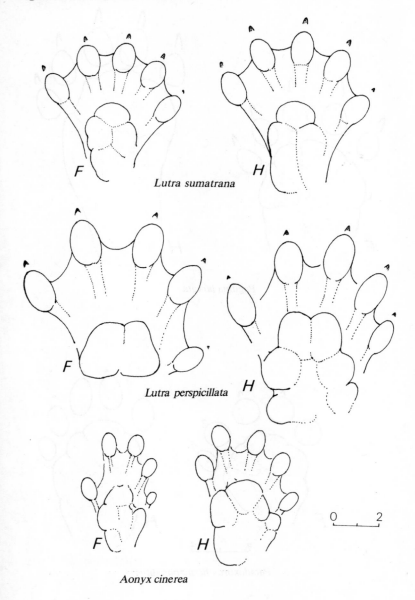

Lutra sumatrana

Lutra perspicillata

Aonyx cinerea

Figure 43. Footprints of viverrids.

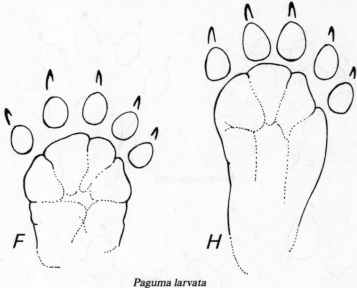

Paguma larvata

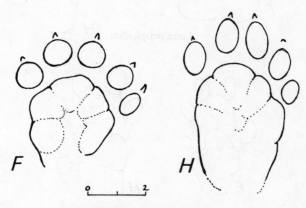

Paradoxurus hermaphroditus

Figure 44. Footprints of viverrids.

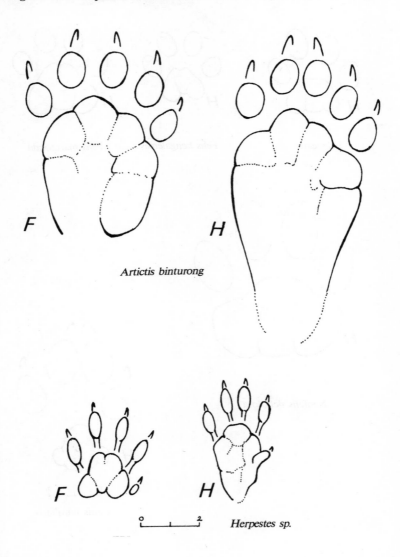

Artictis binturong

Herpestes sp.

Figure 45. Footprints of wild cats and domestic dog.

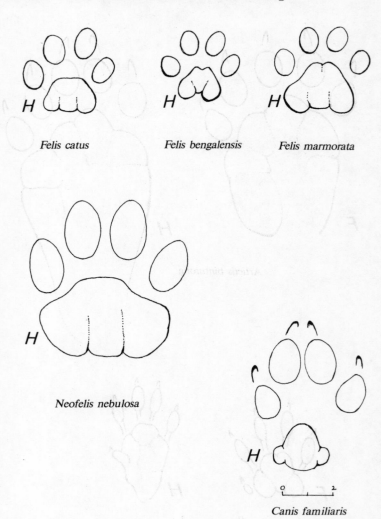

Felis catus

Felis bengalensis

Felis marmorata

Neofelis nebulosa

Canis familiaris

Figure 46. Footprints of ungulates.

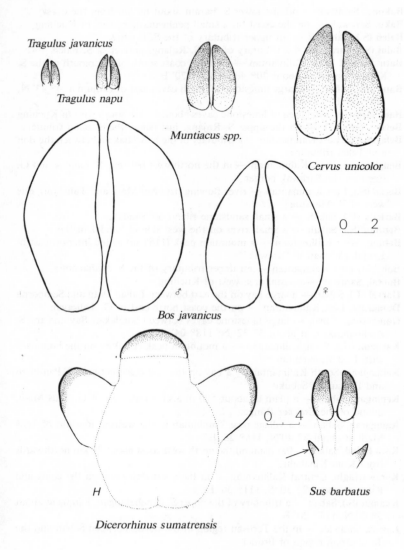

Tragulus javanicus

Tragulus napu

Muntiacus spp.

Cervus unicolor

Bos javanicus

Dicerorhinus sumatrensis

Sus barbatus

311

Appendix 2. **Gazetteer** (Refer also to to Maps 1 and 5).

Bakong, Sarawak — off the lower S. Baram about 60 km from the coast

Bako, Sarawak — on the coast on a small peninsula northeast of Kuching

Baleh (S.), Sarawak — an upper tributary of the S. Rajang

Balui (S.), Sarawak — a tributary of the S. Rajang, upriver of S. Baleh

Batu Jurong, West Kalimantan — near the coast south of the mouth of the S. Kendawangan at about 20° 40' S, 110° 20' E

Baturong, Sabah — a large limestone hill with caves east of Danum at 4° 43' N, 118° 00' E

Bau, Sarawak — an area of limestone caves about 50 km south-west of Kuching

Belaga, Sarawak — on the upper S. Rajang, just below the S. Balui tributary

Belayan (S.), East Kalimantan — a tributary of the S. Mahakam between the Boh and Telen tributaries

Bengkayang, West Kalimantan — in the north-west between S. Landak and G. Pueh on the Sarawak border

Berau (S.), East Kalimantan — river flowing between Mara and Talisayan, due west of P. Maratua

Berhala (P.), Sabah — a small sandstone island off Sandakan

Betotan (S.), Sabah — a small river on the west side of Sandakan Bay

Betung, West Kalimantan — a mountain peak (1151 m) in the interior, east of Lanjak-Entimau in Sarawak

Boh (S.), East Kalimantan — an upper tributary of the S. Mahakam

Buntal, Sarawak — coastal area west of Kuching

Darvel (T.), Sabah — a large bay on the east between Lahad Datu and Semporna

Dumaring, East Kalimantan — on the coast north-east of G. Talisayan

Gomantong, Sabah — large limestone caves between Sandakan Bay and the S. Kinabatangan, at about 5° 32' N, 118° 04' E

Karimun (G.), West Kalimantan — a mountain peak (1960 m) on the boundary with East Kalimantan

Kelumpang, South Kalimantan — a bay on the east coast between T.Pamukan and P. Laut/P. Sebuku

Keningau, Sabah — a plain at about 500 m a.s.l. south-west of G. Trus Madi, inland of the Crocker Range.

Kaingaran, Sabah — a village near Tambunan in the western foothills of Trus Madi at about 5° 40'N, 116° 28' E

Kota Belud, Sabah — flat plain on the north-west coast about 80 km northwards from Kota Kinabalu

Kotawaringin, Central Kalimantan — in the southwest between the coast and Riam at about 2° 30' S, 111° 30' E

Kuamut (S.), Sabah — a tributary of the upper S. Kinabatangan, joining at about 5° 00'N, 117° 20' E

Lawas, Sarawak — in the Terusan region in the north, between Sabah and the Temburong region of Brunei

Limbang, Sarawak — between the two regions of Brunei

Long Petak, East Kalimantan — on the upper S. Telen at about 1° 40'N, 116° 20'E

Madai, Sabah — limestone caves on the east coast about 60 km south of Lahad Datu at about 4° 43' N, 118° 08' E

Martapura, South Kalimanatan — about 40 km east of Banjarmasin

Marudi, Sarawak — the largest town on the lower S. Baram, about 60 km from the coast

Marudu (T.), Sabah — the large bay east of the Kudat peninsula

Menggalong (S.), Sabah — a river in the south-west at about 5° N, 115° 30' E

Mentarang (S.), East Kalimantan — a river between S. Sembakung and S. Kayan

Merah, East Kalimantan — on the S. Telen, north-west of Kutai

Miri, Sarawak — a coastal town south of the S. Baram estuary

Muara, Brunei — the northern most peninsula in the western section of the state

Muara Ancalung, East Kalimantan — on the S. Telen, to the west of Kutai

Muara Teweh, Central Kalimantan — on the upper S. Barito between Tumband Maruwe and Buntuk

Mukah (S.), Sarawak — a river to the south-west of Balingian

Palung, West Kalimantan — a small coastal mountain south-east of T. Sukadena

Pangkalahan, South Kalimantan — inland from T. Kelumpang, between Pamukan and P. Laut/P. Sebuku

Pensiangan, Sabah — south of Sapulut, near the Sabah-Sarawak border, due south of G. Trus Madi

Pleihari, South Kalimantan — near the southern most tip of Borneo, about 80km south-east of Banjarmasin

Poring, Sabah — at 550 m in the eastern foothills of G. Kinabalu, on the south-eastern edge of Kinabalu Park

Puruk Cahu, Central Kalimantan — on the upper S. Barito between Muara Julai and Tumbang Maruwe, at about 0° 30' S, 114° 30' E

Ranau, Sabah — upland plain in the southern foothills of G. Kinabalu at 5° 57' N, 116° 40'E

Ritan (S.), East Kalimantan — a river at about 0° 40' N, 116° E

Sampit (S.), Central Kalimantan — a river between the S. Seruyan and S. Mendawai at about 2°- 3° S, 113° E

Samunsam, Sarawak — on the coast near the western most tip of the state, north-west of G. Pueh

Sandaran, East Kalimantan — the eastern most point of the province, south-east of Labuhan Kelambu

Santubong, Sarawak — to the west of Kuching

Sapulut, Sabah — interior region, south-west of the upper reaches of the S. Kinabatangan, at about 4° 40' N, 116° 30' E

Saribas (S.), Sarawak — a river about 60 Km to the north of Batang Lupar

Sebuku (S.), East Kalimantan — a river north of the Sembakung, at about 4° N

Segah (S.), East Kalimantan — a tributary of the S. Berau to the east of Badang

Segarong, Sabah — limestone caves north of Semporna at about 4° 35' N, 118° 26' E

Sepaku, East Kalimantan — inland from Balikpapan

Sibu, Sarawak — a town on the lower S. Rajang

Sidong (G.), Sarawak — a mountain about 80 km south-east of Kuching

Similajau, Sarawak — on the coast between Bintulu and Niah

Simpang, West Kalimantan — just inland from Sukadana at about 1° S, 110° 10' E

313

Sirik, Sarawak — a swampy headland of the S. Rajang estuary at about 2° 50' N, 11° 10' E

Sukau, Sabah — on the lower S. Kinabatangan at about 5° 32' N, 118° 17' E

Tenom, Sabah — a valley in the south-west between the Crocker Range and Witti Range at about 5° 10' N, 116° E

Tepadong, Sabah — limestone caves on the S. Segama at around 5° 7' N, 118° 8' E

Tingar (G.), West Kalimantan — a mountain between the S. Pasaguan and S. Kendawangan

Tuaran, Sabah — on the coast about 40 km north of Kota Kinabalu

Tutoh (S.), Sarawak — a tributary of S. Baram flowing from the Mulu area

Tutong (S.), Brunei — one of two main river systems in the west, into which drains Tasek Merimbun

Witti Range, Sabah — a low mountain range in the south-west between G. Trus Madi and the Sarawak

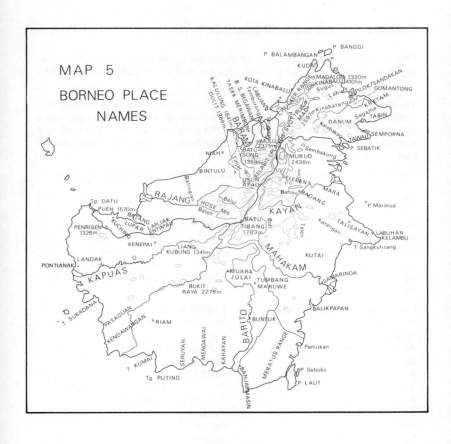

MAP 5
BORNEO PLACE
NAMES

315

Appendix 3. Local names of mammals

This list includes the local names of mammals in the major dialects of Sabah, Sarawak and Brunei including Malay. Names used in the Kalimantan provinces were not available to us.

The spelling of many local languages is not standardized, and several alternative spellings are possible. Some letters and sound combinations are often interchangeable, in particular: 'b' and 'v'; 'f' and 'p'; 'b', 'm', 'mb'. The spelling is generally phonetic, and most letters have a similar pronunciation to English, except that 'c' is pronounced 'ch' as in 'child'.

The following abbreviations have been used to indicate language groups:

Ma — Malay
Br — Brunei

Sabah:
Kz — Kadazan/Dusun
Lu — Lundayah
Mu — Murut
Sg — Sungai (including all east coast dialects
Su — Suluk

Sarawak:
Bi — Bidayuh
Ib — Iban
Ka — Kayan
Ke — Kenyah
Kl — Kelabit

Local name (language group)	English name
Aji Bulan (Ib)	Moonrat
Ambau (Su)	rats
Ambuk (Br, Su, Ib)	Long-tailed Macaque
Ancalau (Br)	muntjak
Angkalit (Br, Mu)	small bats
Angkis (Ib, Kz, Sg)	Moonrat or Long-tailed Porcupine
Apan (Lu, Kl)	Long-tailed Porcupine
Aram (Lu, Kl)	Pangolin
Asih (Mu)	Bearded Pig
Babi Hutan (Ma)	Bearded Pig
Babu or Babut (Kz)	Tufted Ground Squirrel
Bada (Kz)	Pig-tailed Macaque
Badak (Ma)	Rhinoceros
Badan (Kl)	Small-toothed Palm Civet
Bakaa (Kl, Lu)	Bearded Pig
Bakalo (Mu)	Proboscis Monkey
Bakara (Sg, Su)	Proboscis Monkey
Bakas (Kz, Sg)	Bearded Pig
Bambaras (Kz)	Tembadau
Bambun (Ma)	mongooses
Banggat (Ka, Mu)	Hose's Langur
Bangkahakun (Kz)	Sambar Deer
Bangkalit (Br, Mu)	small bats
Bangkatan (Kz, Br)	Proboscis Monkey
Bangkawat (Br, Mu)	Flying Fox
Basing (Br, Kz, Mu, Sg, Su)	squirrels

316

Basuk (Mu)	Pig-tailed Macaque
Bavui (Ka, Su)	Bearded Pig
Bawang (Kz, Mu, Sg)	Sun Bear
Bebas (Kz, Sg)	Long-tailed Porcupine
Bedah (Bi)•	large porcupines
Bedcuk (Lu, Kl)	Pig-tailed Macaque
Begah (Ka)	Giant Squirrel
Bekaleh (Lu)	Proboscis Monkey
Bekul (Ka)	Marbled Cat
Beliai (Kz)	Pigmy Squirrel
Belwot (Kz, Sg)	Sun Bear
Bengkong (Ka)	Slow Loris
Beraguk (Ib)	Yellow-throated Marten
Berang-berang (Ma)	otters
Berangad (Lu, Kl)	Hose's Langur
Beruang (Ma)	Sun Bear
Berud (Kz)	Long-tailed Giant Rat
Beruk ((Ma)	Pig-tailed Macaque
Berukuyan (Ka)	Long-tailed Macaque
Berukutan (Ka)	Pig-tailed Macaque
Bigok (Ib)	Silvered Langur
Bijit (Ib)	Banded Langur
Biladan (Kz, Sg)	Proboscis Monkey
Bilud (Kz, Sg)	Malay Badger
Binangkai (Mu)	Small-toothed Palm Civet
Bohukun (Kz)	Pangolin
Bongan (Sg)	Hose's Langur
Bongol (Kz)	otters
Buang (Ka, Kz)	Sun Bear
Budutlapad (Kz, Sg)	mongooses
Bufang (Kz, Sg)	Sun Bear
Bukah (Ka)	Long-tailed Porcupine
Bukkuh (Mu)	Pangolin
Bulukun (Kz, Mu)	Pangolin
Buri (Ke)	Moonrat
Bungat (Ka)	Banded Langur
Busan (Mu)	Common Palm Civet
Butun (Kz, Sg)	large porcupines
Cemaru (Ib)	Rhinoceros
Cikok (Ka)	Silvered Langur
Cit Tanah (Ib)	rats
Dangen or Dengen (Lu, Ka, Kl)	otters
Dengan Ruit (Kl)	Malay Badger
Dongol (Su)	otters
Dongon (Sg)	otters
Dumbang (Ib)	mongooses
Dungui (Mu)	Proboscis Monkey
Durui (Ka)	Moonrat
Empau (Ib)	Pig-tailed Macaque

Empliau (Ib)	Gibbon
Encalung (Br)	Tembadau
Encimbung (Br, Kz)	mongooses
Engkerabak (Ib)	Giant Squirrel
Engkerampu (Ib)	Tufted Ground Squirrel
Engkuli (Ib)	Clouded Leopard
Enturun (Ib)	Binturong
Falanuk (Lu)	mouse-deer
Fayur (Lu)	Sambar Deer
Fugah (Lu, Kl)	Slow Loris
Futun (Kz, Sg)	large porcupines
Gadingan (Sg)	Elephant
Gajah (Ma)	Elephant
Galing (Ib)	Masked Palm Civet
Gantadun (Kz)	muntjak
Gawir (Kz)	Flying Fox
Gebuk (Br, Kz, Mu, Sg)	Pig-tailed Macaque
Hangangan (Ka)	Yellow-throated Marten
Harimau Dahan (Ma)	Clouded Leopard
Havet (Ka)	Gibbon
Hawat (Ka)	Flying Fox
Hem (Ka)	Pangolin
Hikau (Ka)	Tarsier
Huko (Ka)	pigmy squirrels
Hulun (Ka)	Malay Civet
Ikau (Lu)	Tarsier
Impayutong (Kz, Sg)	Slow Loris
Inanasad (Kz, Sg)	Clouded Leopard
Induyutong (Kz)	Slow Loris
Ingkat (Ib)	Tarsier
Intambah (Ib)	Flying Fox
Ipos (Sg)	Clouded Leopard
Jani (Ib)	Bearded Pig
Jelu Labi (Ib)	Otter-Civet
Jelu Merah (Ib)	Maroon Langur
Jibalau (Mu)	Long-tailed Macaque
Jugam (Ib)	Sun Bear
Kahisan (Mu)	Tembadau
Kahui (Mu)	Orang-utan
Kaitan (Mu)	pigmy squirrels
Kakaa (Kz, Mu, Sg)	Yellow-throated Marten
Kala (Mu)	Long-tailed Macaque
Kalasiu (Ka, Kz, Sg)	Tembadau
Kalio (Lu)	Tembadau
Kalung (Ka)	large porcupines
Kamaya Panas (Ib)	Greater Mouse-deer
Kara (Kz, Sg)	Long-tailed Macaque
Karemuk (Mu)	large porcupines

318

Karui (Mu)	large porcupines
Kasui (Bi)	Malay Civet
Kedurau (Br, Kz, Sg)	Moonrat
Kelasi (Lu, Ka, Kl, Kz, Mu, Sg)	Maroon Langur
Kelawar (Ma)	bat
Kelawat (Br, Lu, Kl, Kz, Mu, Sg, Su)	Gibbon
Kelehiau (Ka)	Tembadau
Keleho (Ib)	Tembadau
Keluang (Ma)	Flying Fox
Kemancur (Mu)	Rhinoceros
Kera (Ma, Ib)	Long-tailed Macaque
Kera Hantu (Ma)	Tarsier
Kerampu (Ib)	Tufted Ground Squirrel
Kesindap (Ib)	small bats
Ketung (Ka)	large porcupines
Kijang (Ib, Ma, Sg)	muntjak
Kikok (Ma)	Hose's or Silvered Langur
Kilabas (Kz)	Small-toothed Palm Civet
Kimayok (Mu)	Elephant
Kisau (Sg)	Orang-utan
Kitan (Ka)	Binturong
Kogiu (Kz, Sg)	Orang-utan
Kolom (Br)	large porcupines
Kongkang (Ma)	Slow Loris
Koyut (Ka)	Pig-tailed Macaque
Kuang (Sg)	Giant Flying Squirrels
Kubung (Ma, Ib)	Flying Lemur or large flying squirrels
Kucing Batu (Ma)	wild cats
Kucing Hutan (Ma)	wild cats
Kuir (Lu, Kl, Mu)	Clouded Leopard
Kukom (Sg)	Slow Loris
Kukung (Ib)	Slow Loris
Kuleh (Ka)	Clouded Leopard
Kulus (Kz, Sg)	Bearded Pig
Kusing (Ib)	small fruit bats
Kuvung (Ka)	Flying Lemur
Kuyad (Lu, Kl)	Long-tailed Macaque
Labo (Lu, Kl)	squirrels
Labo Aping (Kl)	pigmy Squirrels
Lagoi (Kz)	Banded Palm Civet
Laket (Lu)	Lesser Mouse-deer
Lakud (Bi)	Tarsier
Lakuing (Br)	Clouded Leopard
Landak (Ma)	Porcupines
Langah (Kz)	Flying Lemur or flying squirrels
Latak (Sg)	Rhinoceros
Lavau (Ka)	rats
Lavau Siu (Ka)	Pentail Treeshrew

Liman (Sg)	Elephant
Linggahun (Kz)	shrews
Linsang (Sg, Su)	Tembadau
Lisis (Br, Kz, Mu, Sg)	Long-tailed Porcupine
Lisung (Sg)	Tembadau
Longkihai (Kz)	treeshrews
Longoun (Sg)	Rhinoceros
Lotung (Br, Mu)	Slow Loris
Lutung (Ma)	langurs
Maias (Bi, Ib, Lu)	Orang-utan
Makup (Ib)	Sun Bear
Malongkong (Mu)	Binturong
Manggas (Kz, Mu, Sg)	Giant Squirrel
Mangka (Ke)	Giant Squirrel
Mangkotong (Kz, Sg)	Pangolin
Manguluk (Kz)	Masked Palm Civet
Maragang (Kz, Br)	Maroon Langur
Masalong (Mu)	Tembadau
Mayau Tebiang (Ib)	wild cats
Mbegah (Ka)	Giant Squirrel
Memerang (Ma)	otters
Menaleh (Mu)	Yellow-throated Marten
Mihaun (Kz)	Common Palm Civet
Mondou (Kz, Sg)	Clouded Leopard
Mongkolom (Kz)	Mountain Giant Rat
Mongoluton (Kz)	Prevost's or Horse-tailed Squirrel
Monosop (Kz, Mu)	Hose's Langur
Montok (Kz)	small squirrels
Monyet (Ma)	monkey
Monyet Belanda (Ma)	Proboscis Monkey
Mowou (Mu)	treeshrews
Munin (Ka, Kz, Sg)	Common or Small-toothed Palm Civet
Munsang (Ib, Ma)	civets
Musang (Ma)	civets
Mutei (Ka)	treeshrews
Nanansad (Kz, Sg)	Clouded Leopard
Napu (Ma)	Large Mouse-deer
Ngale (Kl)	Malay Civet
Nyamuk (Ka)	Tufted Ground Squirrel
Nyumboh (Ib)	Long-tailed Macaque
Oho (Ka)	pigmy squirrels
Ompu (Kz, Sg)	wild cats
Omunin (Kz, Sg)	Common or Small-toothed Palm Civet
Opoyut (Mu)	Flying Lemur
Padungan Tana (Ka)	Banded Palm Civet
Palang Alud (Kl)	Banded Linsang
Pangkat Tekalung (Ib)	Banded Palm Civet
Pant (Ka)	Banded Langur

320

Paragasu (Kz, Sg)	Masked Palm Civet
Pas Daum (Bi)	Tufted Ground Squirrel
Pasiu *or* Pasui (Kz, Sg)	Binturong
Patut (Sg)	Sun Bear
Paus (Kz)	muntjak
Payau (Bi, Ib, Ka, Kz, Sg)	Sambar Deer
Payou (Kl, Kz, Sg)	Sambar Deer
Payuh (Lu, Kl)	Binturong
Pelandok (Ma)	mouse-deer
Pelanuak (Ib, Lu, Mu)	mouse-deer
Pelanuk (Ka, Kz, Kl, Lu, Sg)	mouse-deer
Pelanuk Balabug (Kz, Sg)	Greater Mouse-deer
Pelanuk Kuleh (Ka)	Greater Mouse-deer
Pelanuk Lireh (Ka)	Lesser Mouse-deer
Pelanuk Pipit (Kz, Sg)	Lesser Mouse-deer
Pelaring (Ka)	Common *or* Small-toothed Palm Civet
Pelih (Kl)	Tarsier
Pendulau (Mu)	Hose's Langur
Penyatat (Bi)	Banded Langur
Peruan (Mu)	mouse-deer
Perukah (Kz, Sg)	muntjak
Perut (Ka)	White-fronted Langur
Posis (Kz)	Malay Weasel
Puan (Ib)	White-fronted Langur
Pugah (Lu, Kl)	Slow Loris
Pukang (Bi, Ib)	pigmy squirrels
Pungit (Kz)	small bats
Purog (Sg)	muntjak
Pusa (Br)	Malay Weasel
Rabuan (Kl)	Masked Palm Civet
Ramo (Br)	Bearded Pig
Rasung (Ib)	Proboscis Monkey
Ringin (Ib)	otters
Rinukut (Kz, Sg)	Tarsier
Rongon (Kz, Sg)	otters
Rukut (Kz)	Tarsier
Runguyan (Kz)	Proboscis Monkey
Rusa (Ma)	Sambar Deer
Sadui (Su)	Malay Badger
Salom (Mu)	Prevost's Squirrrel
Sampong (Kz)	Hose's Langur
Sampuaŋ (Kz)	Prevost's Squirrel
Sangayan (Sg)	Long-tailed Macaque
Santabok (Br)	treeshrews
Sapuan (Kz)	Prevost's Squirrel
Saving Usung (Ka)	Masked Palm Civet
Sengangang (Ka)	Yellow-throated Marten
Sesir (Bi)	Slow Loris
Siga (Lu, Kl)	Giant Squirrel

Sikok (Sg)	Silvered Langur
Simpelili (Mu)	Tarsier
Sinang (Ib)	Malay Civet
Sindukutrukut (Kz)	Tarsier
Singgagar (Br)	Hose's Langur
Singgurutgurut (Kz)	Malay Civet
Singkak (Kz, Sg, Su)	Silvered Langur
Singyat (Ka)	Leopard Cat
Sinrurukut (Kz, Sg)	Tarsier
Sintukadtukad (Kz, Sg)	Banded Palm Civet
Sirukutrukut (Kz)	Tarsier
Sudu (Lu)	Malay Badger
Sungkog (Kz)	small flying squirrels
Tabangan (Sg)	Pig-tailed Macaque
Tabilig (Mu)	Gibbon
Tabirong (Br)	large otters
Tabuan (Sg)	Pangolin
Tagarog (Kz, Sg)	Hose's Langur
Tagaut or Tagawat (Kz)	Flying Lemur or giant flying squirrels
Talau (Mu)	rats
Talom (Kz)	wild cats
Tambang (Kz, Mu)	Sambar Deer
Tambayungan (Mu)	Rhinoceros
Tamdoh (Ka)	Rhinoceros
Tampak (Kz, Sg)	Rhinoceros
Tamparulik (Kz)	Moonrat
Tampu (Kz)	wild cats
Tanduyutong (Kz)	Slow Loris
Tangah (Kz)	Flying Lemur
Tangalung (Ma)	Malay Civet
Tangangansad (Kz)	Clouded Leopard
Tangkis (Kz)	treeshrews and small squirrels
Tantadburui (Kz)	treeshrews
Tantag (Kz, Sg)	Small-toothed Palm Civet or Horse-tailed Squirrel
Tantanion (Mu)	Clouded Leopard
Tatau (Kz, Sg)	Moonrat
Tautung (Mu)	large porcupines
Tebek Banguh (Ka)	Banded Palm Civet
Tekalung Alud (Kl)	Banded Palm Civet
Telau (Ka, Kl, Lu)	muntjak
Telih (Ka)	squirrels
Teludu (Kz)	Malay Badger
Temadcur (Kl, Lu)	Rhinoceros
Tempelili (Br, Sg)	Tarsier
Temuning (Kz, Sg)	Common or Small-toothed Palm Civet
Tenggiling (Ma, Ib, Kz, Sg, Su)	Pangolin
Terutung (Lu, Kl)	large porcupines

322

Tetou (Kz, Sg)	Moonrat
Tigi (Kz)	pigmy squirrels
Tikus (Ma)	rats
Tikus bulan (Ma)	Moonrat
Timbalabug (Kz)	Greater Mouse-deer
Tindukutrukut (Kz)	Tarsier
Tinggalung (Kz, Sg, Su)	Malay Civet
Tingurunurun (Kz)	Malay Civet
Tintukadtukad (Kz, Sg)	Banded Palm Civet
Tirung (Mu)	otters
Tohoroh (Mu)	Hose's Langur
Tokilongun (Lu)	treeshrews
Tokoyon (Lu)	Long-tailed Macaque
Tompin (Kz)	small squirrels
Tompu (Kz, Sg)	wild cats
Tomunin (Kz)	Common or Small-toothed Palm Civet
Toni (Kz)	Yellow-throated Marten
Tubang (Kl, Mu)	wild cats
Tudtu (Sg)	Malay Badger
Tudu (Kz)	Malay Badger
Tuhou (Mu)	muntjak
Tulu (Kz)	Malay Badger
Tuluk (Kz)	mongooses
Tun (Bi)	Binturong
Tupai (Ma)	squirrels *and* treeshrews
Tupai bekarang (Ib)	Prevost's Squirrel
Tupai labang (Ib)	Prevost's Squirrel
Tupai muncung (Ma)	treeshrews
Turu (Mu)	Malay Badger
Ukang (Ma)	Slow Loris
Ulak (Mu)	Bearded Pig
Usa (Su)	Sambar Deer
Using (Ka)	Flat-headed Cat
Utun (Kz)	large porcupines
Uyau Tubang (Ka)	mongooses
Wakwak (Ma)	Gibbon
Wangan (Kz)	Hose's Langur
Yamu *or* Yayamu	Tufted Ground Squirrel

Bibliography and References

The following is a list of some of the more important references on Bornean mammals which have appeared in recent years. Only a few of the older references given in Medway (1977) are repeated here.

Anderson, J.A.R., Jermy, A.C. & Cranbrook, Earl of. 1982. Gunung Mulu National Park. A management and development plan. London: Royal Geographical Society.

Banks, E. 1949 Bornean Mammals. Kuching Press.

Corbet, G.B. & Hill, J.E. 1980. A world list of mammal species. London: British Museum (Natural History).

Cranbrook, Earl of. 1984. New and interesting records of mammals from Sarawak. Sarawak Mus. J. 33(54): 137-144.

Davis, D.D. 1962. Mammals of the lowland rain-forest of North Borneo. Bull. Nat. Mus. Singapore 31: 1-129.

Davis, J. A.1978. A classification of otters. Pages 14-33 in Duplaix, N. (ed). Otters. United Kingdom: IUCN.

Ellis, R. 1982. Dolphins and Porpoises. New York: Knopf.

F.A.O. 1981. National Conservation Plan for Indonesia. Vol. V Kalimantan. Field Report of UNDP/FAO National Parks Development Project. INS/78/061. Bogor.

Francis, C.M., Melville, D.S. & Wong, P.L. 1984. Notes on some bats in Bako National Park and Samunsam Wildlife Sanctuary, Sarawak. Sarawak Mus. J. 33(54): 171-176.

Groves, C. P. & Grubb, P. 1982. The species of muntjac (genus *Muntiacus)* in Borneo: unrecognised sympatry in tropical deer. Zool. Meded., Leiden 56(17): 203-216.

Harrison, J.L. 1964. An introduction to the mammals of Sabah. Jesselton: The Sabah Society.

Hill, J.E. 1983. Bats (Mammalia: Chiroptera) from Indo-Australia. Bull. Br. Mus. nat. Hist. (Zool.) 45: 103-208.

Hill, J.E. & Francis, C.M. 1984. New bats (Mammalia: Chiroptera) and new records of bats from Borneo and Malaya. Bull. Br. Mus. nat. Hist. (Zool.) 47: 305-329.

Honacki, J.H., Kinman, K.E. & Koeppl, J.W. (editors). 1982. Mammal species of the world. A taxonomic and geographic reference. Lawrence, Kansas: Allen Press.

Hose, C. 1893 Mammals of Borneo. Diss, Norfolk: Edward Abbott.

Jenkins, P.D. 1982. A discussion of Malayan and Indonesian shrews of the genus *Crocidura* (Insectivora: Soricidae). Zool. Meded., Leiden56(21): 267-279.

Jenkins, P.D. & Hill J.E. 1981. The status of *Hipposideros galeritus* Cantor, 1846 and *Hipposideros cervinus* (Gould, 1854) (Chiroptera: Hipposideridae). Bull. Br. Mus. nat. Hist. (Zool.) 41: 279-294.

Kobayashi, T., Maeda, K. & Harada, M. 1980. Studies on the small mammal fauna of Sabah, East Malaysia. I. Order Chiroptera and genus *Tupaia* (Primates). Contributions from the Biological Laboratory, Kyoto University. 26: 67-82.

Leatherwood, S. & Reeves, R.R. 1983. The Sierra Club handbook of whales and dolphins. San Francisco: Sierra Club.

Lekagul, B. & McNeely, J.A. 1977. Mammals of Thailand. Bangkok: Association for the Conservation of Wildlife.

Macdonald, D. (editor) 1984. The Encyclopaedia of Mammals: 1. London: George Allen and Unwin.

Marshall, J.T. 1977. A synopsis of Asian species of *Mus* (Rodentia, Muridae). Bull. Am. Mus. nat. Hist. 158: 173-220.

Medway, Lord. 1977. Mammals of Borneo. Field keys and annotated checklist. Monographs of the Malaysian Branch of the Royal Asiatic Society. No. 7. Kuala Lumpur: M.B.R.A.S.

Medway, Lord. 1978. The wild mammals of Malaya (Peninsular Malaysia) and Singapore. Kuala Lumpur: Oxford University Press.

Musser, G.G. 1973a. Species limits of *Rattus cremoriventer* and *Rattus longibanis,* murid rodents of Southeast Asia and the Greater Sunda Islands. Am. Mus. Novit. 2525: 1-65.

Musser, G.G. 1973b. Zoogeographical significance of the Ricefield Rat, *Rattus argentiventer,* on Celebes and New Guinea, and the identity of *Rattus pesticulus.* Am. Mus Novit. 2511: 1-30.

Musser, G.G. 1979. Results of the Archbold Expeditions. No. 102. The species of *Chiropodomys,* arboreal mice of Indochina and the Malay Archipelago. Bull. Am. Mus. nat. Hist. 162: 377-445.

Musser, G.G. 1981. Results of the Archbold Expeditions. No. 105. Notes on the systematics of Indo-Malayan murid rodents, and descriptions of new genera and species from Ceylon, Sulawesi and the Philippines. Bull. Am. Mus. nat. Hist. 168: 225-334.

Musser, G.G. & Califia D. 1982. Results of the Archbold Expeditions. No. 106. Identities of rats from Pulau Maratua and other islands off East Borneo. Am. Mus. Novit. 2726: 1-30.

Musser, G.G. & Newcom C. 1983. Malaysian murids and the giant rat of Sumatra. Bull. Am. Mus. nat. Hist. 174: 327-598.

Strien, N.J. van. 1983. A guide to the tracks of mammals of Western Indonesia. Bogor: School of Environmental Conservation Management, Ciawi.

Tidemann, C.R. & Woodside,D.P. 1978. A collapsible bat trap and a comparison of results obtained with the trap and with mist-nets. Austr. Wildl. Res. News. 5: 355-362.

Tuttle, M.D. 1974. An improved trap for bats. J. of Mammalogy. 55: 475-477.

Watson, L. & Ritchie, T. 1981. Sea Guide to the Whales of the World. New York: Dutton.

World Wildlife Fund Malaysia. 1982a. A Faunal Survey of Sabah. Compiled by A.G. Davies and J.B. Payne. Kuala Lumpur: WWF Malaysia.

World Wildlife Fund Malaysia. 1982b. Lanjak-Entimau Orang-utan Sanctuary. A Management Plan. Compiled by M. Kavanagh. Kuala Lumpur: WWF Malaysia.

World Wildlife Fund Malaysia. undated. A Survey of the Proposed Sungai Danum National Park, Sabah. Compiled by B.H. Kiew. Kuala Lumpur: WWF Malaysia.

World Wildlife Fund. undated. Management Plan for Kutai Nature Reserve, East Kalimantan, Indonesia. Project No. 1524. Unpublished report.

INDEX